SLOVAKIA
BRATISLAVA

LUCY MALLOWS & TIM BURFORD

www.bradtguides.com

Bradt Guides Ltd, UK
The Globe Pequot Press Inc, USA

AUTHOR

Born and educated in the UK, **Lucy Mallows** spent 16 years in Budapest and Brussels, working as a photo journalist, travel writer and translator. An expert on central Europe who spoke seven languages including Russian, Hungarian and a fair attempt at Slovak, her passions were travel, music, swimming, photography and football. Sadly, Lucy passed away in 2018.

UPDATER

Tim Burford studied languages at Oxford University. In 1991, after five years as a publisher, he began writing guidebooks for Bradt, firstly on hiking in east-central Europe and then on backpacking and ecotourism in Latin America. A regular visitor to Bratislava, he has always loved the city and was very happy to have the chance to update this book

– although in very unfortunate circumstances, of course. While working on this edition and the previous one, he spent the majority of his visit walking everywhere (and occasionally using the new bike-sharing system) to check every detail; he also enjoyed delving into the history and culture of central Europe, where he's worked for over 30 years.

FEEDBACK REQUEST

At Bradt Guides we're aware that guidebooks start to go out of date on the day they're published – and that you, our readers, are out there in the field doing research of your own. You'll find out before us when a fine new family-run hotel opens or a favourite restaurant changes hands and goes downhill. So why not tell us about your experiences? Contact us on 01753 893444 or **e** info@bradtguides.com. We will forward emails to the author who may post updates on the Bradt website at **w** bradtguides.com/updates. Alternatively, you can add a review of the book to Amazon, or share your adventures with us on Facebook, or Instagram (@BradtGuides).

AUTHOR'S STORY *Lucy Mallows*

Small but perfectly formed and easily negotiated, Bratislava is the ideal weekend-break destination. The 'little big city' has an amazing ability to regenerate and improve on its already spectacular setting and world-class facilities. I was in town in spring 2015, enjoying the sunshine by the Danube, sipping superb Slovak beer, and I spied the changing skyline: towering five-star hotel, mall and apartment complexes now jostle for space.

However, Bratislava never feels crowded despite the hordes of visitors who pack out the café terraces of the Mediterranean-style Old Town centre. There are many green regions to escape to: from the lush green hills of Koliba-Kamzík and meadows of Železná Studienka to a cycling tour of the Small Carpathian Wine Route – *hic*.

It's a real pleasure to delve into the ever-growing collection of attractions that the city has to offer. I decided, just off the top of my head, to jot down my top ten list of first-class restaurants in Bratislava, should a certain tyre company decide to dish out the stars. I had a collection of 25 fabulous establishments before I'd even drawn breath!

DEDICATION

To the memory of Lucy Mallows.

Fifth edition published July 2025
First published 2005
Bradt Travel Guides Ltd
31a High Street, Chesham, Buckinghamshire, HP5 1BW, England
www.bradtguides.com
Print edition published in the USA by The Globe Pequot Press Inc,
PO Box 480, Guilford, Connecticut 06437-0480

Text copyright © The Estate of Lucy Mallows, 2025
Maps copyright © Bradt Travel Guides Ltd, 2025; includes map data
© OpenStreetMap contributors

Photographs copyright © Individual photographers, 2025 (see below)
Project Manager: Susannah Lord
Copy Editor: Gina Rathbone
Cover research: Pepi Bluck, Perfect Picture

The author and publisher have made every effort to ensure the accuracy of the information in this book at the time of going to press. However, they cannot accept any responsibility for any loss, injury or inconvenience resulting from the use of information contained in this guide. All rights reserved. No part of this publication may be reproduced, stored in a retrieval system, or transmitted in any form or by any means, electronic, mechanical, photocopying, recording or otherwise without the prior consent of the publisher.

ISBN: 9781804692745

British Library Cataloguing in Publication Data
A catalogue record for this book is available from the British Library

Photographs © Individual photographers credited beside images and also those from picture libraries credited as follows: Alamy Stock Photo: (A); Dreamstime.com (DT); Shutterstock.com (S); Superstock (SS)

Front cover Michael's Gate tower (Sorin Colac/A)
Back cover Bratislava Castle (TTstudio/S)
Title page Most SNP (SNP Bridge) and UFO café, over the Danube (BearFotos/S)

Maps David McCutcheon FBCart.S. FRGS

Typeset by Ian Spick, Bradt Travel Guides Ltd
Production managed by Gutenberg Press Ltd; printed in Malta
Digital conversion by www.dataworks.co.in

Paper used for this product comes from sustainably managed forests, and recycled and controlled sources.

ACKNOWLEDGEMENTS *Lucy Mallows*

To Eva Mazuchová and her team at BTB (Bratislava Tourist Board), ever ready with help and ideas, and especially a massive *ďakujem* to Monika Výbochová, whose help, patience, ideas and tireless checking inspired me with confidence during listings compilation.

To Peter and Branislav Chrenka at Authentic Slovakia for insights and a great cycle ride.

To Daniel Kulla at Hotel Devín and David Pobjecky at Crowne Plaza for fascinating chats about Bratislava's past and future.

To Veronika Holečková in Košice for friendship and a superb visit to Slovakia's second city, also Ivana Kavulič and the staff at visitkosice.eu for wonderful hospitality and guidance, also to Miroslava Šeregová Hnatková for guidance around Tokaj and Maria Kočiová for a fascinating tour of Košice.

To Anna Lališova and her expert mapmen at Mapa Slovakia for original orientation and the staff of Bratislava's DPB (Dopravný podnik Bratislava – Bratislava Transport Company) for help with the complicated transport maps.

To Allison Plant for hospitality and advice, to Ľuboš Porada for an amazing trip to Košice Castle, to Tomaš Džadon for showing us his Drevenica (a log cabin perched on top of a tower block) and Viktor Fehér of Street Art Communication and Tabačka for a great tour of the incredible street art of Košice.

To Lucie Fremlová in Brighton for advice on the NGOs and charities and thanks also to Miroslava Robochová for help in Piešťany.

Many thanks also to Olaya Fernández Guerrero, Marie Koksvik Thorsen, Venni Valkama, Giovanni Pompomio, theatre expert Patrik at Obývačka, Lucia in Urban House and Phillip in Devín for their encouraging words during enlightening chats about Bratislava, and all the readers who kindly sent in feedback with hints, tips and suggestions.

FOR THE FOURTH AND FIFTH EDITIONS *Tim Burford*

For this edition, I thank Monika Výbochová at the Bratislava Tourist Board, Daniel Laurinec and Peter Kmeto at the Patio Hostel and all at Bradt, especially Carys Homer and Susannah Lord.

Contents

	Introduction	xi
Chapter 1	**Contexts**	**1**
	Geography 3, Climate 4, Natural history 4, History 5, Government and politics 18, Economy 20, People 23, Religion and beliefs 24, Culture and festivals 25, Cultural etiquette 33, Travelling positively 36	
Chapter 2	**Planning**	**38**
	A practical overview 38, When to visit (and why) 39, Highlights and suggested itineraries 40, Tour operators 43, Red tape 44, Getting there and away 45, Health 51, Safety 54, Women travellers 56, LGBTQIA+ travellers 56, Travelling with kids 56, What to take 58, Money and budgeting 59	
Chapter 3	**Practicalities**	**62**
	Tourist information 62, Local tour operators 62, Embassies and consulates 66, Money 66, Media and communications 67, Religious services 70, Public toilets 71	
Chapter 4	**Local Transport**	**72**
	Public transport 72, Bratislava by bike 74, Taxis 76, Car hire 76, Parking 77, Danube river cruises 77	
Chapter 5	**Accommodation**	**78**
	Luxury hotels 81, Four-star hotels 82, Three-star hotels 84, Pensions 85, Hostels 87, Camping 87	

Chapter 6	**Eating and Drinking**	**89**
	Food 89, Drink 94, Restaurants 95, Cafés and tearooms 104, Bars, pubs and clubs 112	
Chapter 7	**Entertainment, Nightlife, Sport and Shopping**	**120**
	Theatre 120, Music 123, Nightclubs and discos 128, Casinos 129, LGBTQIA+ Bratislava 130, Cinema 130, Sports 132, Shopping 137	
Chapter 8	**Walking Tours**	**146**
	Walk one – Old Town 146, Walk two – castle and beyond 150	
Chapter 9	**Museums and Sightseeing**	**152**
	Major sights 152, Museums 160, Galleries 170, Churches and religious buildings 179, Gardens and parks 181, Squares 186, Bridges 187, Also worth a visit 192	
Chapter 10	**Beyond the City**	**195**
	Devín 195, Ancient Gerulata, Rusovce 197, Senec 198, Small Carpathian Wine Route 198, Červený Kameň 201, Trnava 202, Piešťany 202, Košice 203	
Appendix 1	**Language**	**208**
Appendix 2	**Further Information**	**216**
Index		**226**

LIST OF MAPS

Around Bratislava	196	Highlights		viii
Bratislava: city centre	222	Košice		204
Bratislava: overview	220	Walks		224

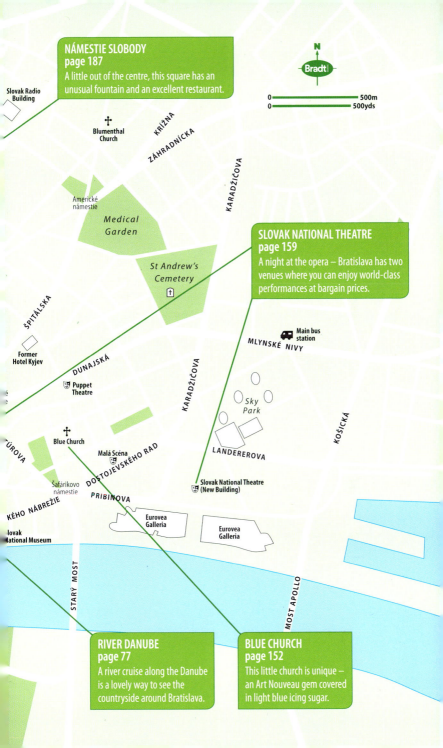

KEY TO SYMBOLS

—	International border
----	Regional border
✈	Airport
🚌	Bus station
P	Parking
🚴	Cycle route/hire
i	Tourist information
	Museum/gallery
	Cinema/theatre
	Ancient city gate
	Castle
	Important building
	Statue/monument
$	Bank/currency exchange
✉	Post office
✝	Cathedral/church
✡	Synagogue
	Cemetery
✚	Pharmacy
	Hotel/accommodation
	Pub
	Bar
♪	Music venue
☆	Casino/nightclub
•	Other point of interest
	Park
	Pedestrian street/area

INTRODUCTION *Lucy Mallows, 2016*

I first visited Bratislava in spring 1982, while studying at Brno University nearby. In the pre-Velvet Revolution, pre-Velvet Divorce days, Bratislava was a charming, if sleepy, provincial town in Czechoslovakia and I stayed with a hospitable Slovak family in what I now realise was a very swanky apartment on a street leading up to the castle.

Ironically, given all my Slavic studies, my fate became intertwined with Hungary from 1986 onwards and I lived in Budapest for 12 years; however, I frequently visited Bratislava to practise my Slovak verbs (over several litres of Slovak beer) and observe its evolution from sleepy and quiet to cosmopolitan and go-getting.

Bratislava's small size is satisfying. You have the sense that you can discover everything in a few days, see all the important sights and get a real feel for the place without the nagging, lingering doubt that you might have missed something secret or spectacular. In spring, the Old Town turns into one giant outdoor café; it has a very Mediterranean feel with endless eating and drinking possibilities and superb quality at extremely reasonable prices. In the last couple of years, Bratislava has transformed itself into a foodie heaven and is getting more so by the hour. The Old Town has many world-class restaurants offering a wide variety of international cuisine. Slovak people are not grim Eastern Bloc types, but instead are unusually relaxed for a country that has seen so much tragedy and trauma.

I mustn't forget the Opera House. Bratislava's opera rivals those in Budapest and Vienna and the ticket prices are astounding – €4 for a last-minute ticket is mind-blowing.

Bratislava is also very green. There are many places to sit back and relax in the sunshine, or for the more energetic, endless opportunities for sports such as hiking, canoeing and cycling. Why not combine exercise with another of Slovakia's natural attributes and sample the excellent wines along the Small Carpathian Wine Route? And have I mentioned the world-beating beer at jaw-dropping prices yet?

So, congratulations for stepping off the beaten track and trying out Bratislava. Your pioneering spirit will pay dividends; think of all the money you'll save on the beer and be sure to tell all your friends about your discovery. Or maybe not; let's keep this our special, Slovak secret.

Bratislava, the 'little big city' is modest, charming and pocket-sized, like its cathedral. It doesn't bellow its beauty like Prague but states its case quietly and insistently, until suddenly you wake up one gorgeous Slovak spring morning and realise you're in love.

Na zdravie! (Cheers!)
Lucy

A NOTE FROM THE UPDATER *Tim Burford*

When I visited Bratislava to update this guide, Lucy's comments remained true. It's still changing, still beautiful, and still building on its natural strengths. It's a city I've loved since the 1990s, and I was delighted and honoured to be able to take over Lucy's excellent guide for its fully revised fourth and fifth editions.

HOW TO USE THIS GUIDE

SYMBOLS
- ✱ Author's favourite
- 🚌 Closest bus stop
- 🚊 Closest tram stop
- 💰 Entrance fee
- 📍 Grid reference

MAPS Find the city maps on pages 220 and 222, and the walks map on page 224.

Keys Alphabetical keys cover the locations of places to eat and drink featured in the book – for the city maps, these can be found on page 225.

Grid references These relate to the colour maps at the end of this guide. For example: 📍 221 H3 refers to the overview map, while 📍 222 C3 refers to the city centre map.

HOTELS Accommodation listings are arranged by price range (not by area), in the Slovak style of stars, from luxurious to one-star (basic). See page 79 or the inside-front cover for an explanation of the price codes used.

RESTAURANTS Restaurant listings are by area – Old Town and Castle District, and Centrum and further afield. See page 98 or the inside-front cover for an explanation of the price codes used.

OPENING HOURS These are included for restaurants, bars, museums and sights. Restaurants and bars are usually open from late morning until 23.00 with last orders for food often at 22.30, while museums are open between 10.00 and 17.00 but closed on Mondays.

MONEY AND PRICES Prices are given in euros (€). Many hotels and shops accept contactless cards, although American Express is not widely accepted.

JOIN
THE TRAVEL CLUB

THE MEMBERSHIP CLUB FOR SERIOUS TRAVELLERS
FROM BRADT GUIDES

Be inspired
Free books and exclusive insider travel tips and inspiration

Save money
Special offers and discounts from our favourite travel brands

Plan the trip of a lifetime
Access our exclusive concierge service and have a bespoke itinerary created for you by a Bradt author

Join here:
bradtguides.com/travelclub

Membership levels to suit all budgets

Bradt GUIDES

TRAVEL TAKEN SERIOUSLY

BRATISLAVA AT A GLANCE

Location In the southwestern corner of Slovakia
Neighbouring countries Poland, Ukraine, Hungary, Austria, Czech Republic
Climate Warm, wet summers; cold, cloudy, humid winters
Population 475,000 (2021)
Life expectancy Total population: 74.5 years; male: 71.1 years; female: 78.0 years (2021)
Languages Slovak (official) 78.6%, Hungarian 9.4%, Roma 2.3%, Ruthenian 1%, other or unspecified 8.7%
Religion Roman Catholic 56%, Evangelical (Lutheran) 5%, Greek-Catholic 4%, Reformed (Calvinist) 2%, Orthodox 1%, others 1%, without religious affiliation 24%, unspecified 7% (2021)
Currency Euro
Exchange rate £1 = €1.18, US$1 = €0.89 (May 2025)
International dialling code Slovakia: +421, Bratislava: 02, Košice: 055
National airport M R Štefánik Airport, 9.5km northeast of central Bratislava. Two more airports at Košice and Poprad.
Time CET (GMT +1 hour)
Electrical voltage 220 volts, frequency 50Hz; two-pin plugs
Weights and measures Metric system
Tourist boards Slovakia w slovakia.travel/en; Bratislava BTB w visitbratislava.com; Visit Košice w visitkosice.org
National public holidays 1 January (New Year's Day and Anniversary of the Establishment of the Slovak Republic in 1993), 1 May (Labour Day), 8 May (Victory against Fascism Day – end of World War II), 5 July (St Cyril and Methodius Day), 29 August (Anniversary of the Slovak National Uprising), 1 September (Slovak Republic Constitution Day), 15 September (Our Lady of the Seven Sorrows), 17 November (Day of Struggle for Freedom and Democracy)

1

Contexts

'The only thing I know about Slovakia is what I learned first-hand from your foreign minister who came to Texas,' George W Bush told a Slovak journalist, shortly after meeting the prime minister of Slovenia. That was in 1999, but Slovakia, it seems, still has a lot of PR work to do.

However, the legendary Casanova knew Bratislava and he knew a thing or two about beauty. He declared it 'the most beautiful city in Europe'. Bratislava is a good-looking place filled with good-looking people who look like they're enjoying life.

Because the city has been conquered so many times, the gene pool has been shaken up, resulting in a handsome population. The economy is thriving, and many low-cost airlines now fly direct to Bratislava, bringing in not only stag parties to appreciate the beer, but also businessmen and women eager to do business in the most vibrant economy in the region.

You would never guess from walking around Bratislava's peaceful, gentle, spruced-up Old Town centre with its pedestrian heart and almost Mediterranean terrace-café culture, but the city's history is more turbulent and traumatised than that of most other countries in the region. After all, what other city in Europe has been capital of two vastly different nations and cultures?

Bratislava sits right at the strategic meeting point of three countries – Slovakia, Austria and Hungary – and played a vital and deeply significant role in the mighty Habsburg Empire. Slovakia was part of Hungary for the best part of a millennium and Bratislava was actually the country's capital for close to 300 years.

Completely refurbished, buffed up and cleaned in 1999, Bratislava's Old Town has never looked so good. However, the city definitely suffers from an identity crisis. It's not exactly an inferiority complex, although it would be forgiven for having one after all the unkind comments. Visiting Hungarians say either 'Oh, we used to own all this', or 'It's just like a small Hungarian country town'. Visiting Czechs say, 'It's not the new Prague', but Bratislava is not Prague, and it's probably quite happy being itself.

And visiting Austrians say it's just a suburb of Vienna, as it sits right at the far western end of Slovakia. Look at the map and Bratislava is much nearer to Vienna (obviously), Budapest, Prague, Zagreb and Salzburg than to most

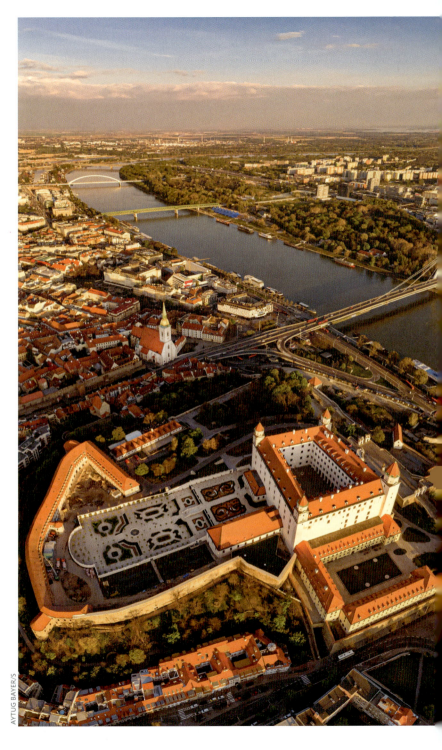

of its own eastern Slovakian cities: Košice and certainly Medzilaborce in the far east of the country, home of Andy Warhol's parents.

To the endless irritation of the two countries, Slovakia is always getting confused with Slovenia. The 2005 Bratislava summit between presidents Vladimir Putin and George W Bush was supposed to put Slovakia firmly on the map, right in the heart of Europe as an important member of the EU. However, putting the country on the map turned out to be a major hurdle. In reporting the summit, CNN's efforts mostly missed off Slovakia entirely, marking just the Czech Republic or incorporating it into a Magyar irredentist's dream of 'greater Hungary'. *USA Today* went one further and placed Slovakia down by the Adriatic, between Italy and Croatia, in Slovenia's position – the only benefit being that it gained a seaside.

Slovaks and Slovenes are equally irritated by the inability of foreigners – even some Europeans – to distinguish the vastly differing countries, 440km and 5 hours' drive apart (and that's bombing down the motorway). It probably doesn't help matters that the Slovak word for Slovakia is Slovensko, which sounds a bit like…oh dear.

GEOGRAPHY

East of Vienna, the Orient begins.
    Austrian statesman Prince Klemens von Metternich

The Republic of Slovakia occupies a territory of 49,035km^2 and is landlocked and surrounded by five countries: Austria, Czech Republic, Poland, Ukraine and Hungary. The border of 1,524km divides up thus: Austria 91km, Czech Republic 215km, Poland 444km, Ukraine 97km, and Hungary 677km. Despite its distance from the sea, Slovakia has many small lakes, streams and rivers and 45km² of its total territory is covered by water. Slovakia is situated at 16°50–22°34'E and 47°42–49°37'N. The mountain peak of Krahule (1,062m), near Banská Bystrica in central Slovakia, is considered the geographical centre of Europe and more than 80% of the country sits at over 750m above sea level.

Bratislava is Slovakia's capital and is situated at the western tip of the country, in a highly strategic position on the mighty Danube River at the meeting point of three countries: Slovakia, Austria and Hungary. The state border with Austria is just over the Danube River, within walking distance of the city centre. The state border with Hungary is 16km away, just beyond the city limits. Slovakia's most important river is the Danube (Dunaj), the river route connecting Slovakia with the harbours of the Black Sea and, through the Rhine–Main–Danube waterway, with west European harbours. It flows

◄ Bratislava Castle and its beautifully restored gardens overlook the Old Town and cathedral.

through Bratislava, dividing the historic Old Town centre from the modern housing district of Petržalka. In the past, two significant trade arteries led through Slovakia: the Amber (Jantárová) and Czech routes, along which not only goods (gold, amber, fur) used to flow, but also information, which enabled mutual knowledge of, and understanding between, peoples and countries. Today, Slovakia is becoming an important junction of economic and commercial relations between eastern and western Europe.

CLIMATE

Slovakia's climate is temperate with warm, wet summers and cold, hard winters. Bratislava is located in a mild climatic zone of continental nature, characterised by wide differences between temperatures in summer and winter and, until recently, by four distinct seasons. Average temperatures in Bratislava for winter are -1–4°C (30–40°F), spring and autumn 9–21°C (49–69°F) and summer 24–26°C (75–79°F), although over the last decade spring and autumn have merged into the more dramatic seasons, meaning that spring, usually a delightful season in the Old Town, has sadly almost disappeared. The average annual temperature in the Bratislava region has risen by almost 2°C since 1951 and will keep increasing, bringing hotter, drier summers. Snow cover on the mountains in the north is less than it has been in the past. The lowest annual temperature is in the mountains at Lomnický štít (peak) (-3.7°C). The warmest zone is the Podunajská Lowland (10.3°C).

For more information before you set off, ie: on whether to pack an extra jumper, look at **w** meteo.sk.

NATURAL HISTORY

Bratislava is very green: a notice board by the castle lists many species of flora and fauna found in the city. Wildlife around the castle includes bats, butterflies, lizards, woodpeckers and red squirrels. There are also many varieties of wildflower and plant: Chinese wolfberry, houseleek, flowering onion, royal knight's spur, wild violets and immortelle.

One of the best non-mountain **birdwatching** areas in Slovakia is Záhorie (the name means 'behind the mountains'), which is conveniently close to Bratislava, beginning just to the north by the D2/E65 motorway and stretching to the Czech border. This is the flood plain of the Morava River along the Austrian border and is a complex of water meadows, marshes, bogs, ponds, pools, reed beds, pine, oak and poplar forest and damp willow and alder woodland. In spring and summer, white storks, red and black kites, collared flycatchers, penduline tits and red-backed shrikes are fairly common here. Though rarer, corncrakes, short-eared owls and white-tailed eagles might also be seen with a little luck and patience. A little further north, the area around Malacky is drier and typified by pine-forested sand dunes where there are nightjars, hoopoe and woodlark.

Bratislava itself has 809ha of **park** and **forest**, and 34 **protected reservations**. Most of this is formed by the Bratislavský lesopark (Bratislava Forest Park), to the north of the city. Despite centuries of deforestation and the effects of acid rain after burning brown coal, 40% of the country is still covered by forest, mainly beech and spruce. Arable land accounts for 30% of the country, while meadows and pastures cover 17%. Slovakia is less industrialised than the Czech Republic and therefore its forests and rivers have been less damaged by pollution.

The **Gabčíkovo-Nagymaros hydro-electric dam**, 40km downstream from Bratislava, has been an environmental disaster on all sides. The Gabčíkovo Dam Project was started in 1977 under the auspices of an international treaty between the then communist brother states Hungary and Czechoslovakia. The goal was to dam the Danube, all the way from Bratislava to Budapest, providing a vital amount of clean hydro-electric energy. The idea was supported by the Austrians, who also looked for cheap energy resources at another country's environmental expense. The Czechoslovak government was desperate to find another source of energy to replace brown coal, whose pollution destroyed most of the country's forests. The Hungarian government pulled out in 1989 after protests by the green lobby, and called for an international inquiry into the environmental effects of the dam on the Danube. They dismantled their dam at Nagymaros (east of Štúrovo, downstream from Gabčíkovo). The Czechoslovak government had already invested huge amounts of money and continued with a scaled-down version of the project (known as Variant C), diverting part of the Danube in 1993. In 1997, the International Court of Justice at The Hague ruled in favour of Slovakia, but that Slovakia had acted illegally by diverting the river. The court ordered both sides to come up with a joint plan for the future of the project but, after years of wrangling, they agreed to discontinue proceedings in 2017. Tragically, the environmental damage has already been done on both sides of the river, according to ecologists. A new channel runs for 10km from south of Bratislava to the Čunovo Dam and the Danubiana Meulensteen Modern Art Museum (page 162), which you can reach either by cycling alongside the channel or on a boat cruise.

HISTORY

THE EARLY YEARS Archaeological finds have shown the existence of man in the area now known as Slovakia from the Middle Palaeolithic era (200,000–35,000BC). The region where Bratislava now stands was visited around 5,000 years ago by Indo-European nomads of the Pit Grave culture and Slovakia was a significant centre for bronze production. Celtic tribes settled here in the 5th century BC and later built fortified settlements on the hilltops of Bratislava and Devín, overlooking the Danube, which were then occupied by the Romans from the 1st century BC. The Romans also built the Gerulata frontier post, which can still be seen at Rusovce, 11km downriver from central Bratislava (page 197), and the philosopher-emperor Marcus Aurelius wrote much of the first volume of his *Meditations* while campaigning against Germanic tribes in the Hron Valley of central Slovakia.

Slavic tribes arrived in the region during the 5th century AD, followed by the Avars, who dominated the region by AD600. A warrior by the name of Samo created a Slavic union that defeated both the Avars and the Franks in the 620s, but the Avars took control again from the 670s, until the start of the 9th century.

GREAT MORAVIAN EMPIRE The Principality of Nitra established itself east of Bratislava by AD828, and the first Christian church in central Europe was built in Nitra during the reign of Prince Pribina (circa AD800–861). This evolved into the Great Moravian Empire, which at its peak, under Svätopluk I (AD870–894), encompassed the lands of modern Slovakia and Moravia as well as parts of Hungary, Austria, Bohemia and the southern part of Poland.

A basilica was built on Bratislava's Castle Hill and in AD863, at the invitation of Great Moravian Prince Rastislav, the brothers and missionaries Cyril and Methodius came from Thessaloniki to Great Moravia and created the Old Church Slavonic alphabet, the origins of today's Cyrillic alphabet. They also translated liturgical books into Old Church Slavonic, which they codified.

THE MIDDLE AGES AND THE MAGYARS In AD907, after much political intrigue, a battle beneath Bratislava's castle, between the East Franks and the Magyars, finally brought an end to the Great Moravian Empire and the region was invaded by the Magyars, whose King St István (Stephen) founded the Christian Hungarian State in the Carpathian Basin in AD1000. By the end of the 11th century, Slovakia had become an integral (and the most developed) part of old Hungary, a relationship which was to last for almost 1,000 years, despite rude interruptions by the Tatars in 1241 and the Turks in 1526.

The territory now known as the Slovak Republic was then called Felvidék ('the Upland' in Hungarian but generally translated as Upper Hungary) and remained so until the end of World War I.

The 11th to 15th centuries were a period of great economic growth and cultural advancement, boosted by German settlers from the 13th century; walls were built around the present Old City in the early 14th century, as it had become a place worth protecting. In 1291, King András III granted Bratislava the privileges of a Free Royal Town and in 1436 King Sigismund of Luxembourg granted the city a coat of arms featuring a castle. During the

Renaissance, and particularly the enlightened rule of King Mátyás Corvinus, cultural life blossomed in Bratislava. The Academia Istropolitana, the first university in what is now Slovakia, was founded in Bratislava in 1465 and you can still see the building, which now hosts the Academy of Performing Arts, at Ventúrska 3.

OTTOMANS AND HABSBURGS Life in the entire region was to change dramatically in 1526 at the Battle of Mohács (in southern Hungary), when the Ottoman forces wiped out the Hungarian army on one tragic day. The Hungarian crown passed to the Habsburg dynasty and ten years later, after the capture of Buda by the Turks, the capital of Hungary was moved to Bratislava (Pozsony in Hungarian, Pressburg in German). Many of the following conflicts, when Hungarian nobles sided with Turks in continuous efforts to dislodge the Habsburgs, were played out on the territory of Slovakia.

In 1536, Pressburg became not only the capital of Hungary, but also the centre of all administrative offices and the seat of the Hungarian archbishop; the city's population, however, remained predominantly German. The Hungarian crown jewels were moved to Pressburg in 1552 and, between 1563 and 1830, a total of 19 Hungarian kings and queens were crowned in St Martin's Cathedral. In 1683, with the help of the Polish king, Ján Sobieski, the Habsburgs defeated the Turks who had almost reached the gates of Vienna; the Turks were then gradually driven out of central Europe for good. At the beginning of the 18th century, Hungarian nobles such as Ferenc Rákóczi II, then Governor (*župan*) of Šariš County and Transylvanian prince (*fejedelem*), rose up against the Habsburgs, challenging their authority in battles carried out mostly on Slovak territory. Many castles were ruined during these uprisings. Rákóczi's band of anti-Habsburg rebels were called Kuruc, while the pro-Habsburgs were known as Labanc.

Habsburg Empress Maria Theresa was crowned in St Martin's Cathedral in 1741 and spent much time in Bratislava, leading the nobility to build grand Baroque palaces in and near what is now known as the Old Town. Towards the end of the 18th century, her reforms and those of her son Joseph II formed the basis of a modern state administration, tax and transportation system, army and schools and made life a little easier for Slovaks.

SLOVAK NATIONAL AWAKENING (SLOVENSKÉ NÁRODNÉ OBRODENIE)
Bratislava's time of prominence came to an end in 1783, when Hungary's capital returned to Buda. By this time the Slovaks were attempting to assert their national and cultural identity and rise up against Hungarian domination, similar to their neighbouring Czechs' reaction against German overlords. In 1792, the linguist Anton Bernolák founded the Slovak Learned Society (Slovenské Učené Tovarištvo) in Modra, near

Bratislava. He was joined by many Slovak intellectuals who saw an opportunity of subverting the Austro-Hungarian monarchy. The lower classes were not inspired until 1843, when Ľudovít Štúr, the son of a Lutheran pastor, codified the Slovak literary language. Previously all literature had been written in Czech, so this made the Slovak nationalist movement more accessible to ordinary Slovaks.

By 1848, revolutions broke out across Europe. The Hungarian uprising against the Habsburgs was inspired by the poet Sándor Petőfi, born in Kiskőrös, Hungary, but with Slovak roots (at his first school his name was registered as Alexander Petrovič). Slovakia was desperate for change and volunteer groups formed in many parts of the country to battle against the Habsburgs.

The Slovak National Council (Slovenská Národná Strana) developed as the first representative Slovak political organ. In 1849, its members endeavoured, through co-operation with Vienna, to effect the separation of Slovakia from Hungary and its incorporation as an autonomous entity within a federal Habsburg monarchy. In 1861, the Martin Memorandum, issued in the town of Martin in central Slovakia, urged the establishment of a Slovak district and language within Greater Hungary, and two years later saw the foundation of a cultural and educational foundation, Matica Slovenská (Little Mother of the Slovaks). This was an important moment for the Slovaks as it confronted the Hungarian oppressors head-on.

From 1823, steamships between Vienna and Budapest called at Bratislava and railways linked the city with Trnava from 1846 and with Budapest from 1850, as the city developed into Hungary's second industrial centre. In 1867, the Austrian Empire, after suffering humiliating defeats against Prussia and Italy, was forced to sign a Compromise (Ausgleich in German or Kiegyezés in Hungarian) with Hungary and create a dual monarchy. For the Slovaks this was nothing short of disaster. Slovakia was still 'Felvidék' (Upper Hungary) and the Slovaks were subjected to an even more ruthless programme of 'Magyarisation'. This policy made Hungarian the only language in schools and large swathes of land were confiscated for use by Hungarian settlers, causing hardship throughout the country. In Bratislava, the majority German population assimilated with the Hungarian culture. By the outbreak of World War I, almost 20% of Slovaks had emigrated, mostly to the USA.

WORLD WAR I When war broke out in 1914, the Slovaks and Czechs decided that they would be better off together, uniting with their Slavic brothers, the Serbs and Russians, and large numbers defected from the Austro-Hungarian armies to fight against them on the Eastern Front.

In 1915, representatives of the Slovak and Czech ethnic organisations went to the USA to sign the Cleveland Agreement, brokered by President Woodrow Wilson, which promised a common federal state. The Pittsburgh

Agreement followed in 1918, proclaiming the autonomous position of Slovakia within a democratic Czechoslovak Republic. By the end of World War I, the notion of establishing an independent Czecho-Slovakia was fully supported by the United States, Britain, France and Italy. On 28 October 1918, the Czecho-Slovak National Committee in Prague proclaimed the existence of Czecho-Slovakia. Two days later, in the Martin Declaration, the Slovak National Council declared its desire for Slovakia to join with the Czech lands in one common state. The skilful Czech politician Tomaš Masaryk became president of the new republic and, during his tenure from 1918 to 1935, did much to defend democracy.

On 1 January 1919, Pressburg (in German, Pozsony in Hungarian) was occupied by Czechoslovak legions and annexed to the new Czechoslovak Republic. The city's name was changed to Bratislava, which had a more Slavic sound and suggested the glory (*sláva*) of Slavic brother (*brat*) hood, while also referring to earlier names of the city (page 12). On 4 June 1920, at Versailles, the Treaty of Trianon returned the territory of Slovakia to the Slovaks and confirmed the controversial new border with Hungary along the Danube River. However, this carving up of central Europe left some 750,000 Hungarians stranded on Slovak soil.

WORLD WAR II The new republic of Czechoslovakia inherited 80% of the Austro-Hungarian industry in the region but also a diverse and tricky blend of peoples in its population.

In the 1930s, as the world plunged into the Great Depression, Czechoslovakia began to crumble under internal tensions. The 1935 elections saw victory for the Hlinka Party, the Agrarian Party and the Hungarian Agrarian Party.

Masaryk resigned from power in 1935 due to bad health and died two years later. On 5 October 1938, after the infamous Munich Agreement had handed not just the Sudetenland (the German-speaking part of the Czech lands) but also Petržalka (the portion of Bratislava south of the Danube) to Germany, Hitler summoned the Slovak People's Party leader, Jozef Tiso, a Catholic priest and staunch nationalist, to Munich and gave him an ultimatum: either declare independence as a Nazi puppet state or we will carve up Slovakia between Germany, Hungary and Poland. In any case, the First Vienna Award of 2 November 1938 handed much of southern Slovakia to Hungary. On 14 March 1939, the Slovak Parliament voted unanimously for independence. German troops took the remaining Czech territories of Bohemia and Moravia.

Wartime Slovakia's 'independence' lasted from 1939 to 1945, during which time Tiso banned all opposition parties, instituted censorship along Nazi lines, and deported Jews to the extermination camps of Sobibor, Majdanka, Treblinka and Auschwitz-Birkenau. Deportation began in March 1942 and in seven months, 74,000 had been taken away. Tiso was very antisemitic and he terrorised the people with the fascist Hlinka Guard whose symbol was a sinister double cross. Subsequently, it was revealed that Tiso struck a deal with the Nazis and paid them 500 Reichsmarks for each Jew taken away. The Nazis promised 'they will never come back'. Tiso fled the country in 1945 but was captured, tried and executed in the June of that year. To this day, he remains a highly controversial figure in Slovak history.

However, not all Slovaks supported the puppet Nazi state and in August 1944, the Slovak National Uprising (Slovenské národné povstanie, or SNP) broke out. It was quashed within two months by German troops, at Tiso's request, but is still remembered in street, bridge and square names throughout the country. Nevertheless, alas, skinheads have made a habit of gathering at Tiso's grave in Martinský Cemetery on the anniversary of the 14 March 1939 declaration of Slovak independence.

POST-WAR AND COMMUNISM In April 1945, Czechoslovakia was 'liberated' by the Red Army. At this time, the Slovak state collapsed and Czecho-Slovakia was once again united, this time as a centralised state based in Prague.

In 1948, the ailing President Beneš (Masaryk's successor, who had spent the war in exile in London) resigned, dying soon after. The Soviets ensured that his place was taken by Communist Party leader Klement Gottwald. A programme of Stalinisation began with five-year plans, arrests, class war and gulags.

THE PRAGUE SPRING On 5 January 1968, the Stalinist First Secretary Antonín Novotný was replaced by a young Slovak reformist, Alexander Dubček. He encouraged civil society and freedom of expression in what was called 'socialism with a human face'. Dubček implemented the 1960 constitution granting Czechs and Slovaks equal rights as separate yet federal states and the optimistic period of 1968 became known as the Prague Spring.

On 21 August 1968, Soviet tanks, supported by Warsaw Pact troops, rolled into Prague, Bratislava and other towns and wiped out all of Dubček's reforms. The Czech and Slovak republics remained separate in name, but the real power stayed in Prague.

The collapse of the communist regimes of eastern Europe in November 1989 enabled the establishment of a democratic government and the restoration of civil freedom and human rights in Czechoslovakia. On 24 November, Dubček appeared on a balcony above Wenceslas Square in Prague alongside playwright, opposition spokesperson and future Czech

1 Visible from all over the city, Slavín Hill is crowned with a magnificent Soviet war memorial to the Red Army soldiers who lost their lives in the battle for Bratislava. **2** The communist-era mural in the main railway station depicts happy workers and peasants. ▶

president, Václav Havel. On 27 November, a general strike was held throughout the country and the people of Bratislava also demonstrated in the streets supporting student movements and the Public against Violence and Civic Forum initiatives. These bloodless demonstrations led to the collapse of the communist government in what was dubbed the Velvet Revolution.

After this, Slovaks were keen for autonomy and in February 1992 rejected a treaty that would have continued with a federal Czechoslovakia. The Czechs and Slovaks could not even agree on whether or not there should be an official hyphen in the name between Czecho and Slovakia.

VELVET DIVORCE AND INDEPENDENCE In June 1992, the left-leaning HZDS (Hnutie za Demokratické Slovensko; Movement for a Democratic Slovakia) won parliamentary elections, led by the populist leader Vladimír Mečiar, a staunch supporter of Slovak independence. Pushed on by Mečiar, the Slovak Parliament proclaimed the sovereignty of the Slovak Republic in July 1992 and the Slovak Constitution was signed on 3 September 1992.

IDENTITY CRISIS

Reflecting the turbulent history and different succession of occupants and occupiers, the city's name has also varied over the centuries. In the Old Town Hall, they have collected all the names:

AD 805 Wratislaburgum
AD 907 Braslavespurch, Bresaulspurch
1038 Breslava Civitas
1042 Brezezburg
1050 Brezalauspurch
1052 Preslawaspurch
1108 Bresburg, Bresburch
1146 Bosonium
1300s–1400s Poson, Posonium
1465 Istropolis (meaning 'City on the Danube')
1500s Posonium Pressburg
1848 Pozsony, Pressburg, Prešporok, Bratislava
1918 Following many centuries of Austro-Hungarian domination, Czechs and Slovaks were so thankful to American President Woodrow Wilson for supporting the establishment of their independent common state, Czechoslovakia, that they renamed Bratislava 'Wilsonovo Mesto' (Wilson City); the new name didn't last for very long
1919 Bratislava – to reflect the brotherhood (*brat* – brother) of Slavs (*slav*)
2006 Young locals sometimes abbreviate the name to 'Blava'
2007 Visiting stag weekenders started calling it 'Partyslava' or 'Bratislover'

On 1 January 1993 Slovakia celebrated the Velvet Divorce, when an independent and sovereign Slovak Republic came into being, followed six weeks later by the election of the first democratic Slovak president, Michal Kováč, once an HZDS ally of Mečiar, but now less of a friend.

For the first years of independence, Slovakia lurked in the shadow of the authoritarian rule of Vladimír Mečiar, a former amateur boxer and inflammatory public speaker. Slovakia became a member of the UN, Organisation for Security and Co-operation in Europe (OSCE), International Monetary Fund (IMF), etc, but the internal politics and economy got into a severe crisis. By 1993 GDP had fallen to 74% of its level in 1989, and previously unknown mass unemployment appeared. Slovak industry, producing until then mainly for the Soviet market, collapsed. Foreign investors also hesitated because of the uncertain political climate. Mečiar carried out a relentless campaign to remove Kováč from office, and rumours abound that he was behind the bizarre 1995 kidnapping of Kováč's son (also Michal), who was blindfolded, given electric shocks to his genitals, forced to drink a bottle of whisky and then driven into Austria in a car boot and dumped.

KEY HISTORICAL DATES Walking around Bratislava's beautiful, peaceful Old Town centre, it's hard to guess its turbulent and busy history, never mind all the different names it has been called. Here is a brief summary of the events which took place within the elegant walls, and for simplicity's sake, the city is always referred to as Bratislava. To check out the ever-changing names, see opposite.

5000BC	Colonisation of the Bratislava region in the late Stone Age
500BC	Illyrians settle in the region now known as Slovakia
100BC	Celts build fortified settlements at Devín and Bratislava and establish a mint producing silver coins called 'Biatecs'
AD100	Gerulata – Roman staging post, today called Rusovce, near Bratislava
AD500	Slavic tribes arrive in the region now known as Slovakia
AD830–906	Great Moravian Empire
AD864	Dowina – the first written reference to Devín Castle in the *Annals of Fulda*
AD907	Braslavespurch – the first written reference to Bratislava in the *Salzburg Almanacs*
AD1000	King St Stephen founds the Christian Hungarian state
1018–1918	Slovakia under Hungarian rule (with brief periods of uprising)
1241	Slovakia invaded by Tatars (1241–42 Tatars plunder Hungary)
1291	The privilege of the Free Royal Town, granted by King András III
1436	King Zsigmond grants a coat of arms to Bratislava (featuring a castle)

1465	Academia Istropolitana, the first university in what is now Slovak territory founded by King Mátyás Corvinus
1526	Battle of Mohács (southern Hungary) – Turks invade the country and Habsburgs assume the Hungarian crown
1536	Buda captured by the Ottomans and the Hungarian capital moves to Bratislava. First session of the Hungarian Parliament in Bratislava (last session in 1848).
1536–1783	Bratislava remains the capital of Hungary, the assembly town and seat of the central administrative offices until 1783 when the capital returns to Buda.
1543	Bratislava becomes the seat of the Hungarian archbishop
1552–1783	The Hungarian royal crown jewels are kept in the Bratislava Castle Crown Tower, then moved to Vienna
1563–1830	Bratislava is the coronation town for 19 Hungarian kings and queens
1683	The Habsburgs defeat the Turks almost at the gates of Vienna
1711	Plague epidemic during which 3,860 people die
1741	Coronation of Maria Theresa in St Martin's Cathedral
1775	Empress Maria Theresa orders the city walls to be pulled down; further development of the city
1776	Establishment of the Theatre of Estates with a permanent company of actors
1780	Establishment of the first manufacturer in Bratislava
1783	Capital of Hungary moves back to Buda
1792	Anton Bernolák founds the Slovak Learned Society in Modra, part of a national cultural awakening in Slovakia
1805	The signing of the Pressburg Peace Treaty in the Primate's Palace after the Battle of the Three Emperors at Austerlitz
1809	Napoleonic troops besiege Bratislava
1811	A huge fire destroys Bratislava Castle
1818	The first steamboat on the Danube River
1840	Horse-drawn railway starts running between Bratislava and Svätý Jur
1843	Ľudovít Štúr codifies Slovak literary language. Before, all literature was written in Czech.
1848	Last session of the Hungarian Parliament in Bratislava
1848–49	Hungarian revolution against Habsburgs
1849	The Slovak National Council developed as the first representative Slovak political body in modern history. Its members spend 1849 co-operating with imperial Vienna to effect the separation of Slovakia from Hungary.
1861	The Martin Memorandum issued in Martin, central Slovakia, urging the establishment of a Slovak district and language within Greater Hungary

1863	Creation of Matica Slovenská (Little Mother of the Slovaks), a cultural and educational foundation
1867	Formation of Dual Monarchy (Austro-Hungarian). Slovaks are subject to ruthless Magyarisation (Magyarosítás).
1886	The present Slovak National Theatre built on the site of the Theatre of Estates
1891	Opening of the first bridge 'Old Bridge' over the Danube
1895	The first tram runs in Bratislava
1918	Bratislava becomes the administrative centre of Slovakia in the first Czechoslovak state, proclaimed a republic on 28 October 1918. Tomáš Masaryk becomes the first president, after the Pittsburgh Agreement in May 1918.
1918	30 October: Martin Declaration. The Slovak National Council votes to federate with the Czechs (they hadn't been informed of events two days earlier in Prague!).
1919	1 January: occupation of the town by Czechoslovak legions and its annexation to the Czechoslovak Republic. The city's name is changed from Pressburg (German) and Pozsony (Hungarian) to Bratislava.
1938	September: Czech President Edvard Beneš lets Germany take Czech lands; Slovaks declare desire for autonomy
1939	14 March: Slovakia forced to declare itself a separate state, the day before Hitler makes Bohemia and Moravia a 'German protectorate'
1941	Jozef Tiso forms quasi-Nazi government, bans all opposition parties and deports 73,000 Jews to Nazi extermination camps
1944	Slovak National Uprising (SNP – Slovenské Národné Povstanie) quashed by German army
1945	Collapse of Slovak State
1945	4 April: Czechoslovakia 'liberated' by Red Army
1946	Foundation of Greater Bratislava by annexing the villages of Devín, Dúbravka, Lamač, Petržalka, Prievoz, Rača and Vajnory
1948	February: the second Czechoslovak state was to be federal, but following communist takeover, administration is centralised in Prague
1968	5 January: Alexander Dubček becomes Party leader (Prague Spring, granting Czechs and Slovaks equal rights). 21 August: Russian tanks roll into Prague, Bratislava and other towns, and quash everything except the declaration on paper of separate but federated Czech and Slovak states. However, the power remains in Prague.
1969	30 October: agreement on the Czechoslovak Federation signed at Bratislava Castle. Bratislava gains official status as the capital of Slovakia.

1971	Bratislava grows as villages of Čunovo, Devínska Nová Ves, Jarovce, Podunajské Biskupice, Rusovce, Vrakuňa and Záhorská Bystrica are annexed
1989	27 November: general strike of citizens of the town, supporting the movements Public against Violence and Civic Forum as well as student movements. Later known as the Velvet Revolution.
1993	1 January: Velvet Divorce – foundation of the Republic of Slovakia
2004	3 March: Slovakia finally joins NATO along with Slovenia, Bulgaria and Romania
2004	1 May: Slovakia joins the EU along with nine other new member states, mostly from central Europe
2006	June: after two terms in office, Mikuláš Dzurinda's right-wing, West-looking government loses the elections to Robert Fico's Smer party
2007	21 December: Slovakia joins the Schengen Agreement, smoothing borders and red tape
2009	January: Slovakia adopts the euro
2013	Košice (page 203), Slovakia's second city, is European Capital of Culture
2016	March: parliamentary elections – Smer remains the largest party but loses its majority; Fico puts together a four-party coalition to remain in power
2018	March: Fico stands down following the murder of a journalist investigating corruption; his deputy Peter Pellegrini takes over as prime minister (but Fico remains leader of the Smer party)
2018	November: independent candidate Matúš Vallo elected as Mayor of Bratislava; re-elected in 2022
2019	March: liberal anti-corruption campaigner Zuzana Čaputová elected president
2020	February: parliamentary elections – Igor Matovič of the OĽaNO party becomes prime minister for three chaotic years
2023	May: technocratic government led by Ľudovít Ódor appointed by President Čaputová; September: early parliamentary elections – Fico becomes prime minister again
2024	April: Pellegrini elected president; May: Fico shot, but survives and returns to work in under two months. He moves closer to Russia and picks disputes with Ukraine and the EU, leading to mass protests.

1 & 2 Bratislava Castle, looking down over the Old Town, and the new Sky Park development encapsulate the city's contrasting historic and modern styles of architecture. ▶

GOVERNMENT AND POLITICS

In May 1997, a referendum was held on NATO membership and also the method of choosing the president. Voting papers were tampered with and Mečiar's boorish replies to reporters resulted in Slovakia being removed from the first group of east European countries lining up to join the EU or NATO.

Many Slovaks blamed the Mečiar government for not doing more to join the EU, by far Slovakia's largest trading partner after the Czech Republic. Slovaks were less upset by the rebuff from NATO; only 46% had voted to join the alliance in the 1997 referendum. Despite calls for early elections, Mečiar managed to hang on until the elections in September 1998, when his HZDS party won the largest share of the vote but was unable to form a government and so lost out to the right-wing coalition of SDKÚ (Slovak Democratic and Christian Union), led by Mikuláš Dzurinda.

In October 2002, Dzurinda won a second term as prime minister, leading a coalition of three centre-right parties in addition to the SDKÚ, which took a liberal, EU-friendly and economically conservative stance.

In June 2004, Ivan Gašparovič was elected president, producing some nervous reactions, as he had been Vladimír Mečiar's right-hand man until just a few years previously. He was re-elected in 2009, but was beaten in 2014 by the independent candidate Andrej Kiska. Kiska is a businessman and philanthropist from Poprad in eastern Slovakia, who founded the charity Dobrý anjel (Good Angel), which helps families in financial difficulties when a relative becomes seriously ill.

Dzurinda's pragmatic West-looking government put the country back on the path to European integration. In March 2004, Slovakia joined NATO along with Slovenia, Bulgaria and Romania, and in May 2004, Slovakia joined the European Union along with nine other states in the largest expansion in EU history. In 2007 Slovakia and eight other states joined the EU's Schengen area for passport-free travel (page 44), and in January 2009 Slovakia leapt ahead of its neighbours and adopted the euro. This has boosted the economy, and Bratislava has benefited from EU funds, with the complete reconstruction of the Old Bridge and brand-new fleets of bright red buses and trams.

NEW FRIENDS, OLD ENEMIES The President of the Republic is elected directly by the citizens and remains in office for five years. The 150 members of the Slovak Parliament and the government are elected for a four-year term. After serving two terms, the Dzurinda government lost the elections of June 2006. Robert Fico's left-wing Smer–Sociálna demokracia (Direction–Social Democracy) party entered into an apparently bizarre coalition with the far-right Slovak National Party (SNS) led by Ján Slota and Vladimír Mečiar's HZDS-LS. The two parties had formed a coalition government between 1994 and 1998 and were criticised for their extreme policies. Mečiar's government had led Slovakia into international isolation in the 1990s, while the SNS is well known for its harsh rhetoric targeting minorities such as Hungarians, Roma and homosexuals. According to Slota, 'Hungarians are the cancer of the Slovak nation', 'Slovaks should jump into their tanks and flatten Budapest' and, 'the best policy for Gypsies is a long whip in a small yard'. In 2003, Slota stirred up controversy again when he suggested that Roma men should be offered money in exchange for undergoing sterilisation. The left-wing Smer's alliance with the extreme-right SNS was without precedent in European politics, and the new government came under attack immediately by European politicians and the economic elites.

Fortunately, as a part of the coalition agreement, neither Slota nor Mečiar obtained a government position. However, they and Fico formed the Slovak Coalition Council, exercising considerable power behind the scenes.

NEIGHBOURLY RELATIONS Mečiar's brutish populist stance did not help relations with the neighbours. A law passed in 1995 recognised Slovak as the only official language, meaning that officially the large Hungarian minority could not use their mother tongue in public places. Equally, on the other side of the fence in Hungary, Viktor Orbán's right-wing government of 1998–2002 did little to endear itself to the Slovaks, especially with the Status Law, which promised dual nationality and extra benefits for all Hungarians living beyond Hungary's borders. Numerous attacks, both verbal and physical, on the Hungarian minority in Slovakia fuelled ethnic tensions.

In the 2010 parliamentary elections, the Fico government was replaced by Iveta Radičová, Slovakia's first female prime minister, and her SDKÚ-DS (Social Democratic and Christian Union-Democratic Party), who led a centre-right coalition government. After only two years in office, Radičová lost a vote of confidence after a dispute on eurozone bailout and, in 2012, Fico and Smer took power again. In the 2016 parliamentary elections, Smer remained the largest party but lost its majority, as a far-right nationalist party, Kotleba – People's Party Our Slovakia (ĽSNS), entered parliament for the first time, while the SDKÚ-DS and centre-right Christian Democratic Movement (KDH) both fell short of the threshold for representation. Fico put together a four-party coalition to remain in office.

In February 2018 a contract killer shot dead the investigative journalist Ján Kuciak and his fiancée, Martina Kušnírová; Kuciak had been investigating tax fraud and possible links to the ruling party. Mass protests led to the resignation of the Fico government; the deputy prime minister, Peter Pellegrini, took over and reappointed some of them, but Fico remained as party leader. In March 2019 the liberal environmental lawyer Zuzana Čaputová was elected president, reflecting continuing anti-government feeling a year after the murder of Kuciak and Kušnírová. The March 2020 parliamentary elections were won by a coalition led by OĽaNO (Ordinary People and Independent Personalities), an anti-corruption movement led by the maverick Igor Matovič. His government became increasingly chaotic, and more populist, stridently opposing civil unions, abortion and drug reform, and even Sunday shopping.

When Covid-19 hit in 2020, it seemed at first that Slovakia had a magic formula protecting its population, with a very low death rate in the first wave, but reality caught up later, with a higher toll, many vaccine refuseniks, and a government thrown into crisis over a secret deal to buy Russian Sputnik vaccines, not approved for use in the EU. Ministerial resignations forced Matovič to swap posts with Finance Minister Eduard Heger (also OĽaNO) in March 2021, but this also fell apart and in May 2023 the president appointed the witty economist Ľudovít Ódor to head a caretaker government of experts.

In September 2023, Fico's Smer–SSD won early parliamentary elections and formed a coalition government with Hlas and SNS. One of Fico's first moves was to confirm that Slovakia would not support sanctions on Russia or supply military aid for Ukraine, although the country's entire fleet of MiG-29 fighters had already been donated, and the private sector can still supply weapons.

In April 2024 Fico's ally (as a rule) Pellegrini was elected president. Shockingly, in May 2024 Fico was shot five times as he left a meeting in Handlova in central Slovakia – with breathtaking aplomb his allies at once blamed journalists for spreading division, when in fact it was the government doing just that, while the 'lone wolf' gunman was probably radicalised on social media.

Fico returned to work in less than two months. He continues to be a boorish figure, presenting himself as pro-Kremlin and anti-migrant, and attacking NGOs. The Special Prosecutor's Office and the National Crime Office, fighting high-level corruption, have been abolished, and the public broadcaster RTVS lost its independence. The Minister of Culture has also purged the heads of bodies such as the National Theatre and the National Gallery. There have been big protests, and in 2024 the European Parliament election was won by the leading pro-European party Progresívne Slovensko (PS), giving some hope to those opposed to the Putin/Orbán playbook.

In the 1970s the communist government planned for Bratislava to be a city of a million people by 2050, although in fact it's now less than half that size. Introduced in March 2024, the *Bratislava 2050* masterplan reflects this reality – in fact over the last two decades about 100,000 residents have moved into nearby villages (in Austria and Hungary, as well as Slovakia), while mobile phone tracking shows that 571,000 people are in Bratislava on an average weekday. The introduction of PAAS car-parking permits has caused those who actually live in Bratislava to register there, and those who have left to similarly regularise their status.

ECONOMY

THE TATRA TIGER Slovakia's economy was a slow starter after the Velvet Divorce from the Czech Republic (1 January 1993; page 13) but in recent

> ## MOTOR CITY SLOVAKIA
>
> Slovakia is the world leader in car production per capita and planned investments and the launch of new models ensures it will stay at number one.
>
> The story begins in 1991 when Volkswagen bought the Czech carmaker Škoda; in 1992 they opened a new factory in Devínska Nová Ves, near Bratislava, to produce Passats and then Golfs. They also produced gearboxes for many VW models, with a new factory in Martin, 230km northeast of Bratislava, opening in 2000. The Devínska Nová Ves plant took on production of the SEAT Ibiza and Porsche and Audi SUVs; when it began manufacturing the Škoda Octavia in 2008 it meant that all four VW brands were represented here, with 5 million cars produced by 2017.
>
> In 2008, a huge car manufacturing plant for PSA Peugeot Citroën (now Stellantis) sprang up in less than a year, in Trnava, just 50km from Bratislava, and was soon joined by Kia Motors Slovakia in Žilina.
>
> In October 2018, Jaguar Land Rover, a division of India's Tata Motors, launched production of Defenders at a new plant in Nitra, 75km east of Bratislava, providing at least 1,500 jobs.
>
> Since 2016, over a million cars have been produced in Slovakia, making the country the world's leading producer per head of population.
>
> These factories were all located in the western part of the country, and there are questions about whether there is enough skilled labour remaining, as Slovaks are traditionally reluctant to travel or move for work. Therefore Volvo is building a large carbon-neutral plant near Košice, where more labour is available, to open in 2026.

years it has become the envy of the region. Dubbed the 'Tatra Tiger' after the mountains that are the country's spiritual symbol (and inspired by the 'Asian Tigers' of the late 20th century), the economy boomed between 2000 and 2008, and GDP growth remained above 3% from 2015 until Covid knocked it back.

Slovakia mastered much of the difficult transition from a centrally planned economy to a modern market economy and came out smelling of roses. The Dzurinda government, spearheaded by Finance Minister Ivan Mikloš, made excellent progress during 2001–04 in macroeconomic stabilisation and structural reform, largely completing the privatisation process. The banking sector is almost entirely in foreign hands, and the government facilitated a foreign investment boom with business-friendly policies, such as the labour market liberalisation.

However, the most attractive measure came on 1 January 2004, when the government cut both income and corporate taxes to a flat 19%, dramatically changing the economic landscape of the entire region and luring many international companies away from neighbouring countries. Slovakia now had one of the best investment environments in Europe, with the lowest overall tax burden of any EU and OECD countries. There were mutterings during the 2006 elections that the Fico government would do away with the flat tax but this did not happen until after the 2012 elections when they introduced a 25% higher rate of income tax, and raised corporate tax to 23%. Since 2011, there are two rates of Value Added Tax: the standard 20% rate and a reduced 10% rate on books and medical supplies.

The labour force is highly educated with 93% of Slovaks benefitting from secondary or higher education, and 18% of the working-age population of Bratislava is active in knowledge industries, a higher proportion than in any other European capital. The infrastructure is good, with both transport and communication easy as Bratislava sits at the geographical crossroads of the new Europe.

Since the end of communism, multi-nationals such as IBM, Johnson Controls, Fujitsu, Samsung, Coca-Cola, Whirlpool, Henkel, Siemens, Heineken and South Africa Breweries launched operations in Slovakia; however, the biggest investments have been in car plants (page 21).

Slovakia's economic growth outpaced most of the EU, and from 2005 to 2011 its GDP grew by 38.3%, the highest rate of any EU country. Due to Covid, the economy shrank in 2020 but recovered to grow by 3.3% in 2021; since then, however, it has underperformed, with growth of 1.8% in 2022 and 1.6% in 2023. The year-on-year inflation rate peaked at 12.1% in 2022, but fell to just below 3% in 2024.

Unemployment rose to 6.9% in 2021 and fell to 5.8% in 2023. The rate is half what it was a decade ago but remains stubbornly high in the far east of the country, which still suffers from poor infrastructure. It takes more than 5 hours to get to the isolated east by bus, whereas Vienna is less than an hour by car and Budapest just under 2 hours. Slovakia hopes to use EU funds to develop the far-east regions. The service industry needs to be overhauled and the country's natural treasures will be improved to develop tourism.

MEMBERSHIP OF THE EUROPEAN UNION Slovakia joined the EU on 1 May 2004 along with nine other mostly central European countries. Countries like Slovakia, Poland, Hungary and the Czech Republic are at present less wealthy than most other EU countries, but they are catching up fast, as more investors look eastwards. In 2024 it was calculated that Slovakia's GDP is 16.2% higher per capita than if it had not joined the EU. From 2004 to 2022, Slovakia received €36.2 billion from the EU, while its contribution to the EU budget was €11.7 billion. In 2024, a survey asked a representative sample of Slovaks whether EU membership was a good or bad thing; 60% said it was good.

PEOPLE

Swamp-and-conifer men they looked, with faces tundra-blank and eyes as blue and as vague as unmapped lakes which the plum-brandy was misting over.
From *A Time of Gifts*, Patrick Leigh Fermor,
recalling his 1934 visit to Bratislava.

It's hard to recognise Leigh Fermor's depiction of Slovaks in the go-getting youth rushing about today's Bratislava from business meeting to business lunch or dancing the night away in fashionable nightclubs. It's impossible to generalise, but many Slovaks share a love for nature and the family. They like nothing better than to escape the city for a trek through the woods, finishing up with a huge, hearty meal washed down with fantastic beer, fiery spirits or quality Slovak wine.

Slovaks embody the stereotype of Slavic hospitality, tempered by a generous portion of dour realism. However, they are neither grumpy like their Hungarian neighbours nor uptight like the Austrians over the river. Slovaks welcome visitors with open arms, and usually an open bottle. Then there's the legendary razor-cheek-boned beauty of Slovak females with their unfeasibly long legs, deriving from a fascinatingly exotic gene pool. Many top models are from Slovakia.

The difference in atmosphere between Bratislava and Vienna or Budapest is marked. It may be because Bratislava is smaller and more manageable, but the people are more relaxed and have more time to sit and enjoy a coffee, beer or glass of Slovak wine at one of the hundreds of terrace cafés in the Mediterranean-style capital. However, it's not all rosé in Bratislava.

Slovaks have chips on their shoulders about the Czechs, and with reason. Only in the past couple of decades has the dynamic Slovak economy allowed them to hold their heads high in the region after years of being treated like a problematic little sister. It still rankles that most people think the greatest stars of Czechoslovak ice hockey, football and Olympic teams of the past were Czech, as many were Slovak.

Bratislava locals are a brainy lot. Imagine living in a town where often old Pressburg families have three first languages, and not the easy ones either: Slovak, Hungarian and German are widely spoken, and nowadays most younger people will speak English, too. Situated strategically at the meeting point of three countries, three cultures and three languages, Bratislava can take the best of everything and has developed a cosmopolitan outlook, adapting well to its position at the geographical heart of the new EU.

There is quite a lot of jealousy from other parts of the country that Bratislava gets the best of everything. It is closer to Vienna than to many other Slovak cities, in terms of both geography and attitude. Towns in the far east feel neglected and there is a problem of demographics as almost all students leave to study in Bratislava then decide to stay there, causing a brain drain in towns further east and a desperate housing shortage in the capital. However, more than 300,000 Slovaks, mostly young people, have left the country in the past 15 years; while the number of foreigners with permanent residence in Slovakia has doubled, rising to almost 60,000.

Around 600,000 ethnic **Hungarians** live in Slovakia, mostly in the south and east of the country. The Slovak Constitution of 1992 guarantees the rights of minorities and most Hungarian children receive education in their mother tongue. Politically, Slovakia and Hungary are always arguing; in private Slovaks and Hungarians get along fine. However, in 1996 the Mečiar government did not help relations by making Slovak the only official language, revenge perhaps for ruthless Magyarisation in the past.

The **Roma** are the second-largest minority group and it is estimated that as many as half a million live mostly in the neglected eastern regions with no amenities, high unemployment and almost no schooling. Under communism, everybody had to have a job, but now potential employers can openly display their prejudices and reject Roma workers. Roma children are tested in Slovak instead of their own language then dumped in 'special schools'. On the Roma side, integration into Slovak society is also difficult because of the complicated caste system and community ties.

In World War II, 80,000 Slovak Roma escaped extermination because the Germans occupied Slovakia only after the Slovak National Uprising (SNP) in 1944. The communists provided homes and jobs for the Roma, but in the process destroyed their nomadic lifestyle.

The remaining **Jewish** population (fewer than 4,000) of Slovakia live mostly in Bratislava and Košice. They are the smallest Holocaust-surviving community in Europe and are mostly elderly. However, many younger people have rediscovered their Jewish roots and the Union of Jewish Youth is fairly active. The **Ruthene** (Rusyn) minority lives in the Slovakian far east and across the border in Ukraine. They have a distinct culture, but it's at risk as many young people leave to find work elsewhere.

The ethnic make-up of Slovakia is 85.8% Slovak, 9.7% Hungarian, 2.3% Roma (although the Roma community is continually under-reported, and estimated at more than 500,000), 0.8% Czech, 0.4% Ruthene, 0.2% Ukrainian, 0.1% German, 0.1% Polish (0.6% other).

RELIGION AND BELIEFS

Some 56% of Slovaks say they are **Roman Catholic**, although in practice they are not as fervent as their northern neighbours, the Poles, but rather more enthusiastic than the Magyars to the south. Young Slovaks are also more devout than the Czechs. The Roman Catholic Church is the largest in Slovakia followed by the Evangelical Church of the Augsburg Confession (the Lutherans) and the Greek-Catholic Church. The first Christian church in Slovakia was founded in AD833 in the city of Nitra. The late Pope John Paul II visited Bratislava in 1990, 1995 and 2002, and the city is one of the few in the world visited by His Holiness three times.

Orthodox and Greek-Catholic believers are found in the north and east of the country, where the Orthodox icons resemble those of Russia. The beautiful wooden churches of Ruthenia in eastern Slovakia hold Greek-Catholic/Orthodox treasures.

Until World War II, the **Jews** played a significant role in Bratislava's multinational, multi-cultural population. According to the Jewish Museum, there is evidence Jewish merchants operated in the Roman province of Kvadia, now Slovakia. After the anti-Jewish riots in western Europe in the 11th century, many Jews found refuge in Bratislava and during the Middle Ages the Jewish community had established itself, with certain privileges and rights. In 1750, some 15,000 Jews lived in Bratislava, in a ghetto between the town walls and Castle Hill. Židovska ulica (Jewish Street) still recalls part of this district. Bratislava was a centre of Jewish Orthodox education, led by rabbi Moshe Schreiber (Chatam Sófer, whose mausoleum can be visited; page 179) and a yeshiva founded in 1806 was the only university in the city.

When Slovakia allied itself to Hitler's Germany, around 74,000 Slovak Jews were deported; the survivors emigrated after the war and today fewer than 4,000 remain in the entire country, with 800 in Bratislava. At one time there were 29 synagogues in Bratislava. The main synagogue and much of the Jewish district was demolished to make way for the construction of Staromestská, the main road leading to Most SNP. Today, one synagogue can be found on Heydukova ulica and there is a large cemetery to the west of town.

Like most post-communist countries in the region, Slovakia has its fair share of **'new' religions**, moving into the supposed spiritual vacuum: Jehovah's Witnesses, Mormons, Baha'is, Hare Krishnas and Scientologists are all active in Bratislava.

CULTURE AND FESTIVALS

Much as it pains them to admit it, Slovak history and culture, including literature, are bound up inextricably with that of Hungary.

LITERATURE From the 10th century until 1918, the country was known as Upper Hungary and during the Middle Ages a dialect of Czech was used alongside Hungarian, German and Latin. **Surviving texts** from the region, the earliest known being the 11th-century *Legends of Saints Svorad and Benedict*, are all in Latin. The earliest specimens of Czech vernacular are 15th-century town documents and devotional texts, such as the *Spiš Prayers* from 1480. Magyar culture blossomed during the enlightened rule of Hungarian King Mátyás Corvinus, who founded the Academia Istropolitana in 1465.

In 1787, Catholic priest and linguist Anton Bernolák published his *Grammatica Slavica* and in 1790 he created a massive six-volume **dictionary** of Slovak–Czech–Latin–German–Hungarian, published in 1827 after his death. In 1792, Bernolák helped found the Slovak Learned Society and stirred a national cultural awakening in the country. The first writer to use Bernolák's *Slovak* was Juraj Fándly, although more successful was another Catholic priest Ján Hollý (1785–1849) who translated Virgil's *Aeneid* and wrote on emotive Slovak–Slav themes such as the *Svatopluk* (1833) about the Moravian prince. Hollý is considered the founding father of Slovak poetry and there's a statue of him seated in a courtyard just behind St Martin's Cathedral (page 158).

In 1843, Ľudovít Štúr **codified** the Slovak literary language. He started a Slovak-language daily paper in 1845 and in literature stressed the importance of local and original writers. Three poets, Janko Kráľ, Ján Botto and Andrej Sládkovič, personified the folk romanticism of the Štúr generation. Kráľ was a strange, solitary figure who battled against the Hungarians. Sládkovič is best known for the long poem *Marína* inspired by an unhappy love affair.

To learn more about life in the Slovak countryside, we can also turn to the eccentric Hungarian author Kálmán Mikszáth (1847–1910) who described life in Felvidék with a gentle ironic humour. His novel *Beszterce ostroma* (*The Siege of Beszterce*) appears surprisingly contemporary in theme. But for many the best author from Slovakia was another Hungarian, Sándor Márai (1900–89), who was born in Košice; *A gyertyák csonkig égnek* (*Embers;* 1942), his first novel to appear in English, is a poignant evocation of the lost multi-cultural Habsburg world but also an insight into the era in which it was written.

Klára Jarunková (1922–2005) is one of the few female writers to be translated from Slovak. Her novels for teenagers have a psychological sensitivity and fresh charm. A book to look out for is by Martin Šimečka (b1957), the son of a well-known Bratislava-based Czech dissident writer, Milan Šimečka. His autobiographical novel *Džin* was translated as *Year of the Frog*.

Oppressed by the Hungarian language, Slovak writers found more success in **poetry**. The lawyer Pavol Országh Hviezdoslav (1849–1921) was the most creative of the period. His acclaimed long narrative poem *Hájnikova žena* (*The Gamekeeper's Wife*) celebrates the freedom of the countryside opposed to the moral corruption of some of the aristocracy. In the years preceding World War I, a group known as the 'Slovak Literary Moderna' appeared with Ivan Krasko at the forefront, describing atmospheric, melancholic moods. After World War II, Stalinism restricted creativity with its emphasis on dreary Socialist Realism. Ladislav Mňačko (1919–94) became the leading Slovak literary dissident describing the life of a corrupt communist politician in *Ako chutí moc* (*The Taste of Power*) in 1967.

ART For visual arts, a trip to the Slovak National Gallery (page 178) reveals the wealth of early religious painting from the region. Pavol of Levoča was the most outstanding Gothic sculptor. Baroque art by painters such as Ján Kracker and Jakub Bogdan is found in churches across the country. The 19th-century Slovak National Revival threw up a crop of Slovak painters. The solitary, strange Hungarian painter Ladislav Medňanský (1852–1919) was born in Beckov in what is now Slovakia. He depicted the vivid Slovak landscapes and lives of tramps and poor people with great power. Many of his powerful paintings can be seen at the Slovak National Gallery. Under communism, statues were chunky Soviet Constructivist. Július Bártfay created numerous World War II monuments, including the Slavín Monument. Nowadays, Bratislava is bulging with private galleries, many of which have artwork for sale. Check out page 170 for a list of places to spot a new Slovak master, or mistress.

CINEMA Slovak cinema is not as well known abroad as Czech. Few films were made in Slovakia before World War II. After the war, the light-hearted *Katka* (1949) by Ján Kadár was a big hit. In 1953, the first film studio, Koliba, opened in Bratislava, creating a backbone for Slovak cinema to this day. The 1960s saw a 'new wave' of Slovak cinema as Kadár joined with Elmar Klos to create *Obchod na korze* (*The Shop on Main Street*) in 1965, which won an Oscar. In the 1970s, Dušan Dušek and Dušan Hanák made powerful, gritty documentaries, and often their films were banned by the communist authorities. The best-loved director is Juraj Jakubisko (b1938) whose films reflect and comment on life in Slovakia. *Tisícročná vcela* (*A Thousand-year-old Bee*; 1983) and *Sedím na konári a je mi dobre* (*I'm Sitting on a Branch and I'm Fine*; 1989) are classics. In 2007, Jakubisko finished filming *Bathory* about the notorious 'Blood Countess' of Čachtice with English actor Anna Friel as the lady Dracula. Slovak cinema has struggled in recent years. However, Slovakia's stunning scenery, the high-quality Koliba and L+S studios, experienced crews and a favourable economic climate make the country a top location destination for film companies. Many Hollywood films use the natural beauty as a bargain-priced backdrop. Orava Castle was used as a setting for *Nosferatu* back in 1922, and more recently Herzog's *Nosferatu the Vampyre* (1979), *Dragonheart* (1996), *The Peacemaker* (1997), *Uprising* (2001), *Behind Enemy Lines* (2001), the fantasy *Eragon* (2006), *The Last Legion* (2007), *Red Sparrow* (2010) and *A Boy Called Christmas* (2021), as well as Mark Gatiss's TV version of *Dracula* (2020), were all filmed in Slovakia, at least partly.

MUSIC As for music, Bratislava was visited by many of the greats: Mozart, Haydn, Bartók, Liszt and Beethoven (page 124), many of whom studied within the Old Town walls and gave concerts. Home-grown music star Johann Nepomuk Hummel (1778–1837) was a pupil of Mozart and Haydn and a friend to Beethoven and Paganini. Composer, teacher and the first great piano virtuoso, he created music in many styles and the house where he was born can be visited at Klobučnícka 2. In the 18th century, Slovaks wanted to redefine their **folk-music heritage** and composers used folk motifs in classical compositions. Mikuláš Schneider-Trnavský and Ján Levoslav Bella were the most well known. Communism stifled **modern music** in the second half of the 20th century, although Eugen Suchoň (1908–93) and Jan Cikkér (1911–89) have solid reputations. There was also a significant jazz movement, led in the 1960s by bands such as Combo 4, the Bratislava Jazz Quartet, the Medik Quintet and Traditional Club Bratislava. Jazz clubs are popular in Bratislava today and there are several places to hear live music. Peter Lipa (b1943), head of the Slovak Jazz Association and chief organiser of the country's largest jazz festival, is an iconic figure, known as the 'father of Slovak jazz'. As a singer, he has made 19 albums including *Beatles in Blue(s)*, which sees him covering songs by his teenage idols. A good introduction to Slovak jazz can be found on his website (**w** peterlipa.com). Rock and pop artists are popular with singers such as Paľo Habera and his former band, Team. Reggae is also thriving in the Slovak capital alongside ambient music, death metal and the inevitable techno.

Perhaps because of the diversity of influences on the land – Celtic, Roman, Hungarian, Slavic German and others – Slovakia has a remarkably varied **folksong** and **dance heritage**, which was particularly common in the 17th and 18th centuries. A popular tale told of a real-life Robin Hood figure, Juraj Jánošík (1688–1713), who led a group of bandits in northern Slovakia and was executed in the main square of Liptovský Mikuláš. The *fujara* is an instrument unique to Slovakia that looks like a didgeridoo but is played like a flute. The folk revivalist Tibor Koblíček uses many folk styles on his album *My Dear Pipes*, using the mournful drone of the *fujara*, the *hurdy gurdy* and other traditional instruments.

FESTIVALS AND EVENTS Bratislava celebrates a range of events throughout the year. Tickets and more information are available online and from the outlets of **w** ticketportal.sk and **w** eventim.sk (page 121).

January

Days of Open Wine Cellars in Svätý Jur
w terroir.sk. Visitors can taste the liquid treasures of the wine cellars at this village close to Bratislava. For more on the Small Carpathian Wine Route, see page 198.

ITF Slovakiatour The International Travel Fair; **w** incheba.sk. This event is held annually at Incheba, Bratislava's huge exhibition & convention site.

Slovak Winter Food Festival
w zimnyfestivaljedla.sk. A month-long

1 The Cirkul'ART International New Circus Festival with its alternative circus acts and street performers is great fun for all the family. **2** Learn about traditional Slovakian crafts during August's ÚĽuv Master Craftsmen Days festival. **3** Traditional costumes are still worn at folk festivals. **4** White Night festival held in October celebrates music and contemporary art. ▶

festival for food lovers with participation from top Bratislava restaurants.
Slovak Winter MTB & Running Trophy w stupavskymaraton.sk. A mountain-biking & forest-running winter marathon in the hills behind Stupava Castle.

February

Convergences Festival w konvergencie.sk. The annual chamber music festival creates space for artists & music lovers to enjoy different music genres & meet chamber music personalities from around the world.
Pezinok Wine Cellars w muzeumpezinok.sk. Annual tasting sessions of the best wines from Pezinok & the surrounding wine-producing region. Organised by the Small Carpathians museum in Pezinok.
Pressburg Ball Prešporský Ball; w presporskybal.sk. The former coronation city has a rich history of balls, but they're less stuffy than the Viennese equivalent.

March

Easter Market w visitbratislava.com. Lots of little stalls selling painted eggs (kraslica), traditional willow whips (korbáč) & other gifts in Františkánske námestie & Hviezdoslavovo námestie.

April

Bratislava City Days Bratislavské Mestské Dni; w bratislava.sk/en. At this time of year, the Bratislava local government arranges a series of open days, so everyone can check up on the work, activities & services of the town & its organisations. The date is historical as the Mayor of Bratislava was traditionally elected on St George's Day (24 Apr), based on a charter by King András III who granted Bratislava many municipal privileges. St George is also the city's patron saint. During the w/end nearest that date (known as Open Bratislava), many historic buildings are open & there is no admission charge for museums & galleries.
Craft Beer Festival w salonpiva.beer. In the Old Market – at the 10th festival in 2024, 40 micro-breweries presented over 200 different beers.
ČSOB Bratislava Marathon w bratislavamarathon.com. On the 1st Sunday of Apr, now established as one of the great sporting events in the Slovak calendar.
Flóra Bratislava w incheba.sk. The international fair of flowers & garden technology at the Incheba exhibition hall on the right-hand embankment of the Danube River. For more than a quarter of a century, Bratislava has been filled with the heady aroma of fresh flowers in mid-Apr.
National Running Race Národný beh; Devín–Bratislava; w devin-bratislava.eu. For the last 72 years, the people of Bratislava have been celebrating the arrival of spring with a national race from Devín to Bratislava, a distance of 11.6km. This is the oldest running race in the country.
Pezinok Wine Show Vínne Trhy Pezinok; w zpvv.sk, pezinok.sk. An international competition, exhibition & enthusiastic tasting of wines at the Culture House of Pezinok, near Bratislava.

May

Bratislava Rag w bratislavskymajales.sk. Free concerts & fireworks by the Danube on the 1st w/end of May.
Cirkul'ART International New Circus Festival Malacky; w cirkulart.sk. Held in Malacky, this brings together modern & alternative circus acts & street performers – great fun for kids in particular.
Creative Streets Festival Artists gather from around the world to paint huge murals on the sides of high buildings.
Festival of Traditional Crafts at Červený Kameň Castle w hradcervenykamen.sk.

Part of the summer season of family-friendly events held at this castle.
Napoleon's Siege of Bratislava
w slovakia.travel/en/the-napoleons-siege-of-bratislava, abbyart.sk. A re-enactment of the 1809 siege in Sad Janka Kráľa.
Night of Museums and Galleries
w nocmuzei.sk. Pan-European event on the occasion of the International Day of Museums.
St Urban's Day in Pezinok w mvc.sk. A celebration of the patron saint of wine-growing in 121 cellars across 20 villages. A wine lovers' meeting with music & homage to the statues of St Urban.

June

Bratislava Beach w visitbratislava.com/places/magio-beach; ⏲ Jun–Sep. The Bratislava Beach opens in Jun on Tyršovo nábrežie on the right bank of the Danube in Sad Janka Kráľa & offers a sandy beach, volleyball, tennis, drinks & snacks, including a fresh fruit market, free Wi-Fi, concerts & an open-air cinema.
Bratislava Castle Festival An international festival of arts & culture. For 13 w/ends, the main courtyard of Bratislava Castle is the scene of a series of concerts, classical & contemporary music. There's also a summer Shakespeare theatre & many other performances.
Bratislava Choir & Orchestra Festival
w choral-music.sk. A w/end in mid-Jun when amateur choirs & youth orchestras from across the world perform, mainly in the city's churches.
Bratislava Organ Festival
w visitbratislava.com/events/bratislava-organ-festival; ⏲ Jun–Jul. Mainly organ recitals, mostly at St Martin's Cathedral.
Coronation Days w korunovacie.sk, visitbratislava.com/coronation-days. An annual event to bring visitors & locals closer to the rituals of the coronation of 19 kings & queens in Bratislava. Participants drink wine from the fountain, shout '*Vivat rex!*' ('Long live the king!'), feast on an ox roast & dance in the streets. Actors in period costumes take solemn vows before making a regal procession through the Old Town, & celebrations end with the dubbing of knights & much merrymaking.
Cultural Summer w bkis.sk; ⏲ Jun–Sep. A feast of music, dance, singing, crafts, amusements & gastronomic delights in Bratislava.
Weekend of Open Parks & Gardens
w vopz.sk. Usually closed gardens open for the w/end, in addition to the public ones.

July

Bratislava Film Festival
w bratislavafilmfestival.com. Replacing Nov's International Film Festival, this is broader-based & less competitive.
Summer Shakespeare Festival Bratislava Castle; w wshakespeare.sk. Open-air performances of Shakespeare plays at Bratislava Castle, some in English & some in Czech or Slovak.
Viva Musica! w vivamusica.sk. The biggest international summer festival of classical music in Bratislava, throughout Jul & Aug.
Wine and Lavender Pezinok; w zpvv.sk. Tasting sessions of wines made by Pezinok wine-growers & a tour of the lavender gardens in the region of Stará hora.

August

Brass Bands in Pezinok w pezinok.sk. The 16th annual international competitive festival for brass bands takes place in Pezinok, with 4 European countries participating.
Festival of Forgotten Crafts
w remeselnyfestival.schatmansdorf.sk. A historic handicrafts show with an accompanying cultural programme at Červený Kameň.

Knightly Games w hradcervenykamen.sk. At Červený Kameň Castle. A presentation of the art of knights, accompanied by more cultural programmes.

Úľuv Master Craftsmen Days w uluv.sk/en. Traditional makers' stalls in the pedestrianised Old Town over the last w/end of Aug. Staged by Úľuv, an organisation that specialises in folk-art production, traditional crafts & specialist collaborations, & has its own network of retail shops with a good selection of embroidered items, colourful folk costumes, woollen fabrics, glass painting, Easter eggs & wooden crafts.

Uprising Reggae Festival w uprising.sk/en. One of central Europe's biggest reggae w/ends, at Zlaté Piesky.

September

Bratislava Music Festival Bratislavské Hudobné Slávnosti; w bhsfestival.sk. Slovakia's most prestigious festival of classical music, now running for more than 40 years, in Sep & Oct. An integral part of the festival is the international tribune of young performers.

Craft Beer Festival w staremesto.sk. Try dozens of beer varieties & different beer specialities while enjoying live music in the Old Market Hall.

Freestyle Kayak w divokavoda.sk. Competitions of rodeo kayaks close the professional sport season at the Divoká Voda Water Park at Čunovo.

Roman Games in Gerulata-Rusovce w muzeumbratislava.sk/anticka-gerulata. Gladiatorial fights (non-fatal) & other games, as well as recreated Roman food & drink.

Slovak Food Festival w slovakfoodfestival.sk. The largest picnic in the city, full of great food, drinks, live shows & competitions, is held at Bratislava Castle.

Small Carpathian Vintage Festivals w pezinok.sk, raca.sk (search 'Račianske hody'). A celebration of wine with a show of grape processing, pressing & tasting. On different w/ends at Pezinok, Modra & Rača, along the Small Carpathian Wine Route (page 198).

Stupava Trophy w stupavskymaraton.sk. The MTB Marathon & mountain-bike races take place in the meadows of Stupava.

October

Apple Feast w moska.sk. A regional event with traditional & new apple specialities. In villages all around Bratislava: Modra, Pezinok, Senec, Svätý Jur, Malacky, Jablonové, Limbach, Dunajská Lužná & suburban areas of the capital.

Biennial of Illustrations Bratislava w bibiana.sk/en/biennial-illustrations-bratislava. Takes place throughout Oct, every other (odd) year. The international competition is an exhibition of illustrations of books for children & young people.

BLAF – Festival of Visual Art w visitbratislava.com/events/bratislava-art-festival. The BLAF (Bratislava Art Festival) takes place in the courtyard of the Slovak National Gallery & showcases contemporary art.

Bratislava Design Week w bratislavadesignweek.sk. The International Contemporary Design Festival takes place at venues throughout Bratislava.

Bratislava in Motion w abp.sk. The International Festival of Contemporary Dance presents the most remarkable achievements of Slovak contemporary dance as well as exceptional talents from neighbouring countries. At the New Thread Factory (Nová Cvernovka).

Bratislava Jazz Days w bjd.sk. Bratislava's main jazz festival runs over a w/end in Oct.

Bratislava Mozart Festival w bratislavamozartfestival.sk. Not only Mozart, but high-class music in beautiful venues such as the Primate's Palace & the cathedral.

Cabbage Days Stupava; w mkic.sk. Dni Zelá – a festival of feasting on cabbage at the village of Stupava, near Bratislava.

One World International Documentary Film Festival w jedensvet.sk. A 6-day programme of films that focus on human rights.

White Night w bielanoc.sk. A big festival of music & contemporary art in Bratislava in early Oct & Košice the following w/end.

November

Christmas Market w bratislava.sk; 20 Nov–22 Dec. One of the most popular events in Bratislava. The Christmas Market fills the Main Sq with stalls offering traditional arts & crafts. See also page 142.

Days of Open Cellars MVC w mvc.sk. The Small Carpathian Wine Region (page 198) holds this annual event for wine lovers.

European Night of Theatre w nocdivadiel.sk. A Europe-wide event including theatrical performances & other events where actors interact with the audience.

Ice skating on Hviezdoslav Square From Nov to Mar, an ice rink appears in the beautiful setting of Hviezdoslavovo námestie, in front of the National Theatre's historic building.

St Martin's Days w bratislava.sk. A celebration of young wine with gastronomic events. The feast day of St Martin of Tours, on 11 Nov, is the traditional day for tasting the new wine; this festival is always held on the nearest w/end.

December

International Festival of Advent & Christmas Music w choral-music.sk/en/Festivaly/listing. Choirs from across the world gather for a w/end of seasonal singing.

New Year's Eve Party in the City w bratislava.sk. New Year's Eve in Bratislava has a unique atmosphere. Around 50,000 people gather in the tiny Old Town centre & are joined by several thousand tourists to enjoy live concerts, open-air discos & other cultural events. The climax is the midnight fireworks show over the Danube & the luminous animations on the river embankment.

New Year's Eve Run across Bratislava Bridges w starz.sk. A running event for those who can't imagine New Year's Eve without sport. The route leads across all the bridges in Bratislava & along the banks of the Danube.

St Nicholas's Day & the Lighting of the Christmas Tree An event to celebrate Svätý Mikuláš (St Nicholas), who visits on 6 Dec, with presents & lots of chocolate for the children.

CULTURAL ETIQUETTE

GET UP, STAND UP On trams, trolleybuses and buses, it is expected that young people and men will stand up and give their seat to an elderly traveller or pregnant woman. If they don't notice, it will be pointed out by all those in surrounding seats and severe chastisement will follow.

CZECHO-SLOVENIA Be sensitive to the fact that Slovakia has always played second fiddle to the Czech Republic (never even getting its own guidebook until Bradt's, in 2007) and remember the difference between Slovakia and Slovenia. Nationals of both are equally irritated by the inability of the Western media (CNN, BBC, USA Today) and even certain US presidents (page 1) to tell these two very different countries apart. The wrong anthem is constantly played at sporting events, but things got ridiculous in March 2018 when the prime ministers of both countries resigned – possibly to troll those who couldn't tell them apart.

FORMALITIES Office workers and civil servants can be very formal when addressing colleagues. Older-generation workers insist on using *Pani* (Mrs) or *Pan* (Mr) plus the surname even if they've known the person for years, and the colleague is younger (but more important).

Slečna' (Miss) is also used. The polite *Vy* (thou) is used instead of the familiar *ty* (you). Foreigners attempting to speak Slovak should use the formal version to be safe, until told otherwise.

NAME DAYS In Slovakia, each day of the year corresponds to one or more personal names (based on the Roman Catholic calendar of saints, still shown on most Slovakian calendars). People celebrate their name day (*sviatok*, or more recently *meniny*) on the date corresponding to their own given name. The name day is not as important as the birthday for a Slovak but still a recognised event, which you should ignore at your peril. Traditionally, friends, family, colleagues and fellow students should be presented with flowers, chocolates, alcohol or a small gift and say *Všetko najlepšie k meninám* ('All the best for your name day').

'-OVA' NAMES You will soon notice that all female surnames end in '-ova' or '-ová'. For example, if the husband's surname is Smith, the wife or daughter is Smithova. In the past, '-ova' meant 'belonging to'. Although the ownership connotation has faded, the use of '-ova' continues today, signifying the person is female. These days, with the rise of feminism, not all Slovak women like the use of '-ova'.

ICE, ICE BABY The older generation of Slovaks have a morbid fear of ice in drinks. Ice cubes in drinks can cause sore throats or, worse still, pneumonia. This seems somewhat illogical when you can get a lovely chilled beer or even ice cream from an outdoor stall in the bleak midwinter.

OXYGEN PHOBIA Don't open a window on the tram, even in the height of summer; fresh air is thought to be dangerous in draught form. Also, if you have a small child, make sure you take a hat and scarf to Bratislava for them, even in midsummer, or you risk incurring the wrath of Slovak grannies berating you for endangering your tiny tot's health.

GREETINGS It is customary to say 'hello' or 'goodbye' when entering/leaving a shop, lift, office or quiet café. To enter without a word is considered ill-mannered. There are many ways of saying hello and goodbye in Bratislava.

Dobrý deň is used with elderly neighbours, business associates, waiters and shop assistants.

Ruky bozkávam ('I kiss your hands') is a very formal greeting which melts grannies' hearts. *Dovidenia* is the polite goodbye, though the more final *zbohom* ('*adieu*') can be used.

Dopočutia ('until I hear you next') is used to say goodbye on the phone.

Ahoj and *čau* (pronounced 'ciao') are the most common informal greetings. These words serve as both hello and goodbye. *Ahoj* ('me hearties') sounds like it came from sailors.

Servus comes from the Latin 'I serve' and is also popular in Hungary and Austria.

HOME VISITS If lucky enough to be invited to a Slovak home, take a gift. Alcohol always goes down well – a bottle of excellent local white wine, *slivovica* (plum brandy) or the gin-like *borovička* (juniper brandy). Chocolates and flowers are welcome with the hostess, but don't take dried flowers or even-numbered bunches as these have a morbid significance. You will also be expected to remove your shoes at the door and don grandpa's old slippers. Slovaks are incredibly hospitable. The Slovak expression *Hosť do domu, Boh do domu* means 'A guest in the home is like God in the home'.

KEEP RIGHT When approaching somebody on a narrow pavement, getting on or off public transport or negotiating a crowd, remember to pass on the right as per driving. Try to pass on the left and you'll throw a local (who goes right instinctively) off balance and you'll probably collide. As for the many tourists who flood the Old Town, it's impossible to judge which way they'll go!

LGBTQIA+ LIFE Bratislava has several gay clubs, although outside the capital LGBTQIA+ get-togethers are few and far between. Old and young Slovaks alike are quite religious and conservative in attitudes and, although they are tolerant by nature, it would not be advisable to stroll through town hand in hand with your same-sex partner.

DRINK AND DRUGS People over 18 can buy alcohol and cigarettes. The consumption of alcohol in public open spaces is forbidden, although you will see homeless people gathering in Bratislava's squares with a bottle or two. Bratislava locals are getting increasingly irritated by groups of UK stags lurching loudly around the Old Town in varying stages of inebriation. In 2006, a band of partiers, fuelled by bargain beer, knocked over and damaged the statue of Schöne Náci. Cannabis is illegal and even small amounts for personal consumption are not tolerated. The law doesn't distinguish between hard and soft drugs when handing out sentences, so think twice before lighting up a joint.

TRAVELLING POSITIVELY

LOCAL CHARITIES

Iniciatíva Inakost Initiative Otherness; PO Box 15, 810 00; 02 5244 4187; e inakost@inakost.sk; w inakost.sk. A voluntary civic initiative to support members of the LGBTQIA+ community with links & activities.

International Women's Club of Bratislava IWC; Hotel Crowne Plaza, room 1757, Hodžovo námestie 2; e charity@iwc.sk; w iwc.sk. Meets from 10.00 on the 1st, 3rd & 5th Mon of the month for coffee at the Crowne Plaza Hotel; they raised over €85,000 for Slovak charities in 2018.

Nota Bene OZ Proti prúdu, Karpatská 10; 02 5262 5962; e protiprudu@notabene.sk; w notabene.sk. A *Big Issue*-style magazine for the homeless to sell. *Nota Bene* (€2.80) is a member of the International Network of Street Papers (INSP; w insp.ngo), a global association of 115 street papers in 36 countries around the world, launched by *The Big Issue* in 1994. In Bratislava, it is supported by local celebrities & actors.

Rómsky Inštitút Roma Institute; Dobrovičova 126/3; 02 5556 3015; e info@romainstitute.sk; w romainstitute.sk. Community centre, library & children's activities for members of the Roma community.

Sloboda Zvierat Freedom for Animals; Pod Brehmi 1A; 02 16 187; w slobodazvierat.sk. Founded in 1992, this organisation provides 2 shelters for the many stray dogs & cats. They also campaign against the long-distance transportation across Europe of live animals, cruel farming methods, bears kept in captivity & animal experimentation.

Slovenský Červený Kríž Slovak Red Cross; Grösslingova 24; 02 5710 2301; e sekretariat@redcross.sk; w redcross.sk

Unicef Michalská 7, PO Box 52, 810 00; m 09 03 770 418; e info@unicef.sk; w unicef.sk

Úsmev ako dar Smile as a Gift; Ševčenkova 21; 02 6381 5209; e info@usmev.sk; w usmev.sk. Slovakia's oldest & biggest voluntary body for the support of abandoned children, aiming to 'let every child have a family'. There is a strange law in Slovakia that doesn't allow a child to be adopted if the real parent visits the children's home at least once a month, preventing many adoptions.

From this angle, there's no sign of the major highway passing within metres of St Martin's Cathedral; instead there's a view to the towers of the Sky Park development. ▶

2

Planning

A PRACTICAL OVERVIEW

Central Bratislava is small, neat and compact and you will not find it easy to get lost. Having said that, the twisting, turning streets of the compact Old Town may get a bit confusing after sampling the excellent local brews!

Bratislava's **Old Town** and the castle are separated by the main road Staromestská leading to the Most SNP (SNP Bridge). To build this bridge and flyover section of the road in 1972, the Jewish synagogue and ghetto were demolished. The Danube (Dunaj, pronounced 'doon-eye') runs along the south side of the Old Town, flowing west to east as it passes through Bratislava on its way from the Black Forest to the Black Sea.

The **business area** of Bratislava lies to the east of the Old Town, as well as to the north, clustered around Námestie SNP, although some banks and offices are found within the Old Town too.

The communist-era housing of **Petržalka** spreads out on the southern side, or right bank, of the Danube, an enclave of Slovakia that lies between the Danube and the borders with Austria and Hungary. This was notorious as a concrete jungle during the communist era, but its apartment blocks have been updated and are now stylish and brightly coloured, and there is in fact plenty of green space.

Five **bridges** (*most*) cross the Danube in Bratislava, the most recognisable being the Most SNP 'Slovenské národné povstanie' ('Slovak National Uprising'). This is also called the UFO Bridge by tourists because of the flying saucer spaceship and UFO café that perches on top of the eastern column. The Most SNP was previously known as 'Nový Most' ('New Bridge') but was usurped by a newer structure, the elegant white arc of the Most Apollo (Apollo Bridge), which opened in 2005.

The Starý Most (Old Bridge) linking the Old Town with Sad Janka Kráľa has been rebuilt to carry only trams, bicycles and pedestrians. Funded by EU money, it opened in time for the Slovak Presidency of the European Union in the second half of 2016. Trams used to run across this bridge all the way to Vienna (page 189).

Bratislava's M R Štefánik Airport is 9km northeast of the city and several top business hotels are found en route. Many people, however, especially those coming from outside Europe, find it just as easy to fly into Vienna's Schwechat Airport then take a 1-hour minibus transfer or taxi ride along the 61km road to Bratislava.

WHEN TO VISIT (AND WHY)

Slovakia achieved independence only in 1993 and, as one of Europe's youngest capitals, Bratislava is also one of its most progressive. There's never been a better time to visit.

It takes only 2½ hours to fly there from London, while on the ground it is an hour from Vienna, two from Budapest and three from Prague. The 'little big city' is a strategic hotspot with a leisure industry to match.

Spring and summer in Bratislava can be really gorgeous. Come during **April** and you'll probably have the place to yourself, apart from the occasional stag party (easily identified and avoided by their matching T-shirts proudly announcing 'Gary's Gang' or 'Plastered in Blava'), but the weather can be glorious. At the end of the month, out come all the terrace tables and chairs outside the pubs, restaurants and cafés, turning the Old Town into 'one big open-air café'.

In the height of **summer**, the Danube River moderates the heat and there are many green spaces such as Devín and the Kamzík Hills to escape to, countless lakes to cool off in (the nearest being Zlaté Piesky, a tram-ride away), and scores of leafy squares.

The **autumn** colours are beautiful. There are many parks in town and it is still warm enough to sit outside a café and contemplate the historic scenery. **Winter** is also atmospheric, with the snow, the Christmas markets and the hills nearby if you want to ski or hike. Do bear in mind that some museums and castles such as Devín may be closed during this season, and shops and bars also have limited opening hours.

WORDS TO GET AROUND

ulica	street	*námestie* (*nám*)	square
cesta	road	*most*	bridge
záhrada	garden	*sad*	park
pešia zóna	pedestrian zone	*les*	forest
veža	tower	*cintorín*	cemetery
mýto	toll gate	*schody*	steps
pošta	post office	*Hlavná stanica*	main railway station
autobusová stanica	bus station	*Dunaj*	Danube

> **POCKET-SIZED, FAIRYTALE CITY**
>
> Bratislava promotes itself as 'the little big city', highlighting the positive attributes of this pocket-sized capital. Promotional films from the last decade depict Slovakia as a 'fairyland' (▶ 'Slovakia fairyland' to watch it) with images that would not look out of place in *Lord of the Rings*. The Slovak Tourist Board in the USA (w slovakia. travel/en) discovered that nature, hiking, historical landmarks and Bratislava are the biggest draws for tourists.

HIGHLIGHTS AND SUGGESTED ITINERARIES

STAYING A WEEKEND

- Walk along the coronation route of Hungarian kings through the **Old Town** (look for the little brass crowns set into the pavement) or, if you're feeling lazy, sit on the tiny Prešporáčik red tour 'train' (page 65).
- Check out the history of the country in the **Slovak National History Museum** (page 167) and take in a breathless view from the Crown Tower. Sit out on the lawn and admire the view of the Danube and the Brutalist concrete blocks of Petržalka (page 192), past the UFO café.
- Travel up the lift to the **UFO restaurant and bar** (page 101) for a spectacular, panoramic view of the Old Town centre, the castle and the Kamzík Hills in the distance.
- Soak up the sun on a pavement terrace in the beautiful Old Town; Bratislava is packed with **cafés, bars, pubs and restaurants** (page 95).
- Walk up to the **Slavín Monument** (page 159) for a view of the business heart of the city and, in the other direction, over to Bratislava Castle and the UFO.
- Take the bus to **Devín Castle** (page 195) for a Sunday afternoon stroll among the castle ruins and along the Danube and Morava riverbanks.
- Work your way through half a dozen excellent **local beers**, finishing off with a shot of *borovička* or *slivovica*.
- Try the Slovak national dish; ***bryndzové halušky*** – gnocchi with sheep's cheese and bacon bits.
- Take in a performance of world-class **opera** at spectacularly low prices; good seats for €19 (page 121).
- Visit the **Blue Church** (page 152), one of the most amazing churches in Europe, seemingly covered in blue icing.

---

1 New Year's fireworks over the castle and St Martin's Cathedral. **2** One of Bratislava's many green spaces, the Medical Garden is a pleasant place for a summer stroll or picnic. ▶

NOT TO BE MISSED – THE TOP TEN

1. OPERA AT THE SLOVAK NATIONAL THEATRE The historical building and the new building by the Danube are both architectural masterpieces, and the performances are world class, too. Page 121.

2. BRATISLAVA CASTLE Bratislava's iconic castle contains an excellent museum and the grounds are the perfect spot for a picnic with a view. Page 153.

3. UFO RESTAURANT AND BAR The restaurant is top-notch and the view from the observation deck is outstanding. Page 101.

4. KOLIBA-KAMZÍK AND VEŽA The revolving restaurant on the top of Kamzík Hill has a spectacular view of three countries: Slovakia, Austria and Hungary. Pages 101 and 116.

5. DEVÍN CASTLE This scenic castle makes a great day-trip destination for walks along the Danube and Morava rivers. Page 195.

6. BLUE CHURCH The lovely little church dedicated to St Elizabeth is an Art Nouveau gem. Page 152.

7. PÁLFFY AND MIRBACH PALACES These historic buildings have fabulous interiors and galleries to match. Both page 157.

8. ST MARTIN'S CATHEDRAL Once the coronation venue for Hungarian monarchs, this little cathedral packs a big punch. Page 158.

9. MICHAEL'S TOWER The historic tower can be climbed for a great view over the Old Town. Page 155.

10. BOROVIČKA AND BRYNDZOVÉ HALUŠKY Don't miss the chance to try these local specialities in a Slovak *krčma*. Pages 95 and 90.

STAYING A WEEK OR LONGER

- Take the trolleybus to **Koliba-Kamzík** (page 184) and, after a tramp through the woods, enjoy a slowly spinning view of Bratislava and its surroundings from the Veža restaurant or café (pages 101 and 116) at the top of the TV tower.
- Hire a **kayak** and paddle along the Danube (page 137).
- Hire a **bike** and do one of the tours along the riverbank, visiting the sights along the old 'Iron Curtain' border (page 62).

- Travel the length of the **Small Carpathian Wine Route** (page 198), sampling along the way.
- Visit the largest medieval cellars in central Europe at **Červený Kameň** (page 201).
- Visit **Košice** (page 203), Slovakia's second city, to get a feel of the east. Don't miss a Tokaj wine-tasting session!
- Visit the **Gabčíkovo Dam wildlife region** and see the **Danubiana Meulensteen Modern Art Museum** (page 162) at Čunovo.
- Take a boat trip to **Vienna** or **Budapest** (page 77), or visit underrated **Brno** by train.
- Try relaxation at its best on a weekend break at **Piešťany Spa** (page 202).

TOUR OPERATORS

Package holidays, city breaks, tailor-made tours and flights are readily available through UK- and US-based tour operators specialising in eastern Europe. See page 62 for local tour operators, some of which can arrange accommodation etc.

UK

Funktion Events Chester CH1 1DA; 0161 341 0052; w funktionevents.co.uk/stag-do/slovakia/bratislava. A palette of stag activities, from drinking & strippers to rafting, shooting & more drinking, but without accommodation included.

Great Rail Journeys York YO1 8NL; 01904 521 936; w greatrail.com. Offers 2 Danube cruises (8 days from £1,195, 11 days from £1,595).

Interhome Ltd Godalming GU7 1EX; 020 8068 9950; w interhome.co.uk. Accommodation in apartments, private houses or villas.

Intrepid Travel UK London N1 0NU; 0808 274 5111; w intrepidtravel.com. Offers 4 trips to Slovakia, including cycling the Danube (8 days for £1,593). There's also a branch in Melbourne, Australia (+0808 274 5111, 1300 854 439).

Last Night of Freedom Gateshead NE8 3AH; 0191 499 8750; w lastnightoffreedom.co.uk. 'For the more sophisticated stag or hen…' Mix-&-match stag parties with accommodation & beer, shooting, etc.

Martin Randall Travel London W4 4GF; 020 8742 3355; w martinrandall.com. High-class cultural tours, including 8 nights in Slovakia for £3,450.

Responsible Travel 01273 823700 (phone lines 09.00–18.00 Mon–Fri); w responsibletravel.com. Independent Brighton-based broker offering dozens of interesting trips to Slovakia (5 days from £580). No shop front.

Tucan Travel London W3 9QP; 0800 804 8435; w tucantravel.com; also in New York (+0800 804 8435; w tucan.travel). Features Bratislava & Slovakia on many tours of the central European region.

IRELAND

Abbey Travel Dublin; +353 1804 7100; w abbeytravel.ie. City breaks & adventure holidays.

USA AND CANADA

Trip Central Hamilton, Ontario L8R 2K3; +1 800 665 4981 (in Canada & USA); w tripcentral.ca. With 2 dozen trips to

Bratislava, including a Central Europe tour (Frankfurt to Prague, Vienna, Bratislava, Budapest & Kraków; 15 days from CAN$3,007).

NATURE SPECIALISTS Paul Stanbury, Naturetrek's Slovakia specialist, writes, 'Slovakia is every bit as exciting for birds as its larger neighbours, yet has attracted little attention from birders or other naturalists. When you consider that Slovakia is home to all of Europe's 9 species of woodpecker, many owl species including Ural, Tengmalm's & Pygmy, eagles, wallcreeper, warblers, wagtails & much more, I'm sure its reputation as a top birdwatching destination will grow. I recommend visiting while it's still virtually untouched by tourism, & discover it for yourself.'

Naturetrek Hampshire GU34 3HJ; 01962 733051; **w** naturetrek.co.uk. Offers a fascinating 'Slovakia – Birds of the Mountains & Plains' tour (8 days from £1,895).
Probirder **w** probirder.com. Based in Budapest, wildlife & bird expert & Bradt author Gerard Gorman & his team specialise in tours of the eastern European states.

RED TAPE

In 2007, Slovakia joined the Schengen Zone, abolishing border controls among participating countries. After entering the Schengen Zone, visitors may travel throughout the now 29-member zone without any other passport or visa control; however, they must be able to prove their visa status on request.

Slovakia now has only five actual border posts (with Ukraine) and three air borders, at Bratislava, Košice and Poprad airports.

ENTRY REQUIREMENTS Note that, from the last quarter of 2026, citizens of visa-exempt countries, including the UK, USA, Canada and Australia, will be required to pay a fee and obtain an ETIAS travel authorisation (**w** travel-europe.europa.eu/etias_en) in order to enter Slovakia. A new Entry-Exit System (EES; **w** travel-europe.europa.eu/ees_en) was also set to be introduced in late 2025, to replace the requirement for stamping passports. Check before you travel.

All visitors to Slovakia need a valid passport for the duration of their stay in the country or, if a visa is required, visitors must present a passport with more than three months left till the date of expiry. Citizens from EU member countries and Switzerland can enter Slovakia with just a valid national identity card (where the country concerned issues such cards).

Citizens of other EU countries (and of the European Economic Area and Switzerland) may visit Slovakia with a valid passport for up to three months, and need a residence permit to stay longer. Nationals from 40 countries worldwide, including Australia, Brazil, Canada, Croatia, Israel, Japan, Malaysia, Mexico, New Zealand, South Korea, the UK and the USA, may also stay in Slovakia, or anywhere in the Schengen area, with a valid passport for up to 90 days out of any 180-day period.

Nationals from all other countries require a visa and should contact the Embassy of the Slovak Republic in their home country before setting off. For more information on Slovak embassies and consulates abroad, see below. Visit **w** foreign.gov.sk/en/web/en for details of current visa requirements.

CUSTOMS REGULATIONS Travellers over 16 can take 200 cigarettes, 100 cigarillos, 50 cigars or 250g of tobacco (or a combination of the respective amounts), 250ml of cologne and 50g of perfume in and out of Slovakia. As for alcohol, you can carry in one litre of spirits or two litres of wine, but you'll find much better prices in the Bratislava supermarkets so why bother lugging over a load of bottles? Save your energy for picking up a nice bottle of *borovička* to take home and tempt your maiden aunts. A maximum of ten litres of petrol can be carried in canisters for emergency use and presents and other items up to the value of €430 can be brought in and taken out of the country. Pets can be transported only with all the necessary pet passports and vaccination certificates. Antiques and works of art require a licence and are subject to customs duty.

If you drive from Slovakia to the UK in your own car, then the booze-cruise limit could apply. In reality, the EU ruling is a guideline rather than a hard-and-fast law, and the key phrase in the debate is 'for personal use', or how much alcohol and nicotine the average person might reasonably consume. In terms of what you can fit into the back of a car, the limits are quite generous. For the record, they are: 800 cigarettes, 200 cigars, 1kg of tobacco, 110 litres of beer, 90 litres of wine, ten litres of spirits and 20 litres of fortified wine. For more information, see **w** gov.uk/duty-free-goods/arrivals-from-eu-countries.

SLOVAK EMBASSIES ABROAD For a list and contact details of all Slovakia's diplomatic missions abroad, go to **w** mzv.sk/en/web/en/ministry/slovak-diplomatic-missions/diplomatic-missions-of-the-slovak-republic.

GETTING THERE AND AWAY

BY AIR Travellers to Bratislava are lucky as they have a choice of two airports – Bratislava and Vienna Schwechat – giving more variety of route, cost, timing and budget flight possibilities. Ticket prices will be higher during peak summer season (June–August) and at Christmas and New Year.

Discount travel websites such as **w** cheapflights.co.uk, **w** expedia.com, **w** lastminute.co.uk and **w** skyscanner.net can offer bargain flights.

Bratislava Airport (BTS; M R Štefánik; 02 3303 3353; **e** information@airportbratislava.sk; **w** bts.aero/en) This is 9km (5 miles) northeast of the city centre.

From the UK Flights from London take around 2 hours 20 minutes.

Ryanair w ryanair.com. Ryanair has a major base in Bratislava, with flights to London Stansted, Manchester, Leeds-Bradford and Edinburgh (from £25 one way, not including baggage allowance, seating, priority boarding, etc) as well as European destinations: Athens, Brussels, Dublin (daily; 2hrs 50mins; from €30 one way), Eindhoven, Malta, Milan, Palma, Paris Beauvais & Rome. The airline now also flies from London Stansted to Košice (page 203) and Poprad.
Wizz Air ❘ 0330 977 0444 (UK call centre); w wizzair.com. One of central Europe's largest low-cost carriers offering cheap flights from London Luton, from £18 one way, not including baggage allowance, seating, priority boarding, etc.

From the US and the rest of the world There are no direct flights from the US to Bratislava; instead fly to Vienna then go by land (45mins by shuttle bus; opposite), or stop somewhere like London & take a low-cost flight from there.

Airport transfers These are operated by the non-stop **Airport Service** (m 09 40 987 600; e info@airportservice.sk; w airportservice.sk), who can also arrange transport to airports in Vienna, Brno, Ostrava, Prague and Budapest. Bus 61 (30mins; €1.10) runs every 20 minutes to Bratislava's main railway station, from where tram 1 or bus 93 will take you to the city centre in 5 minutes. There's one bus ticket machine inside the airport terminal that accepts cards and more basic ones, accepting coins and offering a more limited range of tickets, at the stop outside and to the right; on the bus, there are automated announcements in English and real-time information screens, plus free Wi-Fi. Bikes can be carried, and there's also the N61 night service covering the same route. You can change at Račianske mýto from bus 61 to tram 3 to Petržalka or bus 21 to the bus station. Taxis are also available (20mins) and cost around €20–25; booking in advance with Uber or Taxify will halve the cost. **Aerobus** (❘ +36 70 931 6926; w aerobus.hu) offers transfers to Györ (HUF2,112/€6) and Budapest (HUF4,612/€12) airports. Alternatively, there are also many car-hire firms at Bratislava Airport arrivals (page 76).

Vienna International Airport (Schwechat) (VIE; w viennaairport.com) Vienna International Airport (61km from Bratislava) is the regional gateway for intercontinental travellers. There are more flights (including budget) and a greater range of airlines and flight times than from Bratislava.

Austrian Airlines ❘ 03701 242625; w austrian.com. Flies from London Heathrow to Vienna 5 times a day; fares from £133 return.

Germanwings w germanwings.com. Weekly flights from London Heathrow to Vienna, via Cologne-Bonn or Düsseldorf, with fares from £120 one way.

Ryanair w ryanair.com. Flies from London Stansted & Edinburgh to Vienna, with fares from £22.

Airport transfers Trains from the airport to the city centre run every few minutes and take 15–22 minutes (avoid the expensive Airport Express); there are also bus links to all parts of Vienna. From Vienna's Hauptbahnhof station there are hourly trains to both Petržalka and Bratislava Hlavná stanica, both taking about an hour. A return ticket costs €18 and includes tram and bus travel in Bratislava. For more details, see Austrian Railways (w oebb.at). RegioJet (w regiojet.com), Slovak Lines (w slovaklines.sk) and Flixbus (w flixbus.co.uk) run buses roughly hourly from central Vienna via Vienna Airport to central Bratislava and Bratislava Airport (from £7.50 in advance). **Bratislava Airport Taxi** (↘+421 903 853359; e info@go-limousine.sk; w bratislava-airport-taxi.com) will take up to four passengers from Vienna Airport to Bratislava city centre for €70.

Košice Airport
(KSC; w airportkosice.sk/en) This serves Slovakia's second city, Košice (page 203), and is the gateway to eastern Slovakia. Return flights from London Luton, Stansted, Liverpool and Dublin start from around £15, if booked well in advance.

Lufthansa w lufthansa.co.uk. Comfortable airline, which flies daily from London Heathrow, Manchester, Edinburgh & Birmingham, via Munich or Frankfurt.

Ryanair w ryanair.com. Flights from London Stansted & Liverpool from just £15 – if booked well in advance, with no extras.

Wizz Air ↘UK call centre: 0330 977 0444; w wizzair.com. Flies from London Luton (2hrs 40mins) from £25 one way.

BY TRAIN
If you don't fancy flying, or want to stop off en route, try the train. First cross the Channel by Eurostar (w eurostar.com) to Brussels and on to Köln (Cologne), then take the Nightjet sleeper to Wien (Vienna). Slovak State Railways (w zsr.sk/en) and The Man in Seat 61 (w seat61.com/slovakia.htm) have information in English about train connections. See above for connections from Vienna to Bratislava. You'll arrive at Bratislava's bustling main station, Hlavná stanica, less than 24 hours after leaving London.

Main railway station (Hlavná stanica)
The main railway station is overcrowded but traveller-friendly with signs and announcements in Slovak and English (plus German for the trains to Vienna). In the state railways customer centre (⏰ 07.05–17.35 daily) is a BTB (Bratislava Tourist Board) **information desk** (⏰ 09.00–13.00 & 13.30–17.00 daily). There are several cafés (some with Wi-Fi), snack stalls and waiting rooms (*čakáreň*).

'OH, VIENNA!'

If you fancy popping over to Vienna on the train or boat, or you find yourself in the Austrian capital after a long flight connection, never fear! There's plenty to do. One money-saving idea is to buy the Vienna Card (w viennapass.com), which offers not only unlimited travel on Vienna's efficient public transport (for one, two, three or six days), but also admission discounts on museums, sightseeing trips, theatres and concert halls. Here are some ideas:

ST STEPHEN'S CATHEDRAL In the heart of the city by the Kärntner Strasse and Graben pedestrian streets, this is often the setting for organ concerts. You can also view the reliquary chamber, and Emperor Friedrich III's magnificent red marble sarcophagus can be seen in all its splendour from the organ loft, now open to the public.

MUSEUMS AND GALLERIES Vienna has lots of fascinating museums; see the full list at w wien.info/en/sightseeing/museums-exhibitions/top. In particular, don't miss Klimt's *Kiss* at the Belvedere, or the Brueghels at the overwhelming Kunsthistorisches Museum.

SADDLE UP Vienna is cobwebbed with a network of bicycle routes. Hire a bike (w pedalpower.at) and try a guided tour without wearing out your shoe leather.

VIENNESE COFFEEHOUSES The Viennese certainly take their coffee seriously; after traipsing around the vast museums and never-ending ring roads of the Austrian capital, you will too.

There is also a left-luggage office (*úschovňa batožín*; ⓘ 04.00–23.55 daily with breaks 06.15–06.30, 10.30–11.00, 16.45–17.00 & 21.30–21.45) where you can leave your bags for the set price of €2.50 (up to 15kg) or €3 (over 15kg). Bicycles can be left for €2. There are ATMs, and a waiting room upstairs (with Wi-Fi).

At the ticket counters, many of the staff speak English, and several windows are open 24/7. The private operator RegioJet also has a ticket counter (ⓘ 02 3810 3844; ⓘ 08.00–11.30 & noon–16.30 daily) for its four daily trains to Brno and Prague, as does Leo Express for its trains to Komarno (ⓘ 07.35–20.00 daily). A return ticket to Budapest costs €17.80, to Prague €28, to Brno €10 and to Vienna Hauptbahnhof €18. Tickets can be bought on the day, along with seat reservations, which are required on most fast trains. The website w zssk.sk/en has a user-friendly page in English where you can plan your rail travel, buy tickets and discover special train trips in historic vehicles. For local travel within the Bratislava integrated

The local tradition of coffeehouses goes back to the 17th century, when legend has it that a Hungarian, György Kolschitzky, opened the first coffeehouse, Zum Roten Kreuz, in Domgasse with a stock of coffee beans captured from the Turks. He had bravely taken messages through the enemy lines that encircled the city in 1683, and when they abandoned the siege, he received the coffee as a reward; he had been a Turkish prisoner and knew to add milk and sugar to the bitter brew. Cakes, newspapers and perhaps live music are all part of the Viennese recipe. Coffeehouses became popular during the 18th-century reign of Empress Maria Theresa, but only really established their international reputation at the start of the 20th century, when they became the favourite meeting place for artists, journalists, philosophers, political activists, literati and middle-class socialites. Two of my favourites in Vienna include:

Café Central Cnr Strauchgasse & Herrengasse; +43 1 533 3763; w cafecentral.wien/en. This is one of the most beautiful & serene cafés in Vienna. A favourite of poets Arthur Schnitzler & Peter Altenberg, architect Adolf Loos & revolutionary Leo Trotsky, the interior is like a monastery, with pillars & vaulted ceilings in light yellow stone. Apparently, Trotsky spent many an afternoon dozing over his newspaper & milky coffee; nobody thought he looked the type to lead a workers' revolution. Try the famous Imperial Torte as you gaze around the old Austrian uncles & guess which one will be the most likely to start a riot. €€

Café Hawelka Dorotheergasse 6; w hawelka.at/en. This is a typical artists' hangout, decorated with the original paintings of some of the now-famous fantastical realists who left paintings in lieu of payment. €€

transport area, there are two ticket machines in the station hall, as well as at the tram and bus stops.

If catching a train, be aware that – for instance – if your train is on 4, this means platform 4, not track 4 (which is actually on platform 2). This should become clear when you are in the station.

Transfers From the main hall, turn left and go down the escalator to the **tram** terminus from where tram 1 takes you to the Centrum and Jesenského stops on the edge of the Old Town. Go straight out of the station for **buses** – route 93 heads for Petržalka via the Old Town centre, and route 40 runs to the bus station at Mlynské nivy.

Alternatively, there are banks of **taxis** who'll do the same for a reasonable €10. If you're worried about Bratislava cabbies' undeserved bad reputation, ask about the price first, but you'll probably hurt his feelings and he'll point tearfully to the meter.

Petržalka railway station South of the Danube in the heart of the Petržalka suburb, this station is served by trains every hour to Vienna Hauptbahnhof, taking approximately 1 hour, and every couple of hours to Rajka (20mins), on the Hungarian border. From the platform, go down to the underpass and then to the east side for buses 93/94 to the city centre and the main station, or to the west side for bus 80 to the centre and Kollárovo námestie. It's a small station, but there is an ATM and shops.

Rail passes InterRail (w interrail.eu) offers discount rail travel in 33 countries across Europe, with passes or travellers aged under 28 starting at €171 for four days during a month, to €574 for three months continuous (second-class youth tickets). Adults and seniors can also buy first- and second-class tickets for similar time periods. Possibly more useful are passes allowing four, five or seven days' travel in a one-month period, or ten or 15 days in a two-month period. The **InterRail Global Pass** is not valid for travel in one's home country; however, a one-country pass for Slovakia costs from €47 for three days in one month, to €104 for eight days in one month for a second-class youth ticket, while adult tickets for the same time period cost €48–108 (second class).

The **Man in Seat 61** (w seat61.com/slovakia.htm) is the best source of information on travelling overland from the UK to Bratislava. Booking an afternoon Eurostar to Brussels and the night train to Vienna plus the connection to Bratislava should cost you from £88 one way (plus £20–70 for a couchette or sleeper berth). Through-tickets can be booked online at w thetrainline.com, costing from £133. Slovak State Railways (ŽSR or Železnice Slovenskej Republiky; w zsr.sk) gives information about connections.

Once in Slovakia, EU citizens over 62 years old are eligible for **free train travel** – take your passport and a passport photo to the customer service centre at the main station to be issued a pass. However, you will still need a zero-cost ticket and usually a reservation, as there's a strict quota for free travel on each train.

BY COACH OR BUS It is possible to travel to Bratislava by bus/coach from all major European cities; Eurolines (w eurolines.eu) and Flixbus (w flixbus.co.uk) are the most widely used companies.

Bratislava's **main bus station** is at Mlynské nivy 31 (♀ 221 J4; ☎ 02 5542 2734; w nivy.com/en/buses); it's a modern complex beneath the new Nivy shopping centre. It's a 15-minute walk from here to the Old Town centre, but too far to walk with luggage. Taxis will whisk you into town, or take bus 42 to Hodžovo námestie, bus 21 to the main railway station or bus 50 to Most SNP.

The national bus company, Slovak Lines (w slovaklines.sk), offers tickets, travelcards and timetables, for destinations within Slovakia. RegioJet (w regiojet.com), Slovak Lines and Flixbus (w flixbus.co.uk) run buses roughly hourly via Vienna Airport to central Vienna (from £8 in advance).

In addition, FlixBus and RegioJet both run twice a day to Budapest city and airport (4hrs). These also use the local bus terminal beneath the SNP bridge.

BY CAR It is about 1,500km by road from London to Bratislava and the journey would take at least 17 hours. The route, once on the continent, goes via Brussels, Aachen, Köln (Cologne), Frankfurt and Linz.

You need to buy an e-vignette to use Slovak motorways, at w eznamka.sk/selfcare/purchase (from €12 for ten days; windscreen stickers are no longer used). You'll also need a vignette to cross Austria (€11.50) – best bought from a service station as you approach the border.

For information on car hire, see page 76.

Traffic regulations The road signs correspond to European norms. The speed limit in the cities and villages is 60km/h, outside the cities and villages 90km/h, and on highways 130km/h. Safety belts must be worn. Drivers are strictly prohibited from drinking alcohol.

BY BOAT International connections from Austria and Hungary are possible on the Danube, which also carries passing barges and cruises heading for the Rhine, the Main and the Black Sea. The Slovak company LOD and the Austrian Twin City Liner work together to offer high-speed river services between Vienna and Bratislava, taking just 90 minutes (from €34 each way). These depart from Vienna for Bratislava at 08.30, 12.30 and 16.30 (Fri–Sun, holidays in Mar/Apr/Oct & May–Sep daily), returning to Vienna 2 hours later; and at 09.00 Mon–Thu in Mar/Apr/Oct, returning at 16.00. LOD also offer a day trip to Budapest about once a month, and regular cruises to Čunovo and Devín (page 195).

LOD Fajnorovo nábrežie 2; 02 5293 2226; w lod.sk/en; 08.00–16.00 daily. Their office is 5mins' walk from Hviezdoslavovo námestie, by the Slovak National Museum; walk past the Reduta towards the Danube, cross the main road, then turn left & walk along the embankment. The LOD building has a small bar & 3 souvenir shops. In Vienna, departures are from the Schiffstation Schwedenplatz between Marien & Schwedenbrücke (bridges): +43 1 904 8880; e booking@twincityliner.com; w twincityliner.com.

HEALTH *with Dr Daniel Campion*

The standard of public health in Slovakia is very good and the tap water is perfectly drinkable. Inexpensive mineral water is also available in shops, cafés, restaurants and hotel minibars (€0.75–1 for a 1.5-litre bottle in shops).

No vaccinations are legally required but it is wise to be up to date with routine immunisations such as **diphtheria**, **tetanus** and **polio**. This is now given as an all-in-one vaccine which lasts for ten years. **Hepatitis A**, **influenza** and **Covid-19** vaccines should also be considered for travellers at higher risk. For those who are going to be working in hospitals or in close contact with children, **hepatitis B** vaccination is recommended. The course comprises three vaccines over a minimum of 21 days. Rabies can affect any mammal, but in Slovakia the disease has been eliminated in dogs. Wild animals including foxes and bats can still pose a threat. Pre-exposure rabies vaccine (ideally three doses given over a minimum of 21 days) should be considered for anyone who is going to be working with animals. If you are unfortunate enough to be bitten, scratched or licked over an open wound you should scrub the wound with soap under running water and apply an antiseptic. Seek medical assessment as soon as possible and tell the doctor if you have had the pre-exposure course of vaccine, as this will change the treatment you need.

The **sun** can be very strong in central Europe: take a supply of sunscreen and after-sun care, or look in the local shopping mall.

Many people **smoke** and restaurants can offer separate smoking and non-smoking rooms.

The **cuisine** can be heavy on meat and fat, and locals have unfortunately joined the global trend towards obesity. Raw meat can harbour a variety of microbial threats, from parasites to bovine spongiform encephalopathy (mad cow disease). This risk is probably low, but you may wish to avoid it entirely by declining the often-offered beef tartare, which involves raw meat spread on toast. With excellent local beer and powerful, cheap spirits on offer, it's also sensible to watch your alcohol intake.

Cases of avian influenza or 'bird flu' have been detected in wild birds and hens in Slovakia from time to time since 2016, most recently the H5N1 virus. No human cases have been reported, but birds are culled and protection zones set up following standard EU practice.

People don't **swim** in the Danube because of the strong current and pollution, but there are many local lakes where the water is pretty clean (Zlaté Piesky, Senec and Kuchajda Lake in the Nové Mesto district, for example). Mosquitoes are irritating and the Danube in summer is plagued by the little devils. If you stay on a botel (hotel on a boat), take a good supply of insect repellent. Calamine lotion or hydrocortisone cream can be helpful if you develop swelling or itching after insect bites.

If you intend to go **walking** or **cycling** in the countryside, remember that a tick bite can cause the potentially deadly disease **tick-borne encephalitis** (TBE). This virus has now been detected in 25 European countries, including Slovakia, Austria and Hungary. The disease is most prevalent during the warmer spring, summer and autumn months when the ticks are active. Vaccination against TBE is readily available in the UK and two injections given at least two weeks apart are needed, with a third dose given five to 12 months later if at continued risk. It is available for adults and children aged one and above. Whether you are immunised or not, you should make sure that you wear suitable clothing, such as a hat and long trousers tucked into boots, and use insect repellents containing DEET or icaridin on exposed skin. Ticks should ideally be removed intact, and as soon as possible, to reduce the chance of infection. You can use special tick tweezers, which can be bought in good travel shops; or failing this, with your fingernails, grasp the tick as close to your body as possible, and pull it away steadily and firmly at right angles to your skin without jerking or twisting. Applying irritants (eg: Olbas oil) or lit cigarettes is to be discouraged as a means of removal since they can cause the ticks to regurgitate and therefore increase the risk of disease. Once the tick is removed, if possible douse the wound with alcohol (any spirit will do), soap and water, or iodine. If you are travelling with small children, remember to check their heads, and particularly behind the ears, for ticks. Spreading redness around the bite and/or fever and/or aching joints after a tick bite imply that you have an infection that requires antibiotic treatment. In this case seek medical advice.

HEALTH INSURANCE Slovakia offers high-quality health care at low cost. Tourists with health insurance will be well cared for and those from EU countries should carry a European Health Insurance Card (EHIC), guaranteeing free or reduced-cost health care. UK residents can apply for a GHIC (Global Health Insurance Card) online via the NHS website (w nhs. uk/using-the-nhs/healthcare-abroad). Beware of the many non-official websites, which charge for the (usually free) card.

Visit the UK Foreign, Commonwealth and Development Office website at w gov.uk/foreign-travel-advice/slovakia/health. Advice on all aspects of travel is available at w travelaware.campaign.gov.uk.

TRAVEL CLINICS AND HEALTH INFORMATION A list of current travel clinic websites worldwide is available on w istm.org. For other journey preparation information, consult w travelhealthpro.org.uk (UK) or w wwwnc.cdc.gov/travel (USA). All advice found online should be used in conjunction with expert advice received prior to or during travel.

HEALTH CARE IN BRATISLAVA For minor ailments, a visit to the nearest pharmacy (*lekáreň*) may suffice. There are many in Bratislava, some opening until 22.00. The Comenius University has four big teaching hospitals across the city, and there are various general polyclinics and specialised medical institutions, public and private.

Pharmacies

Lekáreň BENU – Pod Manderlom 222 H4; Námestie SNP 20; 02 2063 4147; w benulekaren.sk; 08.00–19.00 Mon–Fri; 6, 8 or 1, 3, 4 to Centrum; N44, N47, N72 to Hodžovo námestie

Lekáreň BENU – U Zlatého Grifa 222 D5; Sedlárska 2 (cnr Ventúrska); 02 2063 4145; w benulekaren.sk; 09.00–20.00 daily; 1, 3, 4 to Centrum; N44, N47, N72 to Hodžovo námestie. Pharmacists also speak English, German & Italian.

Lekáreň Milosrdní bratia 222 F3; Námestie SNP 11; 02 5788 7802; 07.00–18.00 Mon–Fri; 6, 8 or 1, 3, 9 to Centrum; N44, N47, N72

to Hodžovo námestie. Specialist pharmacy for diabetics.
Lekáreň Pokrok 📍221 G/J1; Račianske mýto 1/A; 📞02 4445 5291; ⏰06.30–21.30 daily; 🚌5, 21, 61, 74, N33, N55 or 🚊3, 7 to Račianske mýto
Lekáreň u Salvátora 📍223 B7; Panska 35; 📞02 2075 2259; ⏰10.00–18.00 Mon–Sun; 🚌50 or 🚊4 to Most SNP; 🚊9 to Kapucínska. In a Neoclassical building facing the cathedral, this historic pharmacy, reopened in 2024, still has all its 1904 equipment plus 18th-century Baroque cabinets.

Hospitals
Academician Dérer Faculty Hospital – Kramáre emergency clinic 📍220 D1; Limbová 5; 📞02 5954 1111; 🚌42, 64, N29 to Nemocnica Kramáre. This is the place to head for children's emergencies.
Faculty Hospital 📍221 K1; Ružinovská 10; 📞02 4823 4113; 🚌50, 9, 50, N70 to Nemocnica Ružinov
Bory Hospital 📍220 D1; Ivana Kadlečíka, Lamač; 📱09 50 105 510; ✉nemocnica-bory@pentahospitals.com; 🌐nemocnica-bory.sk/en; 🚌21 to OC Bory; 🚌216 to Nemocnica Bory. Opened in 2023 by the Penta property development group on the northern edge of the city, this is the country's most modern hospital.
Medissimo 📍221 D8; Tematínska 5/A, Lúky; 📞02 3230 3030; 🌐procare.sk/poliklinika/procare-medissimo; ⏰07.00–19.00 Mon–Thu, 07.00–15.30 Fri; 🚌83, 95, 98, 99, N95 to Technopol. Private clinic in Petržalka with English-speaking staff.

Dentists
Policlinic Drieňová 📍221 K1; Drieňová 38, Ružinov district; 📞02 4342 3433; 🚊9 or 🚌50, N70 to Nemocnica Ružinov. For dental emergencies.
Sydent 📍221 F1; Björnsonova 13; 📞02 5245 3048; 🌐sydent.sk; ⏰surgery 08.00–16.00 Mon–Fri, at other times by appointment; 🚌40, 49, 61, 64, 71, N33, N44, N74 to Karpatská. English-speaking dentists Sylvia Deglovičová & Juraj Deglovič have a private clinic just north of the Slovak Radio building.

SPAS Slovaks are also wildly enthusiastic about the curative powers of spa waters. The nearest spa to Bratislava is just 80km away at Piešťany (page 202), where the waters are particularly soothing for bones and joints, so you could combine a holiday with a water cure and go home not only refreshed but also regenerated.

Piešťany is one of the most popular European health spas and the most important in Slovakia. Its reputation is based on the healing powers of the thermal waters, sulphurous mud and excellent medical care. Piešťany waters are famous for treating locomotor disorders, rheumatological and neurological problems, and it provides excellent therapy after injuries or orthopaedic surgery.

The resort has dozens of hotels, but the best are the four-star **Esplanade** and the five-star **Thermia Palace** (both page 203), which are part of the Ensana Group.

SAFETY

CRIME Bratislava is a safe city for travellers, with a low rate of violent crime. There is, however, a high incidence of petty theft. Pickpockets operate around the main tourist areas, the railway station and in large shopping malls, and foreigners are easily identified and targeted. Cameras, mobile phones and small electrical items (computers, games, etc) are as attractive as cash and credit cards. Take sensible precautions against bag-snatching and mugging. Do not leave valuables unattended or anything on show in a hire car.

You will see quite a lot of homeless people in Bratislava, searching through litter bins or sitting outside Tesco on Kamenné námestie, on Námestie SNP and on Hviezdoslavovo námestie. They are harmless, drinking cheap wine and look too tired to hassle tourists, although I saw one tall homeless man picking on a little Roma lad.

You must carry your passport with you at all times as identification. Keep it safe, in a zipped-up pocket or secure bag and keep a photocopy of the details separately, or a photo on your phone, in case you lose it. Contact your embassy in Bratislava immediately if you do lose your passport; for details on how to contact your embassy, see page 66.

Check restaurant bills; restaurants are legally required to provide a receipt from the electronic till. Taxi drivers have an undeserved reputation for ripping off foreigners. I have taken countless taxis in Bratislava and, with one unfortunate exception, they have been inexpensive and the drivers charming and helpful.

Taking photographs of anything that could be perceived as a military establishment or somehow of security interest used to be a problem but everyone's much more relaxed now. When driving, remember there is a zero tolerance of alcohol and hand-held mobile phone use when driving is also illegal. There are spot fines for speeding or drinking.

When walking around late at night, avoid the stations or deserted parts of town; however, the Old Town is perfectly safe at all times. Travellers with darker skin colour should be aware that there is a nasty rash of nationalist skinheads in parts of Slovakia. They tend to be 'nerds' who focus on what they see as historical injustices but they would not be pleasant to encounter in a dark alley.

For emergency telephone numbers, see page 69.

POLICE Corruption is a problem in Slovakia, and the police are seen as fairly ineffectual, but you're unlikely to be asked for a bribe. Foreigners are allowed to drive in Slovakia as long as they have a valid licence from their home country and have been in Slovakia for less than 30 days. If you have been speeding or have committed a traffic infraction, the police can fine you up to €20 on the spot, or take you to the station and fine you up to €80. Ask for a receipt for the fine; if nothing appears, ask for the policeman's badge number. If you intend to stay in Slovakia for more than 30 days, you must hold an international driver's licence valid for Europe.

TERRORISM Most foreign embassies are right in the centre and security is relaxed, except at the US Embassy on Hviezdoslavovo námestie, next to the

Radisson SAS Carlton Hotel, which has been heavily guarded since the Bush–Putin summit in Bratislava (February 2005). You will only undergo a security check when entering certain government offices, airports and embassies. There have been no terrorist attacks in Slovakia. Slovakia is a very small player on the international scene and there are no cities with more than 500,000 inhabitants. Nevertheless the threat of terrorism is taken seriously and all necessary preventive measures are in place. As a member of NATO and the allied coalition, Slovakia sent troops to Iraq and Afghanistan until 2007.

WOMEN TRAVELLERS

Slovak men are courteous, if a little old-fashioned, regarding women. The concept of feminism is only slowly catching on here, and women on their own are more likely to be pitied than pestered.

LGBTQIA+ TRAVELLERS

Similarly to its former 'Eastern Bloc' neighbours, Slovakia lags behind western Europe in terms of gay rights and attitudes to LGBTQIA+ people. Slovaks are quite conservative and, while not overtly homophobic or aggressive, they would not appreciate kissing, hand-holding or other public displays of affection between same-sex couples. Discretion is advised.

TRAVELLING WITH KIDS

Slovaks adore children and Bratislava is a very safe destination for travellers with young ones. And travelling around the city with children is quick and convenient as the tram–bus–trolley–train network links up efficiently – though British visitors might be surprised to see adults giving up their seat on the tram for a perfectly healthy five-year-old.

The city is packed with many child-friendly venues such as playgrounds and parks (page 181). In terms of activities, boat trips (page 63) can be a lot of fun, and there are several swimming possibilities near Bratislava such as the artificial lake at Zlaté Piesky (page 182) and the Aquathermal Park at Senec (page 198). The main shopping malls (page 143) have adventure playgrounds to keep the little ones entertained. Bratislava is a very green city with many great parks within walking distance, and Bratislava Zoo (page 181) is a fun destination for the whole family. Alternatively, ride bus 44 up to

1 The city has plenty to occupy the kids, including Bibiana children's art gallery.
2 Offering fine views from its revolving restaurant, Kamzík TV Tower dominates the skyline in the hills north of the city. 3 The Art Nouveau Blue Church is an architectural gem – almost good enough to eat. 4 The Small Carpathian Wine Route pairs fine wines and lovely landscapes. ▶

> **INFORMATION ON TRAVELLING WITH A DISABILITY**
>
> The UK's **gov.uk** website (w gov.uk/government/publications/disabled-travellers) provides general advice and practical information for travellers with disabilities preparing for overseas travel. **Disabled World** (w disabled-world.com) is a comprehensive US site written by wheelchair users who have been researching wheelchair-accessible travel full-time since 1985. There are many tips and useful contacts (including lists of travel agents on request) for slow walkers, wheelchair travellers and their families, plus informative articles, including pieces on disabled travelling worldwide. The company also organises group tours. The **Society for Accessible Travel and Hospitality** (w sath.org) also provides some general information.
>
> **Disabled Holidays** (w disabledholidays.com) is a specialist UK-based tour operator that offers accommodation in Bratislava.
>
> For information on travelling around the city for wheelchair users, see page 74.

Koliba-Kamzík Hills (page 184) for a breath of cool, fresh air in the woods and all manner of outdoor activities, or take the lift up to the UFO viewing platform (page 101) and admire the view.

WHAT TO TAKE

Back in the bad old days, visitors to the 'Wild East' had to pack a squash ball to plug the gaping hole in the bathroom sink. Fortunately such brutalities are a thing of the past. If you don't have an adaptor plug, it's best to buy one at your departure airport rather than waiting until you arrive; nevertheless, these and anything else you might need can be found in Bratislava.

Stag-party travellers should pack some sportswear and a swimsuit as there's a huge variety of events on offer. A swimming costume is a good idea for all visitors, as Bratislava is surrounded by plenty of natural bathing possibilities; the lakes and the Small Danube are delightful destinations.

Bratislava is best explored on foot, so pack some comfortable shoes and perhaps an anorak for the occasional, unexpected summer shower. Winters can be chilly and summers stifling so choose clothes accordingly.

There are no restaurants that require a dinner jacket, but some casinos and nightclubs require a certain degree of smartness.

Take out comprehensive travel insurance before your trip to cover lost baggage, theft and medical emergencies, and bring photocopies of the documentation with you. You are supposed to carry your passport or identity card at all times. Take extra passport photos for extended travel passes and make copies of your passport, driving licence and insurance documents to leave in the hotel safe. You'll need a passport for many transactions: mobile phone SIM cards, gym/spa membership and to check into a hotel or hostel.

Eye masks purloined from long-haul flights are helpful as many hotels have flimsy curtains and ear plugs are a good idea if sharing your hotel with stag partyers.

Bear in mind that Slovakia, along with big sister the Czech Republic, is famous for brewing some of the world's best beer. The wines and spirits also merit serious investigation. Pack a penknife with corkscrew and bottle opener but remember not to take such an implement in carry-on hand luggage. Slovak cuisine is hearty and rib-sticking. Bearing all these factors in mind, it might be a good idea to pack extra supplies of headache and indigestion tablets.

MONEY AND BUDGETING

SLOVAK MONEY The Slovak Republic joined the European Union on 1 May 2004, the Schengen Visa Area in December 2007 and on 1 January 2009, entered the Euro Monetary System, losing its home-grown currency, the Slovak koruna, after only 16 years of existence.

Each country in the eurozone contributes its own designs for the euro and cent coins issued in its own country. In Slovakia, the 1, 2 and 5 cent coins feature the mountains on one side and the 10, 20 and 50 cent coins show Bratislava Castle, while the 1 and 2 euro coins display the double cross that features on the Slovak flag.

For information on banks, exchanging currency, ATMs and credit cards, see page 66.

BUDGETING You can find great bargains in Bratislava or you can have a right royal blow-out. Everyone will find something in the 'little big city' to suit their taste and purse, but your money will certainly go further here than in the West. The following guide lists daily budgets for one person, based on two people sharing accommodation.

Penny-pinching You can probably get by on a budget of around €35 for a hostel dorm, eating the daily lunch menu (*denné menu*) available at most restaurants and cafés, visiting a few museums and rounding the day off with a meal in a modest restaurant.

Modest You'll spend about €55 a day for basic accommodation in a two-star hotel, cheered on by occasional treats; the cheapest opera tickets cost just €19, although you can get last-minute tickets for even less.

Comfortable A daily budget of €110 will allow a stay in a three-star hotel, some sightseeing, stops for coffee, cake and beer, a meal in a decent restaurant, late-night drinks in a club and a taxi back to base.

AVERAGE PRICES OF EVERYDAY ITEMS

To give you an idea of what you'd be spending on a trip to Bratislava, here are some average prices:

Cup of tea	€2	Cup of coffee	€2.50
Half-litre of beer	€2.15	Glass of wine	€2
Packet of cigarettes	€5	Big Mac meal	€7
Daily lunch menu	€9.80	Main course in restaurant	€10
1 litre of milk	€1	Loaf of bread	€1.10
1kg of bananas	€1.70	Bread roll	€0.10
Bottle of Kofola	€0.80	1 litre of mineral water	€1.50
1kg of tomatoes	€4.20	1kg of peppers	€1.50
1kg of cheese	€10	1kg of sausages	€8
Single tram ticket	€1.10	1 litre of petrol	€1.63
Milka chocolate bar	€1.60	1kg of apples	€1.40

Luxurious On a daily stipend of €200 you can stay in one of the top four-star hotels in the centre, drink cocktails, eat like a lord, purchase some Modra ceramics, wind down by taking a taxi up to Kamzík Hill and sipping cocktails in the Veža revolving tower, then back to town to a swish restaurant and on to a jazz club for some chill-out sounds.

Splurging It is possible to spend as much as €350 a day if you're going to go berserk in Bratislava. Book into one of the top hotels, take your pick from the designer shops along Michalská and Ventúrska, take a trip out to the Small Carpathian Wine Route, dine out in the UFO café with its sweeping view and splash out on more vintage white wines, including a Slovak version of Tokaj. Get the best seats in the house at the opera and then gamble what's left in your pocket at one of the four classy casinos.

TIPPING Tipping is standard practice in Bratislava. It is called *prepitné* ('for a drink') in Slovak and it is best to round the figure to the nearest 50 cents. The standard rate is around 10–15%. Likewise tipping in taxis, round the figure up to the nearest 50 cents. Still, if you did not like the service, you can refuse to leave any tip.

Leaving tips does not mean leaving the money on the table and simply departing. In fact, when the waiter brings the bill, he/she waits till you pay. When paying, tell the waiter the total sum (the payment plus the tip), or say how much change you want.

JOURNEY BOOKS
CONTRACT PUBLISHING FROM BRADT GUIDES

DO YOU HAVE A STORY TO TELL?

- Publish your book with a leading trade publisher
- Expert management of your book by our experienced editors
- Professional layout, cover design and printing
- **Unique** access to trade distribution for print books and ebooks
- Competitive pricing and a range of tailor-made packages
- Aimed at both first-timers and previously published authors

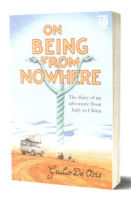

"Unfailingly pleasant"… "Undoubtedly one of the best publishers I have worked with"… "Excellent and incredibly prompt communication"… "Unfailingly courteous"… "Superb"…

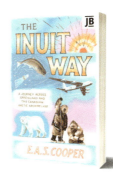

For more information – and many more endorsements from our delighted authors – please visit: **bradtguides.com/journeybooks.**

Journey Books is the contract publishing imprint of award-winning travel publisher, Bradt Guides. All subjects are considered for Journey Books, not just travel. Our contract publishing is a complement to our traditional publishing, not a replacement, and we welcome traditional submissions from new and established travel writers. Please visit bradtguides.com/write-for-us to find out more.

3

Practicalities

TOURIST INFORMATION

The **Bratislava Tourist Board** (BTB; **w** visitbratislava.com) is the main source of information for the city – pop into any of their branches for information on guided tours, advice on accommodation, entertainment, eating and drinking, and trips around the Bratislava region. The Bratislava City Card (page 71) is also available here giving many discounts on museums, public transport and other services.

BTB OFFICES In addition to the 2 year-round offices, there are summer-only information desks at the airport, the bus station & on Hviezdoslavovo námestie.

Bratislava main railway station 220 E1; Námestie Franza Liszta 1; 09.00–13.00 & 13.30–17.00 daily (page 47)
Main office 223 F4; Klobučnícka 2; 02 16 186, 02 5441 9410; **e** btb@visitbratislava.com; 09.00–12.30 & 13.00–17.00 Mon–Sat, 10.00–12.30 & 13.00–16.00 Sun; guided tours: **m** 09 05 848 407; **e** guides@visitbratislava.com; Bratislava City Card: 02 5935 6651; **e** bratislavacard@visitbratislava.com; **w** card.visitbratislava.com

OTHER TOURIST INFORMATION SERVICES

Bratislava Region Tourism Sabinovská 16; 02 4319 1685; **w** bratislavaregion.travel. Offers useful information for exploring the county-sized (2,053km^2) area surrounding the capital.
Slovakia.Travel w slovakia.travel/en. The national tourist board has an excellent website but no offices.

LOCAL TOUR OPERATORS

Organised tours can take you around town on foot, by bicycle or even on a little bus/train contraption.

Authentic Slovakia m 09 08 308 234, 09 15 705 392; **w** authenticslovakia.com. A brilliant tour company, started by 2 brothers, Peter & Branislav Chrenka, & their enthusiastic team of guides who offer an insight into the real Bratislava & its surroundings. Tours include a 'Post Communist City Tour' in a 1970s Škoda around off-the-beaten-path places of Bratislava's communist past & subsequent transformation (2hrs from €25), & a 'Bratislava Identity Bike Tour' that visits the Old Town & Socialist housing areas (2½hrs from €25; a 2hr extension to the bunkers on the border with Austria costs another €25). An all-day 'Castle Ruins Tour' travels to ruins in & around Bratislava (6/10hrs from €50/90), while a 'Village Pub Crawl' is a great way to meet the locals & share a drink or 2 (4–5hrs from €50). The cost depends on the number of participants: less for more people. Tours can also be booked at the BTB office at Klobučnícka 2 in the Old Town. The Bratislava City Card (page 71) gives a 10% discount on tour prices. Highly recommended.

Boat trips Fajnorovo nábrežie 2; 02 5293 2226; w lod.sk/en. Day trips from Bratislava to Devín (€21), Gabčíkovo (€49) & Vienna (€34), plus trips once or twice a summer to places such as Tulln, Krems, Esztergom & Budapest. Visit the LOD office (page 51) for more details on private boat hire.

Bratislava Free Tours m 09 44 568 055, 09 19 346 428; w befreetours.com. A free guided tour of the Old Town, setting off at 11.00 daily from the statue of Hviezdoslav in the square of the same name. Guides operate on a tips-only basis, & are therefore highly motivated to deliver an entertaining & high-quality tour. Other (not free) tours include a 'Communist Bunker Tour' (€20, min €100/group) or 'Adventure Bratislava' with rafting (€59), paintball (from €30), go-karting (€50) & bridge jumping (€35). A 'Pub Crawl' tour takes place every Fri & Sat (€13) & they also offer a slightly disturbing AK-47 shooting trip (from €50), advertised as 'Don't escape the Eastern Bloc without firing the world-famous Kalashnikov'.

Bratislava Sightseeing m 09 07 683 112; w bratislavasightseeing.com. Organised by Luka Tours, this offers bike tours, bike rentals (page 133), plus trips to Devín Castle, the Small Carpathian Wine Route, Piešťany, Vienna, the Záhorie region & a cycle tour along the Eurovelo13 Iron Curtain Route (w eurovelo13.com).

Bratislava Stag Obchodna 68; m 09 07 709 637; w bratislavastag.com. Shooting, karting, rafting, mud-wrestling & a lot of drinking.

BTB Guided Walking Tour 02 5935 6651; m 09 08 705 070; e citycard@ visitbratislava.com; w card.visitbratislava. com/discount/guided-walking-tour-of-the-city-centre. A 75min guided walking tour of the historic city centre in English, German or Slovak. Sets off daily at 14.00 (make reservation at BTB, Klobučnícka 2 at least 2hrs in advance; €16) & is free with the Bratislava City Card (page 71).

Discover Bratislava w freetourbratislava. com. A free guided tour of the Old Town & castle, setting off at 10.00 & 15.30 daily (Nov–Mar 11.00 & 14.30) from the fountain on Františkánske námestie, & lasting at least 2½hrs; also possible extensions to Slavín, Devín or Kamzik. The guides only receive tips, & therefore take care to provide a highly interesting & entertaining tour. Also Hidden Gems (Apr–Oct noon), a 20th-century tour (€1.20 bus fare; Apr/May 15.00 Thu–Sat, Jun–Oct 15.00 daily) & a 'Spooky Legends' evening tour (Apr–Oct 19.00 Thu–Sat, Nov–Mar 19.00 Fri & Sat).

Enjoy Bratislava m 09 49 683 882; w enjoy-bratislava.com. A stag-do operator. Sporting activities, beer tours & pseudo-military activities such as firing Kalashnikovs & destroying cars by driving over them in a tank, all with sexy guides & strippers.

Flora Tour & Travel Ltd Kúpeľná 6; 02 5443 5803; m 09 03 505 505; w floratour.sk; 09.00–17.00 Mon–Fri. Offers everything from sightseeing tours of Bratislava & all over Slovakia, to plane tickets & bike & boat trips.

Golden Express Nám. Suchoňa 2; m 09 03 768 543; w goldenexpress.eu/en. White-and-gold road trains leaving from Nám. Suchoňa for a castle tour (€15; 60mins) & a panoramic tour (€19; 90mins), with multilingual headsets.

Jewish Bratislava m 09 07 683 112; w bratislavasightseeing.com/176/6-Jewish+Bratislava. Organised by Luka Tours, a 3hr walking & tram tour (€135) visiting the Chatam Sófer Memorial, the Museum of Jewish Culture & the last remaining synagogue. A tour with private transport (€87/64 adult/child) visits the same sights. Tours depart 10.00 Sun–Fri.

Omega Tours Námestie SNP 13; 02 5443 1367; m 09 05 566 009; w omegatours.sk. Founded in 1993 by Juraj Chrenka, father of Authentic Slovakia's Peter & Branislav (page 62). Offers tailor-made tours, Danube cruises, 'Discover Slovakia' tours, day trips such as Bratislava half-day sightseeing tour, Danube Cruise & Devín Castle, the Small Carpathian Wine Route, wellness & spa holidays, a typical Slovak dinner with live music, plus trips for groups & individuals.

One Day Trips from Bratislava m 09 03 302 817; w tour4u.sk. Trips out of town run by the people who bring you the Prešporáčik® 'Old Timer' red bus tours (see below), as well as speedboat trips on the Danube. Wine tasting in the Small Carpathians; tours to Devín Castle; to Driny Cave & Smolenice Castle; to Trenčin, Beckov and Bojnice castles; to the historic mining centre of Banská Štiavnica; visits to Prague, Budapest & Vienna; & a 15hr trip to the gorgeous High Tatra mountains.

Prešporáčik® Old Timer Panská 37; m 09 03 302 817; w presporacik.sk/en. The Prešporáčik® Old Timer city tours (open-topped, vintage-style red buses, with audio guide in English, German, French & 20 other languages) chug around the Old Town (09.00–17.00 daily, year-round). Leaves from Námestie Suchoňa for 3 different routes: the 60min Castle Tour, with a 20min break at the castle (€16/8 adult/child), the 60min UFO & Blue Church Tour, with a break at the UFO observation deck (€26/16 adult/child), & the 95min Panoramic Tour, with breaks at Slavin & the castle (€24/12). The Bratislava City Card (page 71) gives a 20% discount on tour prices.

Segway Tours Laurinská 3; m 09 03 416 410; w bratislavasegway.sk/en. Discover Bratislava in a different way; tours include training, rental & instructor. The 1hr 'Riverside Tour' (€40 pp) sets off from the Park Inn Danube & rolls along both banks of the river. The 1½hr Castle Tour (€50 pp) takes you up to the Hrad & also lets you admire it from across the Danube. The 2hr 'City Segway Tour' (€60 pp) visits all the major sights in the Old Town & Castle District. The Bratislava City Card (page 71) gives a 10% discount.

The Stag Company Nile House, Nile St, Brighton BN1 1HW; 01273 225 070; w thestagcompany.com/bratislava-stag-weekends. Various types of entertainment, including karting, rafting, shooting, beer bike tour & other bar crawls, & more.

Wine Tour Flora Tour; Kúpeľná 6; 02 5443 5803; m 09 03 610 716; w floratour.sk. Flora Tour organises trips along the Small Carpathian Wine Route with the opportunity to visit the ceramic-making village of Modra (4hrs; from €75 pp). Also check at the BTB office at Klobučnícka 2 for day trips.

◀ 1 A new initiative from the same company that runs the iconic little red 'Old Timer' bus tour is speedboat jaunts on the Danube. 2 Cruise along the Danube for a day trip to nearby Devín. 3 Learn more about Bratislava's communist past and recent transformation on a city tour in a 1970s Škoda. 4 The Prešporáčik® 'Old Timer' buses chug around the city all year round (in the background, the famous inverted pyramid, home to Slovak Radio).

EMBASSIES AND CONSULATES

For a full, updated list of embassies both overseas and in Bratislava, visit **w** embassypages.com/city/Bratislava.

MONEY

BANKS Banking services are provided in Bratislava by both Slovak and foreign banks. Inside banks, visitors can use the exchange offices during office hours, which are usually open between 08.00 and 17.00 on Mondays to Thursdays, and between 08.00 and 15.00 on Fridays. The major banks (below) also have branches in the major shopping centres which are open seven days a week. ATMs are normally on the outer walls or within a secure room reached with a swipe card. The most frequently accepted credit cards are Mastercard and Visa.

ČSOB 222 F3; Námestie SNP 29; 0850 111 777, 02 5966 8844; **w** csob.sk; 09.00–17.00 Mon–Thu, 09.00–16.00 Fri; 1, 3, 4 to Centrum. ATM outside.

Slovenská sporiteľňa 221 F6; Obchodná 51; 0850 111 888 (help desk); **w** slsp.sk/en; 0800–noon, 13.00–16.00 Mon–Fri; 1, 9 to Vysoká. ATM outside.

Tatra Banka 222 H4; Dunajská 6; 02 5919 1000, 800 00 1100; **w** tatrabanka. sk; 08.30–16.30 Mon–Fri; 1, 3, 4 to Centrum

EXCHANGING CURRENCY Since adopting the euro in 2009, the number of bureaux de change booths in the Old Town has dwindled. However, you can easily buy euros in banks and hotels, at the airport or main railway station, or can use your debit card to take out euros at any of the ATMs dotted all over town. ČSOB is the most expensive place to change money as they charge a 2% fee; Tatra Banka and Slovenská sporiteľňa usually offer the best rates. There are links to bank and ATM locators at **w** transferwise.com/gb/blog/atms-in-slovakia.

Hotels can also give somewhat worse rates outside banking hours. Visitors arriving at the main railway station are immediately warned 'Do not change money in the street', but there's no need to invest in the dodgy-looking fellow with a wad of euros; there are still two **currency-exchange offices** (*zmenáreň*) just outside the Old Town: Currency Exchange Pekr at Dunajská 2 (222 H4; **m** 09 17 689 662; 10.00–18.00 Mon–Fri) and Zmenáreň Exchange at Obchodná 39 (221 F4; **m** 09 48 969 110; 10.00–18.00 Mon–Fri).

> **OPENING HOURS**
>
> Businesses are usually open 09.00–17.00 Monday–Friday. Shops are open 08.00–18.00; supermarkets and chain stores 08.00–20.00. Shops close at noon on Saturday, and some chain stores are open on Sunday.

VISA TRAVELMONEY The Travelex Money Card (020 7837 9580; w travelex.co.uk/travel-money-card; TravelexUK) is a convenient, safe alternative to carrying piles of cash. The system uses a pre-paid card that allows 24-hour access to your money in any local currency. You load it up with funds before your trip and draw cash as you go along from an ATM, or use the card for contactless payments. When you've used up your funds, you can simply throw the card away.

CREDIT CARDS Major credit cards (Diners Club, Visa and Mastercard/Eurocard) and debit cards (Maestro and Visa Electron) may be used to withdraw cash from ATMs of major banks (ČSOB, Tatra Banka, Slovenská sporiteľňa) and for payments in larger hotels, restaurants, shops and petrol stations. Smaller shops, museums and ticket offices may be reluctant to accept credit cards, so keep some euros handy. American Express is not widely accepted so it is advisable to take other cards.

Contactless payment is widely accepted, with minimal fees for international transactions – sometimes as little as £0.02.

MEDIA AND COMMUNICATIONS
PRINT MEDIA
Slovak press The Slovak press is independent (foreign and locally owned) and suffers from hangovers of the past suffocating regime combined with an excess of magazines. Thousands of trees have been pulped to produce the vast range, covering every genre under the sun, but particularly lifestyle and women's.

Kam do Mesta (*Where to Go in Town*; w kamdomesta.sk) is a handy pocket-sized free listings guide. It comes out once a month and you can get copies in the BTB office at Klobučnícka 2. It is all in Slovak but the information on bars, concerts, films, etc, is quite easy to decipher, using the 24-hour clock. The first page lists all the name days for that month, so you won't miss an opportunity to wish Angela (11 March), who just brought you a beer, a happy name day (*Všetko najlepšie k meninám!*).

Nový Čas (*New Time*; w cas.sk) is the best-selling Slovak daily tabloid, published by Ringier Slovakia, a subsidiary of the Swiss Ringier company, which also publishes various television and women's magazines in Slovakia.

The Slovak daily ***Pravda*** (*Truth;* w pravda.sk) is a colour tabloid, second in popularity only to *Nový Čas,* and is available free if you are walking around the Old Town as there is always a teenager handing out complimentary copies. Alternatively, you can buy it in the newsagents for €0.80. ***Týždeň*** (*Week;* w tyzden.sk) is the newest weekly on the stands.

Sme (w sme.sk) is a daily paper and flagship of Petit Press, backed by the German Verlagsgruppe Passau company. ***Plus 7 dní*** (*Plus 7 Days*; w plus7dni.pluska.sk) is the greatest success of the 7 Plus group, which also publishes ***Šarm*** (*Charm*) and **Báječná žena** (*Wonderful Woman*).

English-language press *The Slovak Spectator* (w spectator.sme.sk) is a monthly newspaper aimed at the expat community with 16 to 20 pages of news, features and some culture. The paper costs €2, although you can pick up a complimentary copy in most hotel foyers; you can also sign up on their website for a free daily news email. *The Spectator* also publishes a large number of offshoots: the annual *Largest in Business* (€7) and several other magazines on real estate, investment and employment.

TELEVISION The only TV networks (*televízne siete*) you can watch in Slovakia with just an aerial are the two state channels and half a dozen commercial terrestrial ones (plus the Czech channels ČT1 and ČT2 and Hungarian stations RTL Klub, TV2, MTV1 and MTV2).

The state channels **Jednotka** (formerly STV1; w rtvs.sk/televizia/live-1) and **Dvojka** (formerly STV2; w rtvs.sk/televizia/live-2) are run by STVR (Slovenská Televízia a Rozhlas – Slovak Television and Radio), and compete with the commercial stations with popular shows such as *SuperStar Search Slovakia* (*Slovensko hľadá SuperStar*).

As an antidote to the dry, dull programmes of the Socialist era, the commercial stations offer fairly dumbed-down evening entertainment, with a ratings-winning selection of game shows, reality TV and soap operas. **Markíza** (w markiza.sk), a privately owned commercial station, is the most popular in the region; its **TV Doma** ('At Home') channel is aimed at young women with lifestyle chat shows and endless soap operas, while **Dajto** targets young men, showing repeats of *Charlie's Angels* and *Breaking Bad*. **JOJ** (w joj.sk), a local Bratislava station, has cheap programmes, attempting to challenge Markíza. For news, try **TA3** (w ta3.com).

Being right in the heart of central Europe, Slovak televisions can also pick up broadcasts from TV stations in Poland, Germany and Austria.

RADIO **Rádio Europa 2** (w europa2.sk; 104.8FM) is part of the TV Markíza group, set up a few years back under the name Radio Koliba, and is now the most popular station in Bratislava. **Rádio Slovensko** (w rtvs.sk/radio/radia; 96.6FM) is broadcast by Slovenský Rozhlas from the wonderful inverted pyramid building on Mýtna just north of Námestie Slobody. Slovak Radio operates five national networks (Slovensko, Devín, FM, Regina, Patria) and an international service. **Radio Slovakia International** (w rsi.rtvs.sk) started broadcasting in English in 1993. In the daily 30-minute spots, they broadcast news and extensive information on all aspects of life in Slovakia. Listeners can tune in on shortwave via the World Radio Network or the internet (w encompass.tv/solutions/radio).

Private radio stations competing for listeners in Bratislava include **Rádio Expres** (w expres.sk; 107.6FM), doing well after purchase by an American communications group in 2007, **Fun Rádio** (w funradio.sk; 94.3FM) and **Rádio Viva** (w radioviva.sk; 94.9FM).

USEFUL TELEPHONE NUMBERS

IN AN EMERGENCY
Ambulance ☏ 155
Assistance for motorists ☏ 18 124
Autoclub helpline (ASA Slovakia) ☏ 18 112
City police ☏ 159
Emergency road service ☏ 18 154
English-speaking contact for police, ambulance & fire ☏ 112
Fire ☏ 150
Police ☏ 158

OTHER USEFUL NUMBERS
International directory enquiries ☏ 12 149
Slovak directory enquiries ☏ 1181 (w telefonny.zoznam.sk)

TELEPHONE Cheap local calls can be made from any phone, but for international calls use a card phone; you can buy a card (*telefonná karta*) from a tobacconist or post office.

Bratislava's area code is 02 (remove the zero when calling from outside Slovakia) and telephone numbers are eight digits long (after the 02). Mobile numbers usually begin with 09 03, 09 04, 09 05, etc and 09 10, 09 11 etc, followed by a six-digit number. For calls out of the country, dial the international access code '00', listen for the second burring tone, and proceed with the relevant country code and number.

Mobile phones GSM (global system for mobile communication) signals cover virtually all of Slovakia and travellers must use a triband GSM mobile phone. Major international providers include Orange, O2 and T-Mobile. EU member states benefit from roaming call charges being capped; since Brexit, most British providers have maintained the cap, but this could change. Check with your provider before travel.

POST OFFICES Slovenská Pošta (w posta.sk) delivers a reliable, helpful service throughout the country and most post offices (*pošta*) are open 08.00–17.00 Monday–Friday. You can also buy stamps (*známky*) from some tobacconists (*tabak*), street kiosks or when you purchase your postcards. The **main post office** is at Námestie SNP 35 (♀ 222 E3; ⏰ 07.00–20.00 Mon–Fri, 07.00–18.00 Sat; 🚌 1, 3, 4 to Centrum). There are plenty of others, for instance Posta 14 outside the western end of the main station, Posta 15 at the southern end of the Ministry of Transport and at the Aupark Shopping Center (♀ 220 D8; ⏰ 10.00–20.00 Mon–Fri, 09.00–20.00 Sat & Sun). See page 213 for Slovak letter-sending vocabulary.

INTERNET Many hotels either offer wireless connections or broadband data ports in rooms or have free Wi-Fi zones in their cafés and lobbies; just ask the waiting staff for the password and join their network. If you are staying in a hotel that charges for access, you may be better off sitting in a café, accompanying your correspondence with a cold beer, or using data on your phone, assuming roaming charges are still capped.

Almost all cafés, bars and bistros now offer free Wi-Fi, so the 'purely internet' cafés have all but disappeared.

RELIGIOUS SERVICES

The Bratislava International Church 220 D4; Little Lutheran Church (Malý Evanjelický Kostól), Panenská 28 (near the Crowne Plaza Hotel); 02 5443 2940; **w** bratislavainternationalchurch.org; 93, 203, 207 to Hodžovo námestie. English-language worship every Sun at 10.00 & fellowship & refreshments every Sun at 11.00.
Bratislava Synagogue 222 G1; Heydukova 11–13; 02 5441 6949; **w** synagogue.sk; Jul–Sep 10.00–16.00 Fri & Sun; 1, 3, 4 to Centrum. Bratislava's only remaining synagogue was built in 1926. Regular Orthodox services are held on the Shabbat & during major Jewish festivals. Those wishing to attend should first email **e** memorial@znoba.sk. For group tours & enquiries about the museum (page 164), email **e** synagogue.sk@gmail.com.
The International Baptist Church of Bratislava 221 K5; Súľovská 2; **w** ibcb.baptist.sk; 71, 72 to Gagarinova. English-language worship every Sun at 10.15 & Bible study every Tue at 18.30. For more information contact **e** pastor@bratislavafaithcommunity.org.

WEIGHT AND GRAVITY

There is an obsession in Bratislava with weight and gravity. Meat dishes (but also vegetables, fish, pasta and rice) are all listed in restaurants with their weight given in grams, which is actually quite helpful if you are following a strict diet! Whole fish, like trout and carp, are listed with prices for an average fish, then €0.20–0.30 added on for each extra decagram weight of raw meat. So, unless you specify that you want only a little fish, you may end up paying a couple of euros more than you expected, as chefs may overestimate your appetite or capacity.

Beer is always listed with its specific gravity measured in degrees Plato (the German engineer, not the Greek philosopher), usually 10° or 12°. This is **not** the same as the percentage of alcohol, otherwise we'd get very drunk very quickly – in fact a 12° beer is about 4% (or 1040 Original Gravity), the same strength as red wine.

BRATISLAVA CITY CARD

For getting the best out of the city, the Bratislava City Card (02 5935 6651; e citycard@visitbratislava.com; w card.visitbratislava.com) is a great idea. Produced by BTB (Bratislava Tourist Board) and supported by the municipal government (w bratislava.sk), it offers a free guided city tour, free entry to all the branches of the City History Museum and discounts of about 20% on others, plus discounts at the zoo, swimming pools and some restaurants as well as on taxis, other guided tours and trips. Cards are valid for one (€23), two (€27) or three (€30) days, or for €26/32/36 with free public transport included. It also now comes as an app, which works online or offline. Paper cards are available from all the BTB offices: at the airport, ferry port, Slovak Rail customer services office at the railway station and at Klobučnícka 2 (the Central Tourist Point, in the Old Town centre). Some hotels and also the Flora Tour travel agency (page 63) also offer the card. The card is validated by filling in the dates and other details; alternatively you can buy online and print a receipt to be exchanged at one of the tourist offices.

PUBLIC TOILETS

Apart from nipping into a pub, you'll find there is a dearth of places to spend a cent, and you'll need one after all that lager. The subway under Hodžovo námestie, and the bus and railway stations all have public toilets, some better than others, and there's an underground public loo in a corner of Hviezdoslavovo námestie (the corner is now officially named Námestie Eugena Suchoňa, after the Slovak composer) between the Reduta and the Notre Dame Church. The bus station (page 50) has clean, free public conveniences with an attendant keeping an eye on matters. Some pubs and restaurants are not too grumpy about people using the loo without buying a drink. McDonald's at Gorkého 1, at the corner of Hviezdoslavovo námestie, charges (€0.50) to use the bathroom (downstairs and to the left). Out of the centre, the modern shopping centres all have excellent facilities.

4

Local Transport

PUBLIC TRANSPORT

The transport system is impressively well organised with buses, trams, trolleys and trains all linked up in the Bratislava Integrated Transport (BID) system, with a unified zonal fare structure. Vehicles are comfortable and clean, real-time information is displayed at stops (although services generally run on time) and prices are low. On all methods of transport, most stops are request only, so you'll probably need to ring the bell to get off. The Bratislava Transport Company website is at **w** dpb.sk; but for timetables, downloadable maps of the city's main public transport routes and a route planner in English, as well as a brief history of the city's transport, you're best off going to **w** idsbk.sk/en. For information on **airport transfers**, see page 46.

TICKETS **Ticket machines**, found at all stops (some are in English and German as well as Slovak), offer 16 ticket type possibilities. The main options are listed here. It's increasingly easy to pay with card (including contactless); otherwise you may struggle to find a shopkeeper or ticket seller who will change a large-denomination note to give you coins for the ticket machines.

Alternatively, an **office** in the Hodžovo námestie pedestrian underpass (⏰ 06.00–20.00 Mon–Fri, 08.00–16.00 Sat) sells tickets and travel passes.

Fare zones are based on concentric circles, but the two in central Bratislava (100 & 101) are treated as one for most tickets. A 30-minute ticket will suffice for most journeys, including to Gerulata/Rusovce, Zlaté Piesky and the airport; the main exception is Devín which requires a 60-minute ticket. The standard 30-minute fare is currently €1.10, but an e-ticket via the app is only €0.97. You can also use a contactless card (on the yellow box in the bus); this costs €1.20 (but includes a transfer and is capped at €4.80 per day). Those aged 6–17 or 63 and over pay half, as do students – but this doesn't work if you use a contactless card. You also need a half-price ticket for baggage. Plain-clothed inspectors can impose an on-the-spot fine of €50–70 if you don't have a ticket.

Ticket types
Basic 15mins Zones 100 & 101; €1.20
Basic 30mins Zones 100 & 101; €1.60
Other basic tickets Options range from 60mins (any 3 zones; €1.60) to 150mins (any 10 zones; €3.10)

Tourist 24hrs Zones 100 & 101; €4.80
Tourist 3 days Zones 101 & 101; €9.80
Tourist 7 days Zones 100 & 101; €14.40

TRAMS There are five tram routes running all around town, numbered 1, 3, 4, 7 and 9. They generally run between 05.00 and 23.00. Note that route 3 is currently being extended south through Petržalka from Jungmannova to the southern edge of the borough.

BUSES There are 69 bus routes, numbered 20–192 (with numerous missing numbers plus the trolleybuses; below), and 20 night-bus routes (below). Buses run generally between 05.00 and 23.30 and all link up well with the trams and trolleybuses, and services run on time. The bus route you are most likely to use is the number 29 to Devín. Stops are announced in both Slovak and English; you should press a request button when you want to get off. Most buses are modern, equipped with USB chargers and Wi-Fi.

Buses heading south across the river mostly leave from the city bus station beneath the SNP bridge; other regional buses mostly leave from the main bus station – pay the driver.

Night buses There are 17 night-bus routes, numbered from N21 to N95, with a lot of missing numbers. These run between 23.00 and 03.30 and link the city centre, the main railway station and many of the outer suburbs such as Rača, Čunovo and Devínska Nová Ves. Hodžovo námestie, between the Crowne Plaza Hotel and the president's Grassalkovich Palace, is the night-bus hub, with eight routes meeting here. The most useful are the N33, which runs from the main railway station through the town and west by the river; the N61, from the station through the centre to the airport; and the N93, from the station through town to Petržalka.

TROLLEYBUSES There are 12 trolleybus routes, numbered from 40 to 72, plus 33 and 64 (which use a diesel engine off the wires), running mostly in the hills and northern parts of town. Trolleys run generally between 04.00 and 23.00 and can also go around in a loop and come back on a different route from the way you went.

TRAINS Trains are now included in the integrated transport system, but are not much use for journeys in the city centre. Even so, Bratislava bus/tram tickets will get you to Devínska Nová Ves, Senec and Pezinok (but validity ceases one stop short of Trnava).

GETTING AROUND BY WHEELCHAIR Bratislava, with its pedestrianised Old Town centre is – for a central European city – pretty wheelchair-friendly. The pavements are smooth and the route up to the castle has been properly paved, making access tiring but doable. Every bank and most hotels have an entrance ramp and lifts to upper floors; however, some restaurants are situated in inaccessible cellars. The spa hotels are designed for visitors with limited mobility and have a range of facilities and treatments.

Nevertheless, public transport is tricky. It is virtually impossible to get wheelchairs on to the older trams, but the modern low-floor trams, built by Škoda in the Czech Republic, which appear on all routes in the city, are fine; the newer buses also have ramps. Increasingly, there are raised platforms at the stops, and lifts were installed in 2019 to reach the platforms at the main railway station. The Prešporáčik little red bus (page 65) has a space for wheelchairs. Newer trains have wheelchair spaces, but many stations have low platforms, so you should request assistance in advance.

For further, general, information on travelling with a disability, see page 58.

BRATISLAVA BY BIKE

Bratislava is gripped by a cycling craze with new cycle routes appearing regularly and trendy bike shops popping up around town. Two companies offer bike rental (page 133) and there are two bike-sharing schemes, Slovnaft BAjk (w slovnaftbajk.sk), Rekola (w rekola.sk) and ANTIK Smartway (w antiksmartway.sk). All are very popular and easy to sign up to. Similarly, e-scooters are available from Bolt (w bolt.eu/en/cities/bratislava), Svist (w svist.sk) and Tier (w tier.app/sk). In fact, the Old Town, once a haven for pedestrians and tiddly, tottering stags, is now much more hectic with silent bikes and e-scooters whooshing past (beware the food delivery riders, in particular).

Both banks of the Danube have cycle routes and it is possible to cycle to Devín. However, the direct road along the river is busy and narrow in places (and cycle lanes can't be added because it's a protected area) – you might prefer the hilly tracks through the forest inland or to take a train to Devínska Nová Ves and cycle south from there for 3km along the excellent Morava Valley route. Another excellent route heads south from Petržalka to Čunovo and beyond. There's also the Stefanikova Cyklomagistrala, a ridge route along the hills north from Kamzík.

1 Accessible modern Czech trams have been running on Bratislava's streets since 2014. **2** Bratislava boasts numerous walking trails and cycle paths, such as in Sad Janka Kráľa park, pictured. **3** An evening cruise along the Danube is a relaxing way to end a busy day of sightseeing. ▶

GELIA/S

BRATISLAVA TOURIST BOARD ARCHIVE

BRATISLAVA TOURIST BOARD ARCHIVE

TAXIS

Some say local taxi drivers are a brat pack, who rip off foreigners at every possible occasion. There may be some truth in this at the airport and main rail and bus stations, but mostly the drivers are courteous, extremely friendly and helpful. App-based services such as Uber and Bolt have been permitted in Bratislava since 2019. Taxis around the city should cost €8–15, while from the city to the airport it is €20–25. From the city to Vienna Airport costs €70. Some reputable firms include:

Airport Taxi Bratislava m 09 03 718 787; w taxibratislava.sk
Bratislava Airport Taxi m 09 03 853 359; w bratislava-airport-taxi.com
EasyTaxi m 09 18 555 555, 09 07 440 440; w easytaxi.sk/bratislava
Hello Taxi 02 16 321; m 09 05 222 333; w hellotaxi.sk

Taxi Bratislava 02 16 300; m 09 07 930 300; w taxibratislava.eu
Taxi-Taxi 02 16 901; m 09 10 467 999; w taxitaxi.sk
Taxi Trend m 09 11 030 399; w taxibratislava.eu

CAR HIRE

As the city centre is car-free and the public transport system is excellent, you only really need to hire a car if you're looking to explore the surrounding region, or visit Košice. Slovak car-hire agencies are substantially cheaper than those of Western firms, ranging from €23 to €50 per day, and the process is marked by much less red tape. There are many car-hire companies at M R Štefánik Airport.

Ab-Wickam Kopčianska 65, Petržalka; m 09 03 655 390; w rent-cars.sk/autopozicovna/ab-wickam. Offering short- & long-term car hire since 2001, with Peugeot 207s from €40/day or €26/day for a week or more, or Škoda Octavias from €36/30. The office opens specifically for clients after a phone or email reservation.
Avis 02 5341 6111; m 09 00 200 200; w avis.sk; 08.30–20.00 daily. Cars available from Bratislava M R Štefánik Airport, Schwechat Airport Vienna, Košice Airport & Poprad Airport. Peugeot 208s from €26/day.
Budget Car Rental M R Štefánik Airport; 02 3303 6231; w budget-cz.

com; 07.00–midnight daily. Offers car rental for €32/day for a Škoda Fabia & also one-way rental eg: to Vienna Airport for an extra €91.
Europcar M R Štefánik Airport, Ivánska cesta; 02 5556 6666; m 09 15 748 692; w europcar.sk; 08.00–17.00 Mon–Fri, by reservation at w/ends. From €35/day for a Fiat 500.
Sixt M R Štefánik Airport, Terminal C; 02 4824 5178; m 09 11 833 133; w sixt.co.uk; 08.00–22.00 daily, with 24hr return. From €30/day for a Škoda Fabia.

PARKING

As Bratislava centre is car-free and the surrounding streets clogged with cars, it's useful to know where to leave the motor safely. Bear in mind it's very expensive to use car parks attached to hotels, and costs slightly less in lots in back streets. As well as those listed, places can also be found at the shopping malls (page 143), the passenger river port (Osobný pristav; ⓘ 08.00–22.00 daily), and at the main railway station (Námestie Franza Liszta; ⓘ 24/7), where prices will be slightly less than at the hotels. A residents' permit scheme was introduced from 2022.

Carlton Garage Hviezdoslavovo námestie 3; ⓘ 24/7. €5/hr Mon–Fri, €3.50/hr Sat & Sun (max €50/40). 430 spaces.
Garáž Centrum Uršulínska 2; ⓘ 24/7. €4.90/hr, €3.90/hr Sat, Sun & overnight. 163 spaces.
Garáž Opera Palackého; ⓘ 24/7. €2.60/30mins, €2.60/hr Sat, Sun & overnight; daily max €35. 400 spaces.
IPP Park Hrad Zámocká 1A; ⓘ 24/7. 270 spaces on 4 levels under the castle, €3/hr (€1.50 for castle visitors; max daily charge €18; accessible space free), & also a bargain €1 for the entire night (19.00–08.00).
Tatracentrum Vysoká 7; ⓘ 24/7. €3.50/hr (1st 15mins free), nights & w/ends €2/hr (1st 15mins free). 313 spaces.

DANUBE RIVER CRUISES

Taking a river cruise upstream to Devín, or heading further to Vienna is a lovely way to spend an afternoon (except in winter). LOD and Twin City Liner operate fast services to and from Vienna (page 51) and LOD also offers a variety of cruises (**w** lod.sk/en). As well as the options below, you can charter cruise vessels and catering services for parties or trips to Vienna, Hainburg, Devín, Čunovo or Gabčíkovo by calling ☎ 02 5293 2224 or emailing **e** charter@lod.sk.

Bratislava sightseeing boat ⓘ mid-Apr–30 Aug Tue–Sun, Sep & Oct Sat & Sun; 45mins round trip; €13/10 adult/child; 10% less for seniors, students & travellers with a disability. Sails under the 5 bridges of Bratislava.
Devín ⓘ 25 Apr–30 Aug Tue–Sun (depending on weather), Sep Sat & Sun; 90mins one way; return tickets €21/16 adult/child; 10% less for seniors, students & travellers with a disability, bicycle transport €2.

5

Accommodation

For a relatively small city, Bratislava has more than its fair share of hotels competing for tourists, business visitors and local travellers. This makes for a healthy atmosphere with each hotel, pension and hostel trying to outdo the others in terms of facilities, prices and bathroom freebies. There is still a wide variety of accommodation, however, giving the visitor a good choice when considering location, amenities, even theme, as with the gimmicky-yet-fun Film Hotel (page 84). Virtually all hotel and restaurant staff now speak good English.

Like many in the region, the Slovak hoteliers are fixated about the star system of grading hotels, a hangover from the communist-era mania for points-scoring, be it ice skating or extra marks for those creepy welcome messages that spring into life on the TV screen when you enter your new bedroom. The starring system is a pretty complicated business, depending on whether the hotel in question has a swimming pool or separate bathroom and loo. Apparently, it gives an indication as to services, amenities and standard of interior, but it can at times appear quite arbitrary.

There are some excellent four-star hotels in Bratislava and the city now has several **five-star hotels**: the Arcadia (page 81) in the Old Town; the Grand Hotel River Park (page 81), part of a luxury retail, apartment and entertainment complex hanging right over the Danube west of town and the Sheraton (page 82) adorning the Eurovea luxury complex by the Apollo Bridge. Hotel Albrecht (page 82) is a five-star boutique hotel in an elegant manor house located in the hills above the castle.

As far as **four-star hotels** are concerned, there is something to suit all tastes, with a range of facilities, styles and locations. Some of the established, more traditional top-class hotels are situated on the banks of the Danube, with a view of the river. Some smaller, yet no less chi-chi, guesthouses are found in the hilly residential area north of the city's Old Town heart.

At the other end of the price spectrum, Bratislava has a relatively good choice of **budget** pensions and hostels, as well as Airbnb private apartments (**w** airbnb.com), which are really taking off. You may also come across the *garni* hotel, meaning a hotel with no restaurant, but which offers breakfast. Hotels in the largely residential districts towards the airport tend to cater

> **ACCOMMODATION PRICE CODES**
>
> These price codes indicate the cost of a room in high season. The top ranking (€€€€€) suggests a really swanky hotel, while the lowest (€) signifies a more modest hostel. The price bands given are walk-in rates for single and double rooms during high season – generally May to October and the period over New Year. During low season, rates drop by around 30%.
>
> | | |
> |---|---|
> | €€€€€ | €110+ |
> | €€€€ | €90–109 |
> | €€€ | €75–89 |
> | €€ | €60–74 |
> | € | less than €60 |

for business travellers, but offer bargain rates at weekends for the leisure traveller and are popular with young families on a tighter budget; they have a good range of services such as high-speed internet connections and fitness centres.

The problem with accommodation in Bratislava is that there is little on offer in the reasonably priced range. The city is well served for luxury and budget options, but there is a lack of **mid-range** hotels – although we have tried to find and list them all in this chapter. Those within this category usually lurk around the three-star level and are found outside the Old Town in less attractive parts of the city. They can be fun if you don't mind negotiating a tram ride each morning and evening and also give a glimpse of Slovak life beyond the tourist belt.

For something a little different, you could try camping in the city, at the Zlaté Piesky lake (page 88) at the end of the number 4 tramline. It's a fun option with kids, but there may be mosquitoes, so take precautions.

The hotels in this chapter have been sorted into price range, beginning with the luxury hotels and following on with the four-star, three-star, then pensions, guesthouses and hostels. This guide divides Bratislava's hotels into stars; however, the first group includes the five-star hotels, plus several four-star hotels, which stand out from the crowd and give that little extra pampering. If my budget allowed, I'd plump for a pillow in one of these any day, or night. The listing of hotels within each category is purely alphabetical, by descending price code. Bratislava is not a huge city so hotels, pensions, hostels, private apartments and campsites are not divided into district, and only the hotel section is separated into five price categories. Bus, tram, trolleybus and night bus numbers are also shown.

As for paying, all the hotels listed of three-star status and above accept the major credit cards; check with others first about methods of payment. The

19% VAT (DPH) is often added to the charge, and there is a city tourist tax (€3 pp/night) which some hotels add on after and some include. Advance reservations, group bookings, and stays of more than one night will bring room charges down, and with the hot competition for guests, almost all hotels above three stars offer discounted deals on weekend breaks. If travelling independently, keep an eye on websites like w lastminute.com and w expedia.com.

The facilities you can expect in each category are laid out below. Breakfast is a buffet spread of cereal, fruit, bread, salami and cheese, tomatoes and peppers, scrambled egg, frankfurters and hot spicy sausage, with a selection of tea, coffee and juice. Many hotels can arrange bike hire, opera trips and other excursions.

LUXURY HOTELS

This collection of hotels includes 5- & 4-star options that soar so high above all others they deserve a separate category. These all have great – if varying – locations near the centre, en-suite rooms with a bath &/or shower; TV, minibar, room safe, AC, internet access or business centres, restaurant & bar, fitness facilities & saunas; they may also have a swimming pool, solarium, shops & café.

Arcadia Hotel ♀ 222 D3 (21 rooms, 4 suites, 9 maisonettes) Františkánska 3; 02 5949 0500; w arcadia-hotel.sk; N61 to Centrum; N31, N34, N44, N47, N53, N55, N70, N72, N80, N93, N95 to Hodžovo námestie; 1, 3, 4 to Centrum. Stylish 5-star boutique hotel right in the heart of the Old Town in a 13th-century listed building. Superbly appointed rooms feature every comfort & the maisonettes give a real feeling of home on 2 floors. Elegant lobby lounge & cocktail bar, plus wellness & relaxation area & conference facilities. The only hotel in Slovakia to win Small Leading Hotels of the World status. €€€€€

Crowne Plaza Hotel Bratislava ♀ 220 E4 (209 rooms, 15 suites) Hodžovo námestie 2; 02 5934 8111; w cpbratislava.sk; 42, 44, 47, 83, 84, 93, 94, N31, N34, N44, N47, N53, N55, N70, N72, N80, N93, N95 to Hodžovo námestie. Good location just north of the Old Town, opposite the Presidential Grassalkovich Palace, where the busy Staromestská highway zooms across Hodžovo námestie. With its state-of-the-art equipment, excellent business services & superb restaurants, the hotel attracts both business folk & those seeking a little extra pampering while on holiday. 6 floors of luxurious, well-appointed rooms, business accommodation on the 5th floor with its own reception & executive meeting rooms, 14 conference rooms with more than 1,200m^2 of meeting space, cigar lounge, hairdresser, gift shop & limousine service. The Zion Spa wellness centre (w zionspa.sk) has a small pool, sauna & steam room as well as a gym. The Banco Casino (page 129) offers poker, roulette & fruit machines in a classy setting. €€€€€
Grand Hotel River Park ♀ 220 A6 (231 rooms) Dvořákovo nábrežie 6; 02 3223

◀ 1 For location alone, the vast, imposing Radisson Blu Carlton Hotel overlooking Hviezdoslavovo námestie wins hands down. 2 The Grand Hotel River Park luxury hotel offers five-star opulence right on – or over – the Danube. 3 Nestled in the Old Town, the Arcadia Hotel occupies a 13th-century listed building.

8222; w marriott.com/hotels/travel/btslc-grand-hotel-river-park-a-luxury-collection-hotel-bratislava; 🚌 29, 31, 39, N31, N33, N34 or 🚋 4 to Chatam Sófer; 🚋 9 to Kráľovské údolie. The Grand Hotel River Park, a luxury collection hotel, offers 5-star opulence & comfort right on the Danube. Ask for a room on the riverside for the best views. The River Bank Restaurant (w riverbank.sk; €€€€€) offers international cuisine with local, seasonal produce, & the stylish bar has an extensive wine selection. Enjoy a smoke at the cigar club or on the terrace, while keep-fit enthusiasts have a huge, top-floor Zion Spa & Fitness Centre to work out or relax in. These luxuries don't come cheap, & locals aren't too happy with the modern apartment block spoiling their panoramic river view or the helicopters landing on the roof. €€€€€

Hotel Albrecht 220 A4 (11 rooms) Mudroňova 82; m 09 07 666 600; w hotelalbrecht.sk; 🚌 44, 47, N47 to Červený Kríž. 5-star boutique hotel in an elegant, historic manor house in the hills above Bratislava Castle. All rooms are different, but all have king-size beds, plasma TV screens, high-speed internet & L'Occitane toiletries. No lift. The day spa has a 10m pool with a counter current, massage treatments & a dry & steam sauna. The wellness zone is also open to the public. Classy, comfy bar & light, airy Albrecht Restaurant (€€€€) with a good view of the gardens. €€€€€

Sheraton Bratislava 221 H7 (186 rooms, 23 suites) Pribinova 12; 02 3535 0000; w sheratonbratislava.com; 🚌 40, 78 to Nové SND or 🚌 50, N33 to Malá scéna. In the Eurovea shopping mall complex on the banks of the Danube, opposite the elegant New National Theatre (Nové SND), the Sheraton has spacious, fully equipped guest rooms & luxury suites, & several lounges & bars. The Zion Spa has a pool, sauna & steam bath, & offers a range of treatments & massage. Dog- & cat-friendly, if you want to take your pet. €€€€€

Radisson Blu Carlton Hotel 223 D8 (168 rooms, 9 suites) Hviezdoslavovo námestie 3; 02 5939 0500; w radissonblu.com/hotel-bratislava; 🚌 50, N33 or 🚋 1, 4 to Námestie Ľudovíta Štúra. For location alone, this vast, imposing hotel overlooking Hviezdoslavovo námestie wins hands down. The present building dates from 1912, when hotelier Henry Pruger created a Carlton–Savoy complex on the site of the Three Green Trees Inn. It opened in 2001 (after 9 years of reconstruction) as part of the Radisson Blu group. Only 1min from the Opera House & Reduta & 2mins from the Old Town. Plush, chintzy furnishings & original glass atrium ceilings. Bedrooms in 2 styles: warmer, traditional golden hues or modern, cooler colours. The bar has an open fire & shelves of leather-bound books, & the renovated Savoy Restaurant (page 101) has changing foodie concepts. Great summer terrace restaurant (⏰ 11.00–22.00 daily; €€€€) & fabulous buffet b/fast. Small in-house fitness centre & free vouchers for gyms at Park Inn by Radisson (opposite). €€€€

Marrol's 223 H7 (51 rooms, 3 apartments) Tobrucká 4; 02 5778 4600; w hotelmarrols.sk; 🚌 50, N33 or 🚋 1, 4 to Námestie Ľudovíta Štúra. Marrol's is a gem of a hotel, hiding away in a modest terraced building on a back street, a 5min walk from Hviezdoslavovo námestie. The Houdini Restaurant (€€€€) emphasises seasonal produce & locally rooted cuisines, along with *sous-vide* cooking, & the Jasmine spa offers a retreat from the hectic business of the day. B/fast extra. €–€€€€

FOUR-STAR HOTELS

4-star hotels have the same features as those in the luxury section, but may not have such good locations or restaurants.

They have en-suite rooms with a bath &/ or shower, sat TV, telephone, minibar, room safe, AC, business centre with internet access, restaurant & bar, & many also have fitness facilities. However, there are some top-class centrally located hotels available, some of them right in the Old Town. Others are located on a hill north of town in a calm, green residential area, yet still very close to the Old Town & accessible by both car & public transport.

* Hotel Devín ♀ 223 C9 (90 rooms) Riečna 4; ☎ 02 5998 5111; w hoteldevin. sk/en; 🚌 50, N33 or 🚋 1, 4 to Námestie Ľudovíta Štúra. For many years, Hotel Devín stood alone as the only 4-star hotel in Bratislava, & it still retains a traditional self-assured ambience & a classic, opulent style. Renovated in 2012, it's one of the best in town & good enough for the Dalai Lama & Václav Havel who have both stayed here; though not together. The buffet b/fast is superb, with great local sausages & cheeses. Good-sized rooms with very beige marble bathrooms, a woody bar, & café & a bistro. The Spa Centre (🕘 09.00–21.00 daily) offers Thai massage, Finnish sauna, pool, gym & massage tables. €€€€€

Hotel & Residence Roset (27 suites) Štúrova 10; m 09 17 373 209; w rosethotel.sk/ en; 🚌 50 or 🚋 1, 3, 4 to Šafárikovo námestie. The most architecturally distinguished of Bratislava's hotels, in the charming Art Nouveau Tulip building, this all-suite hotel also has a gym, spa & a terrace tucked away at the rear. €€€€€

Park Inn by Radisson ♀ 223 B9 (240 rooms) Rybné námestie 1; ☎ 02 5934 0000; w parkinn.com/hotel-bratislava; 🚌 50, 91, N33 or 🚋 4 to Most SNP. This reopened in 2018 as a less grand alternative to Radisson's nearby Carlton. An unattractive exterior conceals a smart hotel with good views of the river & castle. Rooms all have cable TV & internet access. Non-smoking, family & accessible rooms also available. 8 meeting rooms & access to the Freja Sports Club available. The stylish Bocca Buona Restaurant (€€€) offers a good buffet b/fast & excellent Italian food, & the MOW (My Own World) bar sprawls across the square on sunny days. €€€€€

Falkensteiner ♀ 222 A2 (162 rooms & suites) Pilárikova 5; ☎ 02 5923 6100; w falkensteiner.com/en/hotel/bratislava; 🚌 80, 83, 84, 93, 94, N31, N34, N80, N93, N95 to Zochova; 🚌 44, 47, N47 to Kozia. New business hotel not far from the centre. Rooms have coffee machines, free Wi-Fi & minibar. There's a café & bar, and the Aquapura spa on the top floor has a great view with a sauna, cardio workouts & massage treatments available. 5 conference rooms with state-of-the-art presentation equipment. €€€€–€€€€€

AC Hotel Bratislava Old Town ♀ 220 E4 (199 rooms) Vysoká 2A; ☎ 02 2002 0000; w austria-trend-bratislava.h-rez.com; 🚌 42, 44, 47, 83, 84, 93, 94, N31, N34, N44, N47, N53, N55, N70, N72, N80, N93, N95 to Hodžovo námestie. Just behind the Crowne Plaza on a pedestrian street leading to the Staré mesto, this offers free Wi-Fi, minibar & safe in all rooms, plus 6 meeting rooms, a wellness area & gym. Restaurant (€€€) with good 'Morgenstund' b/fasts (buckwheat porridge with fruit & seeds), café & bar. €€€€

Beigli Hotel & Garden ♀ 222 B3 (14 rooms) Baštová 4; m 09 10 749 242; w hotelbeigli.sk; 🚋 9 to Kapucínska. A small boutique hotel on a remarkably quiet old-town street; its most attractive feature is the lobby bar & garden café; there's an excellent b/fast too. €€€€

Hotel Danubia Gate ♀ 221 G5 (29 rooms) Dunajská 26; ☎ 02 2066 5500; m 09 17 232

000; w danubiagate.sk; N61 or 1, 3, 4 to Centrum. Compact modern business hotel 10mins' walk east from the Old Town. Named after the medieval gateway in the outer city walls, rooms have free Wi-Fi, minibar, computer, CD, DVD & MP3 players. The 'De Luxe' rooms have private hydromassage in the bathrooms. The hotel's Street Coffee & Restaurant (€€€) offers steaks, vegetarian & healthy lunches. The concierge can book tickets for the Opera House nearby. Free parking in the yard if you book direct; there's also a bike store & workshop. €€€€

Hotel Lindner 221 K1 (222 rooms) Metodova 4; 02 3993 0000; w lindnerhotels.com/en/hotels/lindner-hotel-bratislava; 49, 61, 63, 71, N53, N74 or 4, 9 to Trnavské mýto. A stylish modern business hotel (opened in 2013) above the Central shopping centre in Ružinov, with great views from the 13th-floor bar. A good restaurant (€€€€), swimming pool & parking (from €20/day). €€€€

Hotel Loft Bratislava 220 E2 (122 rooms) Štefánikova 4; 02 5751 1000; w lofthotel.sk; 42, 83, 84, 93, N31, N34, N61, N70, N80, N93, N95 to Pod Stanicou. Loft Hotel Bratislava is a modern independent hotel (not at all loft-like) just off the main road from the railway station to the Old Town, almost opposite the Archbishop's Summer Palace. All rooms are well equipped with modern décor, minibar, coffee- & tea-making facilities, TV & safe. The on-site Fabrika Beer Pub brews its own fine beers & has a good range of international dishes. €€€€

Skaritz Hotel & Residence 222 C4 (20 rooms, 6 apartments) Michalská 4; 02 5920 9770; w skaritz.com; 1, 3, 4 to Centrum; N31, N34, N44, N47, N53, N55, N70, N72, N80, N93, N95 to Hodžovo námestie. Old Town boutique hotel where you're right in the heart of the action, on the busy street, lined with bars & restaurants, that leads down from Michael's Gate with its iconic tower towards the main square (Hlavné námestie). All rooms are stylishly furnished & well equipped with safe, DVD, CD, MP3 player, Wi-Fi & coffee maker; the apartments have kitchen & dining facilities. Lounge, meeting room, lift, Thai massage & free sauna. €€€€

Best Western Hotel West 220 D1 (41 rooms, 3 apartments, 6 penthouses) Cesta na Kamzík; 02 5478 8693; w hotel-west.sk; 44, N44 to Koliba terminus then 20mins' walk uphill; 15mins by car or taxi from the town centre. Beautiful location on top of wooded hills north of the city. Close enough to town for business folk, yet peaceful & separate from the city. A young, modern hotel surrounded by great hiking hills. Individually furnished apartments for those staying a little longer, with kitchen & direct phone lines. The Schoppa Restaurant (€€€) is in a mountain hut nearby & offers traditional Slovak dishes. There's also a sauna, small pool, sunbathing studio & nightclub for meetings. Mountain biking & tennis courts are nearby. €€€

THREE-STAR HOTELS

3-star hotels range from cheaper places offering good value for money to more expensive ones trying to attract average 4-star hotel guests. All have en-suite rooms with bath &/or shower, AC, TV & internet access in a business centre. Many also have gyms, fitness centres & eating & drinking venues.

Film Hotel 220 F4 (13 rooms) Vysoká 27; m 09 11 941 140; 1, 9 to Vysoká; N53, N55, N70, N72 to Kollárovo námestie. An elegant townhouse just off Obchodná ('Commercial') street leading northeast out of town. Aside from bumping into the occasional giant Oscar statue or walking over star names on the tiled floor, the experience is not as tacky as it sounds. Rooms are comfortable & spacious & the building is quite elegant from the outside, apart from the neon. Spacious & well-appointed rooms are named after film stars. €€€

Aplend City Hotel Perugia 223 C6 (14 rooms) Zelená 5; m 09 02 411 111; w aplendcity.com/en/hotel-perugia; 1, 3, 4 to Centrum; N31, N34, N44, N47, N53, N55, N70, N72, N80, N93, N95 to Hodžovo námestie. Right in the heart of the Old Town, the building was built in 1926. Rooms are plush with period furniture & original artwork. Restaurant Koliba Kamzík (page 99) offers Slovak dishes. In the pedestrian zone, so there's no traffic noise, but parking can be problematic. €€

Hotel Arcus Garden 221 H3 (12 rooms) Moskovská 5; 02 5557 2522; w hotelarcus. sk; 47, N53, N70 or 3, 4 to Americké námestie. Intimate, friendly pension just northeast of the charming Medical Gardens (Medická záhrada), within walking distance of the Old Town. Slightly old-fashioned décor, with TV, radio, minibar, telephone & Wi-Fi. It's a *garni* hotel so there's no restaurant, but you can get b/fast. €€

Hotel Divoká Voda map, page 196 (24 rooms) Čunovo; 02 6252 8002; w divokavoda.sk/en; 90 from Nové SND to Areál vodných športov. Areál Divoká Voda (Whitewater Resort) is 15km south of Bratislava on an artificial island in the Danube; it's adjacent to the Danubiana gallery (page 162). At the resort, there are bungalows, a campsite (page 87), & the Hotel Divoká Voda, with 18 dbl, 3 superior & 3 4-bed rooms. All come with AC, TV, Wi-Fi, bathroom & toilet. There's also a dry sauna, infra sauna & jacuzzi. The restaurant (€€) provides b/fast, lunch, barbecues & seasonal menus for hotel guests & the general public; there's also a floating restaurant across the road to the west (€€). €€

Hotel Elisabeth Old Town 221 G5 (41 rooms) Klemensova 2; m 09 48 636 260; N61 or 1, 3, 4 to Centrum. An unassuming but friendly hotel in a period building that's fairly handy for the bus station. Rooms are small but clean; b/fast extra. €€

Hotel Ibis Bratislava Centrum 220 C5 (120 rooms) Zámocká 38; 02 5929 2000; w accorhotels.com/gb/hotel-3566-ibis-bratislava-centrum/index.shtml; 9 to Kapucínska; 31, 39, 80, 83, 84, 93, 94, N31, N34, N80, N93, N95 to Zochova. Calling itself an 'economy hotel for business & leisure', the location is certainly excellent, right next to the tram tunnel under Castle Hill – the trams are not too noisy. Between the Old Town & the castle, it's part of the French Accor group – rooms are simple & somewhat impersonal but with good, smart bathrooms. 2 rooms are equipped for visitors with disabilities. Also has a business corner, restaurant (€€), wine bar & free Wi-Fi access. B/fast extra. €€

Hotel Nivy 221 K1 (250 rooms, 4 apartments) Líščie nivy 3; 02 5441 0390; w hotelnivy.sk; 50, N70 or 9 to Líščie nivy. A 1970s block in the Ružinov district by the Štrkovec Lake (Štrkovecké Jazero, popular with anglers & sunbathers), the rooms are basic but comfortable; however, the main attraction is the 25m pool & wellness centre, which has 5 kinds of sauna, a whirlpool & a chill-out area – see page 136 for details. Restaurant (€€€) & café. B/fast extra. €€

PENSIONS

Pensions are popular with many travellers as they are often smaller & cheaper than regular hotels, but they also have a family atmosphere missing in a big international venue. The selection listed here is all either in the centre or within easy walking distance. Some are more basic, others quite luxurious, but all provide clean, modern rooms with en-suite bathroom &/or shower. Some have restaurants attached, which can hold their own against the best in town.

Bastion Apartments 221 G1
(6 apartments) Smrečianska 6; **m** 09 17 595 497; **w** bastion.sk/apartmany; 🚌 49, 61, 63, 64, 71, N33, N55, N74 or 🚋 3, 7 to Račianske mýto. Bastion's apartments come with split-level rooms; living room & bathroom below & bedroom on the gallery, with 2 TVs, AC & minibar. Free parking. €€

Downtown Bratislava B&B 220 D4
(16 rooms) Panenská 31; **m** 09 02 072 942; **e** downtown@senger.sk; 🚌 42, 44, 47, 83, 84, 93, 94, N31, N34, N44, N47, N53, N55, N70, N72, N80, N93, N95 to Hodžovo námestie. Recently refurbished, but still with small, simple rooms, this period building has rooms on 3 floors without a lift – but top-floor rooms have AC. B/fast available. €€

Garni Hotel Virgo 220 D4 (11 rooms) Panenská 14; ☎ 02 3300 6262; 🚋 44, 47, N47 to Kozia. A newish guesthouse near the city centre. Rooms are stylish & well appointed, each with a private terrace. Check in at Panenská 5 (**m** 09 48 944 780). €€

Hotel Orlan 221 K5 (19 rooms) Strojnícka 99, Ružinov; ☎ 02 4363 3704; **w** orlan.sk; 🚌 42 to Strojnícka. 2-star *garni* pension on the far side of Ružinov, so convenient mainly for car owners. Rooms are cheap & cheerful with TV, Wi-Fi, sauna & free parking; as a *garni*, they offer b/fast (€7) but no other meals. €€

Penzión Grémium 222 G5
(8 rooms) Gorkého 11; ☎ 02 2070 4874; **w** penziongremium.sk; 🚋 1, 4 to Jesenského; 🚌 N33 to Námestie Ľudovíta Štúra. This 3-star pension in the centre of town used to be a fairly grungy student hostel but it's been given a makeover & the comfortable rooms are stylishly decorated with wooden furniture, TV & Wi-Fi. The pension is 'cycle-friendly', with information about cycle tours. €€

Penzión Portus 223 C8 (6 rooms) Paulíniho 10; **m** 09 02 431 230; **w** portus.sk; 🚌 50, N33 or 🚋 1, 4 to Námestie Ľudovíta Štúra. On a tiny back street behind the US Embassy, Portus plays on a nautical theme,

PRIVATE APARTMENTS

Self-catering apartments are another good accommodation option, and there are a lot of both short-term and long-term lets available. Advantages include privacy, choice of hours and cuisine as well as lower prices (apartments can be booked for a minimum stay of two nights with prices starting at €50/apartment/night), while disadvantages include the necessity of arriving at an agreed time to pick up the keys. Some apartment owners also insist on full or partial payment in advance via a bank transfer or PayPal as well as a deposit against damage. A private room in a central location can be rented for as little as €40 and long-term rentals are also possible for an even lower rate. Airbnb (**w** airbnb.com) has around 400 excellent options in Bratislava, with private rooms, shared rooms or even the entire apartment for reasonable prices.

The Bratislava Tourist Board (BTB) (page 62) has a list of the best apartments and can also suggest places to stay if you want to do your own cooking and cleaning. Most of them are in the Old Town and equipped with Wi-Fi, cable TV, phone, washing machine, oven or microwave.

with 3 dbls, 2 trpls & a quad, all of which have Wi-Fi, sat TV, bathroom & toilet. A little bistro (⏰ 08.00–18.00 Mon–Fri; €€) offers pizzas & tasty local dishes. There's a smoking terrace & a wine cellar with space for 10 drinkers. Check in at the Bluebell B&B immediately to the west. €

HOSTELS

Bratislava has a good selection of hostels near the centre of town so, if you don't mind bunking in with students, you can find great prices. Hostels also offer the opportunity for meeting people from all parts of the world, with social activities such as cycle trips, concerts & pub crawls often available.

CHORS – like a Hotel 📍 221 F4 (40 rooms) Obchodná 43; m 09 10 127 878; w cho.rs/en; 🚋 1, 9 to Vysoká; 🚌 31, 39, 42, 47, 80, 94 to Kollárovo námestie; 🚌 N31, N34, N44, N47, N53, N55, N70, N72, N80, N93, N95 to Hodžovo námestie. A shiny new capsule hotel – not in the Japanese sense, but rather with dorm beds arranged in box-like pods to give more privacy than you'd normally expect – this is a stylish, centrally located option ideal for those not accustomed to hostelling. B/fast, towel & soap are included, & there's good AC & Wi-Fi, a kitchen, plus art by local artist Marek Ormandík. *From €37.* €

Hostel Folks 📍 222 D2; (12 rooms inc dorms) Obchodná 2; m 09 03 725 252; w hostelfolks.com/en/hostel; 🚋 1, 9 to Poštová; 🚌 N31, N34, N44, N47, N53, N55, N70, N72, N80, N93, N95 to Hodžovo námestie. Wonderfully spacious, clean & friendly, & very close to the Old Town; bring ear plugs & eyeshades for dorms (the private rooms are on the quiet side of the building). There's a huge common room with free tea/coffee & biscuits, but no real kitchen. *Dorm beds from €10, dbls from €35.* €

Patio Hostel 📍 221 F4 (16 rooms) Špitálska 35; ☎ 02 5292 5797; w patiohostel.com; 🚌 3, 4 to Mariánska; 🚌 N61 to Centrum. On the road from Tesco up to the Medical Garden, Patio is a friendly, long-established hostel with accommodation in quiet & colourful twin & trpl rooms & 4- to 12-bed dorm rooms with lockers. Common room with cable TV, bar with table football, fully equipped kitchen, lift, Wi-Fi, parking (€10) & bike rental & storage. €

Schöndorf Hostel 📍 221 F4 (8 rooms inc dorms) Obchodná 48; m 09 48 437 397, 09 05 730 756; w schoendorfhostel.com; 🚋 1, 9 to Vysoká; 🚌 31, 39, 42, 47, 80, 94 to Kollárovo námestie; 🚌 N31, N34, N44, N47, N53, N55, N70, N72, N80, N93, N95 to Hodžovo námestie. A modern but frankly robotic hostel (only online booking, access by PIN, no staff at check-in) with 6- & 8-bed dorms, 3 dbls & a 4-bed room. In the courtyard is the lovely Bio Café (f biocafeschondorf). €

Urban Elephants 📍 222 G3 (4 dorms) Kolárska 8; m 09 40 568 810; w elephants.sk/urban; 🚌 N61 or 🚋 1, 3, 4 to Centrum. Attractive central hostel with an age cap of 40; there's a full kitchen, an excellent common room with table football, & 4 dorms. There's a nightly pub-crawl, but the nearby Wild Elephants Hostel (w elephants.sk/wild) is more of a party place. €

CAMPING

Camping is not necessarily the most obvious accommodation option for what is essentially a city destination; however, families with young children, & especially those on a budget, will enjoy the old-fashioned resort charm of 'Golden Sands' (Zlaté Piesky). Areál Divoká Voda is the perfect place to stay if you enjoy watersports, but it is too far from Bratislava to make it a convenient base.

Areál Divoká Voda 📍 map, page 196 (16 bungalows, 50 tent pitches) Čunovo; ☎ 02

6252 8002; **w** divokavoda.sk; 90 from Nové SND to Čunovo – Areál vodných športov. Areál Divoká (Whitewater Resort) is a large watersports complex on an artificial island in the Danube, 15km south of Bratislava. There is a large campsite where you can pitch a tent for €3–8/night plus €3 pp; cars cost €3/night & campervans €15/night. Bungalows cost €50/night for 4 people. For information on the hotel at this site, see page 85; its restaurant (€€) provides b/fast for €8. €€

Autocamp Zlaté Piesky map, page 196 (45 chalets, 20 bungalows, 1 apartment, 300 tent pitches) Senecká cesta 2; 02 4425 7373; May–Oct; N53 or 4 to Zlaté Piesky (25mins), then walk over bridge. Cheap but basic campsite at the delightfully old-fashioned 54ha lake resort in the northeast of Bratislava. Camping costs (/night): €4 adult; €2.50 child; €4 3-person tent; €8 campervan; & €6 caravan. Besides the campsite, small cabins can be rented. The bungalows have a shower, kitchen & small fridge. The apartment sleeps up to 4, with separate bedroom, family room & equipped kitchen area, also TV, private shower, own parking place & picnic area. *Chalets €, bungalows & apartment €€*

6

Eating and Drinking

Láska ide cez žalúdok ('Love goes through the stomach')

Slovak cuisine is a mélange of central European influences, taking a bit of everything from its neighbours: goulash from the Magyars, strudels from the Austrians, and home-kneaded dumplings from the Germans – not to mention beer from the Czechs.

Slovak chefs grew up in the meat, potato and cabbage school of cooking; however, it's easy to find something lighter in the many restaurants with international menus, offering cuisine from Italy to India, France to Vietnam. Many traditional Slovak restaurants also offer lighter versions of the sturdy, traditional dishes, and veganism is now widespread. Slovak cuisine is not as stodgy and bland as that in the Czech Republic and due to the culinary influence of southern neighbours, it has a perkier, spicier tang. A hundred years ago, most Slovaks lived on and from the land and robust peasant cooking still dominates the national psyche. This is the land of cabbage, caraway seeds, cheese, wheat flour, potatoes and endless variations on the theme of pork. However, after a day cycling along the Small Carpathian Wine Route or visiting castle ruins, such hearty fare can be just the thing.

After 1,000 years under Hungarian domination and 40 years of communism, Slovakia's restaurant culture remains in its infancy, although in Bratislava they have caught on quickly with new, exciting restaurants opening every month. This guide to restaurants offers a selection of both traditional and international places so you can try the local dishes or stick with something you know.

FOOD

Breakfast (*raňajky*) at home is bread with butter, cheese, ham, sausage, eggs, peppers and tomatoes, jam and yoghurt, washed down with tea with lemon or strong coffee. Some new cafés serve pastries or local versions of croissants (*lúpačky*). On the way to work, some people nibble on frankfurters (*párky*) and crescent rolls at a café (🕐 early Mon–Fri only is pretty much the rule), followed by elevenses early at 10.00. Bratislava is in the midst of a quality coffee craze, with various trikes tempting passers-by with aromatic brews for €1.50–2.50 (page 115), and many cafés and patisseries offer coffee to go (*káva so sebou*).

Slovakia has excellent **milk products**; the yoghurts are creamy and the cheeses are also much better than in most other countries in the region. Look out for local RAJO brand yoghurts, which knock spots off the bland multi-national products. Sheep's cheese, *bryndza*, is tangy and definitely worth trying, usually served with dumplings in the traditional *bryndzové halušky* dish, with optional bacon bits on top. *Tvaroh* is like a blend of cottage and cream cheese, while *parenica* is a stringy, rubbery hard cheese, wound up like a snail and often smoked.

Slovaks love to **snack**, and the Old Town is filled with hole-in-the-wall eateries and little pop-up snack bars offering pies (*buchty*), potato pancakes (*lokša*) with savoury fillings such as cabbage, poppyseed or garlic, and giant deep-fried doughnuts (*langoše*) topped with sour cream or grated cheese. Filled baguettes (*bagety*), pizzas and kebabs are also available everywhere throughout the city. Pancakes (*palacinky*) can arrive with either sweet or savoury fillings.

Lunch (*obed*) is the main meal of the day, a serious event of soup, followed by a substantial main course and dessert. Unless eating out, the Slovak **dinner** (*večera*) is a bit like breakfast; a do-it-yourself affair with bread and cold meats, cheeses and pickles.

Back to the main event – *obed*. This should begin with a soup (*polievka*), although some locals might claim that meals actually begin with a shot of plum brandy (*slivovica*). Slovak cooking is so robust that appetisers (*predjedlá*) are rarely necessary. For those with a healthy appetite, a slice of ham rolled around horseradish cream (*šunková rolka s chrenovou penou*) could fill a gap. The tangy fresh sheep's cheese (*bryndza*) or raw onions and lard sometimes appear on simpler menus as a beer accompaniment, served with bread (*chlieb*), a Slovak staple. Soups are usually thick; no watery gruel here, but often very salty. Cabbage soup (*kapustnica*) is one of the best-known soups (and renowned as a hangover cure), livened up with smoked pork, cream, mushrooms and sometimes plums. Garlic soup (*cesnaková polievka*) is great and often arrives in a huge, scooped-out bread roll (*bosniak*).

Slovak **main dishes** tend to be heavily based on meat (*mäso*). Pork (*bravčové*) is king here. It comes as ribs (*rebierko*), chops (*karé* or *rezy*) or steak (*roštenka*). A slab of pork is quite often stuffed with ham and/or cheese.

Fried, grilled or roast poultry (*hydina*) is popular, with turkey (*morka*) and chicken (*kuracie*) leading the way. In the autumn, roast goose (*husia*) and duck (*kačica*) are traditional treats, served with *lokše* (potato pancakes) and cabbage. Beef (*hovädzie*) appears on many menus but is more expensive (especially tenderloin steak) than the other meats. Fish, such as carp (*kapor*) and trout (*pstruh*), from local rivers can be bony but tasty. Restaurant menus

---

1 Cafés, bars and bistros line every pavement in the Old Town. **2** Pressburg croissants (*Bratislavské rožky*) – crescent-shaped pastries filled with walnuts. **3** Sample traditional dishes of *bryndzove halušky* (potato dumplings with sheep's cheese), and roast duck served with potato pancakes and cabbage, all washed down with locally brewed beer. ▶

SLOVAK GRAPE VARIETIES

Kde niet vína – niet lasky ('Where there's no wine, there's no love')

Slovak winemaking history dates back to the 7th century BC when Celts grew vines on the hilly land northeast of Bratislava, though it's often attributed to the Romans and specifically the emperor Marcus Aurelius. The continental climate makes Slovakia, like Hungary, ideal for producing fruity whites (favoured by German and Austrian drinkers) and robust reds. The white wine is more reliable than the red and the Tokaj could be taken home as an excellent gift to sweeten up your mother-in-law. To be sure to get something drinkable, stick to wines above €8. Superior quality wines sell for €12–18.

Since the 1950s, Slovak winemakers have created 14 totally new grape varieties, by blending local grapes and exploiting the unique quality of Slovakia's climate and soil. The white grapes are named after Slovak castles such as Devín, Hetera, Breslava and Milia, while the blue (red) grapes are named after local rivers: Dunaj (Danube), Hron, Váh, Rimava and Rosa. In 2015, only four (Dunaj, Hron, Váh and Devín) of the new grape varieties were planted, covering 3% of the total vineyard area. The most popular of the new wines are the white Devín and the blue Dunaj.

In the last decade or two, Slovakia has acquired a niche reputation for its orange and natural wines. Natural wines, made without pesticides, preservatives, chemicals, sulphites or added sugars, are well established, but orange wine (*oranžové víno*) is a more recent development. Based on ancient Georgian techniques, it's like a white wine with elements of red wine, with the grape skins being left in the vat during fermentation. This gives a full peachy flavour and more tannins, making it an ideal pairing with seafood, salads and light pasta dishes. The best-known Slovakian orange wine is Slobodné, notably their dry young Cutis Deviner, and the best-known natural wine is Vino Magula Carboniq, both from the Trnava area.

Words to look for on the label are *červené* (red), *biele* (white), *ružové* (rosé), *oranžové* (orange), *suché* (dry), *sladké* (sweet), *akostné* (quality), *výber* (choice) and *vina s privlastkom* (wine with a special attribute). The website w wineshop.sk sells Slovak wine online. See also page 143.

THE WHITES
Chardonnay This French variety is a popular grape in Slovakia & often used for the production of local sparkling wines.

Devín A new full-bodied, acidic variety with a hint of spicy grapefruit & lemon balm, leaning towards Muscat. Devín is a cross between the Tramín *červený* (Gewürztraminer) & Veltlínske *červenobiele* varieties. This variety was created in 1958 by Dorota Pospíšilová & Ondrej Korpás at Bratislava's Wine Research Institute, & produces dry wines as well as naturally sweet ones.

Müller-Thurgau The most widely planted white grape in Slovakia (& Germany). Created by Dr Hermann Müller from the Swiss canton of Thurgau in 1882 by crossing Riesling & Silvaner grape varieties.
Pálava Another new variety developed in the Czech Republic; it's a cross between Tramín & Müller-Thurgau.
Rizling Rýnsky German Riesling, with a crisp, fruity finish.
Rizling Vlašský Welsch Riesling from the Champagne region of France.
Rulandské Biele French Pinot Blanc with good acids.
Sauvignon Blanc French variety popular with Slovak winemakers.
Tokaj This legendary grape variety, called 'the wine of kings, the king of wines' by Louis XIV, is usually associated with Hungary, but after the Trianon Treaty of 1920 10% of the total vineyard area was left in Slovakia. It's usually a sweet dessert wine like a Sauternes. Wine cellars such as **J & J Ostrožovič** (w ostrozovic.sk) in Veľká Tŕňa & Tokajská spoločnosť Viničky (w vino-tokaj.sk) in Viničky can be visited easily on a day trip from Košice (page 203), 71km northwest of the wine-growing region.
Tramín Gewürztraminer & very flowery.
Tramín červený Not red, despite the name (*červený* means 'red') but the grape's skin has a reddish tinge. Very flowery yet dry, a great accompaniment to Slovak cheeses or trout.
Veltlínske zelené (Grüner Veltliner) One of the most consistently delicious wines; flowery, crisp & fresh.

THE REDS
Alibernet Cabernet–Sauvignon hybrid (developed in Ukraine in 1950) with notes of blackcurrants & blackberries.
Dunaj (Danube) This variety was created in 1958 by Dorota Pospíšilová when she first crossed the Muškát Bouchet grape with Oporto & then mixed in Svätovavrinecké (St Laurent). With its early ripening, it is a very suitable variety for Slovak climatic conditions. It has good resistance to frost & is as robust & distinctive as its river namesake.
Frankovka Modrá Also known as Blaufränkisch, this is common on the Small Carpathian Wine Route & often turns up as the house wine in Bratislava's restaurants; it's less light than the Austrian version & is soft & well rounded with concentrated bouquets of fruit & berries. This was the empress Maria Theresa's favourite wine; she gave it the royal seal of approval in 1767 & called it the 'pregnancy wine' as she thought it helped her fertility. Sample this with caution; the empress had 16 children!
Modrý Portugal Blauer Portugueser is lighter than most. An easy variety to grow, it ripens early & has a lovely, light ruby colour.
Neronet Like Alibernet, it's a Cabernet hybrid. It's juicy & tannic with cherry aromas.
Rulandské Modré Pinot Noir, an ingredient of Burgundy. This grape variety produces rich, velvety wines with hints of plums.
Svätovavrinecké St Laurent – a French variety like a darker Pinot Noir, with good body, dark red colour, yet light & fruity with well-structured tannins.

often give a base price for 150g then add on a charge for every 10g over. When ordering fish, tell the waiter the general size of fish you fancy. Carp is a traditional Christmas Eve dish throughout the Slav world, which can be simply fried (*vyprážaný*), grilled (*na rošte*), served with nuts (*s orechami*) or heaps of garlic (*s cesnakom*). Magyar neighbours gave Slovaks goulash (*guláš*), a stew with meat (pork, beef, or both), potatoes and carrots, laced with onions, caraway seeds and paprika. The Viennese lent their schnitzels and the Istrian coast offered a delicious stew of smoked pork and sauerkraut.

After selecting a main course, you then have to choose a **side dish** (*príloha*): potatoes (*zemiaky*), rice (*ryža*) or a portion of veg. Slovak restaurants charge extra for side dishes, and waiters can look disturbed if you don't order one. The potatoes are always reliable and arrive baked (*zapekané zemiaky*), boiled (*varené zemiaky*), mashed (*zemiaková kaša*) or fried (*opekané zemiaky*). Chips or French fries (*hranolky*) are everywhere.

The star of **dessert** (*dezert*) menus is the pancake (*palacinka*). These have sweet fillings: chocolate (*s čokoládou*), jam (*s džemom*) or a ricotta-esque cheese (*s tvarohom*). Sweetened noodles (*rezance*) topped with poppy seeds and melted butter are also popular. Slovaks love cakes and pastries – see page 105 for a few pointers.

In the last decade or so **vegetarian** and **vegan** food has become widespread; until then, the only vegetarian option (apart from pizza and pasta) was fried cheese (*vyprážaný syr*) with chips (*hranolky*) and tartare sauce. Now there are at least half a dozen exclusively veggie and vegan restaurants in or near the centre of town, and many other places do fabulous salads (*šalát*) and incredibly imaginative veggie dishes. Broccoli baked with smoked cheese (*zapekaná brokolica*) is an old favourite, and another reliably good option is *lečo*, a delicious concoction of tomatoes, peppers and onions, a kind of ratatouille eaten across central Europe, often with rice or a stirred-in raw egg.

Many restaurants and cafés provide **gluten-free** options and the supermarkets have a range of products if you are on a restricted diet. I even found a delicious lactose-free chilli-chocolate ice cream at the famous Luculus ice-cream parlour (page 110).

If you are on a tight **budget**, or simply want to lunch the local way, look out for the daily lunch menu (*denné menu*) on offer at almost every restaurant. This will usually be a soup and a main (rarely meat-free), although some places also include a soft drink and a dessert. As these are intended for locals, there may not always be an English version of the menu. Ask your waiter for suggestions or take pot luck. The average price for this is a bargain €8, so you really can't go wrong.

DRINK

Slovak **mineral water** (*minerálna voda*) is delicious and contains many life-enhancing properties. Also popular are **soft drinks** like Kofola (Czech cola) that's mixed with soda water and often available on draught in half-litre mugs. *Vinea* is a refreshing red or white grape juice drink sold in tall glass bottles and local fruit juices are excellent, with unusual choices like peach, pear or lip-puckering quince.

These days, the most popular drink served in Bratislava is **homemade lemonade**. It often arrives in a jam jar, half-litre jug or some other funky glass and will have added orange zest, ginger, nettles, cucumber, watermelon, lavender, cardamom, elderflower, rose petals, mint and stevia, or something else that the bartender has dreamed up that week. This is a delicious alternative to beer, especially in the often-overpowering heat of a summer's day.

For centuries under Hungarian rule, the peasant population had little access to **wine** (*vino*), which went to nobles throughout the kingdom, although the lower-quality stuff did serve as an everyday drink in wine-producing areas. Beer (*pivo*), the beverage of the rising burgher class, cost too much for most peasants and it was illegal to make it without a royal licence. *Burčiak* is a young wine, cloudy and still fermenting, which is produced in September, doesn't last long and can explode in the bottle. Try it at the Pezinok and Modra wine festivals (page 30).

Slovaks used to distil at home the produce from their orchards, creating the famous, fiery plum brandy (*slivovica*), and similar paint-stripping brews from pears (*hruškovica*), cherries (*čerešňovica*), apricots (*marhuľovica*) and even beetroot (*repovica*). Devín specialises in a less fiery currant wine (*ríbezlák*). *Borovička* is made from juniper berries and tastes a bit like gin. It's said to be the best cure for a cold. *Demänovka* is another bittersweet herbal liqueur while the cinnamony *Becherovka* is Czech but also worth a try.

Honey wine (*medovina*) used to be made in nearly every village home. This custom has dwindled nowadays, but most villages still have at least one beekeeper. This mead-like drink is still served hot at Bratislava Christmas market and there is another bizarre festive drink which the brave can try there. *Hriatō* is an alcoholic 'speciality' made from heated honey and bacon or goose fat, giving off a powerful aroma. It makes a good cough mixture, if you can get it down.

RESTAURANTS

Many restaurants place copies of the **menu** by the front door on the outside wall, so you can get an idea of the food and the prices before you venture in. This is not compulsory, but because of a 'good local habit' to be helpful. It also gives restaurants the chance of showing their wares in the hope of tempting visitors to enter.

All restaurants in Bratislava are required by law to issue a printed **receipt** from the electronic cash register, so if you have any concerns over the bill, make sure you get one. Major **credit cards** are usually accepted, but check first, before launching into the chateaubriand steak for two and champagne supper.

SLOVAK BEER

Although not as well known as the Czech Republic for their brews, Slovaks really love their beers and in the 1950s and 1960s Slovak beer production increased dramatically. It fell after the fall of communism due to tax and the introduction of alternative drinks, but is now stable. Recently, there has been an explosion of micro-breweries, with 20 in Bratislava alone and 90 more across the country, producing pilsners and IPAs, of course, plus porters, stouts, sour beers, wheat beers and other styles. However, the Slovak market is dominated by two big brewers: Heineken (with their cheap Kelt lager) and Topvar (with the Czech brand Kozel).

Below I've mentioned only the most frequently encountered beers – some pubs will have more varieties. Look out for light lager (*svetlé ležiak*), amber lager (*polotmavy ležiak*), dark beer (*tmavé pivo*), or draught/on-tap beer (*výčapné pivo*). There'll be lots of foam, just accept it. In touristy pubs and bars, particularly in stag-friendly Bratislava, specify what brand of beer you'd like, otherwise they'll just plonk down a half-litre of the cheapest (or the most expensive) brew, which probably won't be Slovak and will thus render your 'research' meaningless. If the waiter is impressed with your Slovak skills he might enquire whether you'd like a *desatka* (10° – about 4% alcohol), a *jedenástka* (11° – about 5% alcohol), or a *dvanástka* (12° – about 6% alcohol), as many of the beers come in different strengths. Shandy (*radler*) is a popular and refreshing summer drink.

Corgoň Produced by Heineken at the Hurbanovo brewery (halfway to Budapest) & named after a statue in the town of Nitra. 'Corgoň' means 'champion', making it an appropriate sponsor for Slovakia's national football league (2003–14). A very popular beer with a high level of bitterness giving a well-balanced brew.

Kaltenecker A well-established commercial brewery in the Rožňava suburb of Bratislava, producing good pilsners, Brokát dark lager, IPAs & stouts, & also renting its vats to various wandering brewers without premises of their own, such as Damian Gypsy Brewery, Hopfanatic & Horizont Sörök.

Bratislava Old Town is a wall-to-wall eat-out city with cafés, bars, cocktail venues, restaurants, self-service canteens, stand-up buffet stalls – you're totally spoilt. Slovak, international, Mediterranean, Mexican, Japanese – there's a great choice and it's doubtful that you'll need to book (apart from at the 'flavour of the month'), as if your intended eaterie is full, just totter two yards along the pavement and you'll find another option.

A few interesting restaurants are dotted about in the tightly packed district beneath the castle; others **outside the Old Town walls** are more spread out. Restaurants line up on the north side of leafy Hviezdoslavovo námestie and along the Danube promenade at the Eurovea shopping centre, and there

Kelt A smooth, fruity 10° (4.2%) brew produced at Heineken's Hurbanovo brewery.
Komín From the Bratislava borough of Ružinov, this produces a full range from lager to IPA, summer ale & amber & alcohol-free beers; always available at the Alzbetka pub (page 115).
Martiner Original Delicious dark beer from Martin, now produced by Heineken in Hurbanovo.
Šariš Brewed in Veľký Šariš near Prešov in eastern Slovakia. In 1997, Šariš was bought by SABMiller, who merged it with Pivovary Topvar, creating Slovakia's largest brewery; in 2016 it was sold to Asahi Breweries of Japan. Their flagship beer is Šariš 12° Premium, & Smädný Mních (Thirsty Monk) is a refreshing light 10° beer with a rich, dense foam. The Šariš 11° Tmavý is a fine dark beer using 4 kinds of hops, with a nutty, full taste.
Steiger The refreshing 'Hell' (clear) beer & dark varieties, from a brewery founded in 1473 in Vyhne, near Banská Štiavnica. The Steiger Radler is lemony & very low alcohol.
Stein Light & dark. Opened in 1873, Stein moved production to the Steiger Pivovar in Vyhne in 2007. The Stein 10° draught is a Bohemian pilsner with a fine, bitter hop flavour.
Stupavar Brewing since 2017 in Stupava, north of Bratislava, they boast of their honest, unpasteurised, unfiltered beers – lagers, IPA, black IPA, Weizen, porter, even pumpkin ale.
Topvar Founded in 1957, production was moved to Veľký Šariš in 2010 & the company is now owned by Asahi Breweries of Japan. Light, dark & alcohol-free. The dark Topvar 11° Tmavý tastes of caramel coffee & has won many awards.
Urpiner A successor to the historic Banskobystricky brewery in the mining town of Banska Bystrica in the centre of Slovakia, the Urpiner brewery was opened in 1971, & has been expanded & modernised since 2007. It produces particularly flavourful lagers (especially the 12° version).
Zlatý Bažant (Golden Pheasant) Light & dark. Started in 1968 in Hurbanovo, near Komárno, as a state-owned enterprise supplying beer to western Slovakia; bought by Heineken in 1995. The best-known Slovak lager with a crisp, spicy, well-rounded flavour. Very refreshing on a summer's day.

has been a resurgence of café and bistro life in the up-and-coming district surrounding the Blue Church and east towards the main bus station. Basically, all restaurants, with the exception of Veža on top of Kamzík Hill (page 101), are within walking distance. A trio of restaurants is located south of the river in Sad Janka Kráľa park, and walking back to your hotel across Most SNP or Starý Most on a fragrant spring evening is a lovely way to round off the day.

Regarding **opening hours**, Bratislava restaurants do not show any signs of life until 10.00, but then usually stay open until 23.00/midnight, although they may stop serving at 22.00. Unfortunately, health/veggie cafés generally only open for lunch on weekdays.

> **RESTAURANT PRICE CODES**
>
> The following price codes indicate the average cost of a main course in restaurants, ranging from top-of-the-range *haute-cuisine* establishments, to more modest canteen-style lunch bars.
>
> | | |
> |---|---|
> | €€€€€ | €22+ |
> | €€€€ | €16–21.99 |
> | €€€ | €12–15.99 |
> | €€ | €6–11.99 |
> | € | less than €6 |

An interesting development is that many of the flashier, more expensive restaurants are now closing, along with many tourist traps and leery, beery stag pubs; the grander hotel restaurants closed during the Covid-19 pandemic and haven't reopened. These are being replaced by reasonably priced, trendy bistros, cool cafés and brunch joints, and high-quality bakeries, frequented by hip, young locals who want to enjoy all the interesting new drinks and dishes.

With a third of the population **smoking**, it can get pretty stuffy, though in 2009, a ban was introduced on smoking in all establishments serving food. If the restaurant has two rooms, it can set aside one for smokers, but cannot serve food there. If they only have one room, then it's strictly non-smoking. Cafés and pubs often have smoking areas, although they cannot if they offer food. Many tea houses have sprung up in Bratislava, and they are almost always non-smoking.

The sections on restaurants, cafés and pubs have all been divided into two main districts: **Old Town and Castle District** and **Beyond the Old Town gates, Centrum and further afield**. Only occasionally will you have to take a taxi to your choice of chow venue, as the majority can be reached on foot.

OLD TOWN AND CASTLE DISTRICT

Modrá Hviezda 220 C6; Beblavého 14; 02 5443 2747; w modrahviezda.sk; 17.30–22.00 Wed–Fri, noon–22.00 Sat–Sun; 203, 207, N47 to Hrad. The 'Blue Star' restaurant serves Slovak specialities in a stable setting in a historic, 18th-century late Baroque building on a narrow passage under the castle. A good place to try expertly prepared traditional dishes such as venison, duck, zander, & Mangalica game casserole. €€€€–€€€€€

Reštaurácia Hradná 220 C6; Námestie A Dubčeka 1; m 09 49 015 016; w hradna.com; 10.00–22.00 daily; 44, 47, N47 to Hrad. Visitors to this restaurant in the castle grounds enjoy local wines, a lighter modern take on traditional favourites & a terrace with a smashing view of the Old Town centre & the Danube. €€€–€€€€€

Enjoy Bistro 222 C4; Michalská 3; m 09 18 461 004; w enjoybistro.sk; 08.30–21.00 Mon–Thu, 08.30–22.00 Fri–Sat, 08.30–20.00 Sun; 1, 3, 4 to Centrum; N31, N34,

N44, N47, N53, N55, N70, N72, N80, N93, N95 to Hodžovo námestie. Right on the main street of the Old Town, this attractive modern café-bistro has a busy terrace on the street & a popular kids' area. It's one of the best brunch spots (until noon), with pasta, risottos & salads to follow. They also specialise in organic English teas (€3.70). €€€–€€€€

Koliba Kamzík 223 C6; Zelená 5; m 09 03 703 111; w zelena.kamzik.sk/en; 11.00–23.00 daily; 1, 3, 4 to Centrum; N31, N34, N44, N47, N53, N55, N70, N72, N80, N93, N95 to Hodžovo námestie. Part of the Aplend City Hotel Perugia (page 85), this offers Slovak country cuisine in a rustic barn setting, with 4 vegetarian main courses. There's a similar branch at Michalská 16 (222 C4; w michalska.kamzik.sk/en). €€€–€€€€

Jasmin 220 D6; Zidovska 7; 02 5441 5182; w jasmin1.sk; 11.00–22.30 Mon–Thu, 11.00–23.00 Fri–Sat, 11.00–21.30 Sun; 9 to Kapucínska. Founded in 1996, this remains the best Chinese restaurant in town (as opposed to the more fast-foody pan-Asian places in the city centre). €€€

Nibble & Sip House 222 C5; Ventúrska 9; m 09 48 488 480; ; 11.00–22.00 daily; 1, 3, 4 to Centrum; N31, N34, N44, N47, N53, N55, N70, N72, N80, N93, N95 to Hodžovo námestie. A trendy tapas & cocktail place in the historic Zichy Palace, or in summer in its elegant courtyard, with a gargoyle spouting up out of the flagstones. Flashy but reliable. €€€

Primi 221 H7; Eurovea; m 09 14 346 952; w primieurovea.sk/en; 11.00–midnight daily; 40 to Nové SND; 50, 70, N33 to Malá Scéna. Large slick restaurant on the Danube promenade with a mile-long menu offering pasta, pizzas, salads, risottos, cocktails & teas. Resident DJs at w/ends until the wee hours. €€€

Lux Flavour 222 C5; Zelená 2; m 09 15 515 122; w luxflavour.sk; 10.00–23.00 Mon–Thu, 11.00–01.00 Fri–Sat, 11.00–23.00

RESTAURANT NAMES

In Slovakia, eating and drinking venues announce themselves with words that may not be immediately recognisable. Apart from *reštaurácia* and *bufet*, the signs on establishments can leave visitors confused. Here is an explanation of some of the places to check out for food and drink.

Reštaurácia Restaurant
Jedáleň Canteen
Bufet Stand-up snacking venue
Samoobsluha 'Self-service' dining
Cukráreň Patisserie (from the word *cukor* – sugar)
Piváreň Beer hall
Vináreň Wine tavern (literally 'wine cellar')
Kaviareň Coffeehouse
Koliba Rustic country restaurant offering grilled meats (literally 'a hut')
Krčma Pub
Hostinec Pub in the countryside, the centre of all village life

Sun; 🚋 1, 3, 4 to Centrum; 🚌 N31, N34, N44, N47, N53, N55, N70, N72, N80, N93, N95 to Hodžovo námestie. A trendy place, with bright lights, creative cocktails & occasional DJ sets, so it's a bit surprising that they specialise in Slovak cuisine. €€–€€€

Urban Bistro 📍 222 C4; Michalská 5; **m** 09 48 569 003; **w** urbanbistro.sk; ⏱ 09.00–22.00 Mon, 09.00–midnight Tue–Thu & Sun, 09.00–02.00 Fri & Sat; 🚋 1, 3, 4 to Centrum; 🚌 N31, N34, N44, N47, N53, N55, N70, N72, N80, N93, N95 to Hodžovo námestie. A delightful place (hipster in the right way), with fine coffees & beers & a great range of food, with brunch served until 14.00 & lunch only from 14.30! Bare concrete pillars & beams, white tiles & zinc ducts, & an open kitchen at the rear. €€–€€€

✷ **Urban House** 📍 222 F5; Laurinská 14; **m** 09 11 755 205; **w** urbanhouse.sk; ⏱ 09.00–midnight Mon–Thu, 09.00–02.00 Fri & Sat, 09.00–23.00 Sun; 🚋 1, 3, 4 to Centrum; 🚌 N31, N34, N44, N47, N53, N55, N70, N72, N80, N93, N95 to Hodžovo námestie. Wonderful, cavernous & cool place to chill out right in the heart of the Old Town. Excellent brunch options are followed by a largely American-style menu, with burgers, pizza, tacos, fish & steaks. Enjoy a homemade lemonade (€5.90) while swaying gently in the hammock. See page 108. €€–€€€

✷ **Alchymista u veľkých Františkánov** 📍 222 D4; Františkánske námestie 10; **m** 09 18 575 443; 📘 alchymista.pub; ⏱ 11.00–midnight Mon–Sat; 🚋 1, 3, 4 to Centrum; 🚌 N31, N34, N44, N47, N53, N55, N70, N72, N80, N93, N95 to Hodžovo námestie. Locals & visitors mingle on junk-shop chairs in a shabby-chic setting, enjoying the pork ribs with homemade pickles. €€

✷ **Da Vinci Bistro&More** 📍 222 B4; Klariská 8; **m** 09 01 708 488; 📘; ⏱ 11.00–midnight Mon–Thu, 11.00–02.00 Fri, noon–02.00 Sat, 14.00–midnight Sun; 🚋 1, 3, 4 to Centrum; 🚌 N31, N34, N44, N47, N53, N55, N70, N72, N80, N93, N95 to Hodžovo námestie. A great place to chill out just 1 street away from the crowds, Da Vinci lines the walls with works by the polymath artist & offers superb salads, pasta & pizza plus local beers in a sophisticated yet friendly setting. Great service from multi-lingual locals; pub quiz on Mon. €€

Foodstock 📍 222 F4; Klobučnícka 6; **m** 09 05 456 654; **w** foodstock.sk; ⏱ 11.00–22.00 Sun–Wed, 11.00–midnight Thu–Sat; 🚋 1, 3, 4 to Centrum; 🚌 N31, N34, N44, N47, N53, N55, N70, N72, N80, N93, N95 to Hodžovo námestie. Brilliant vegan/vegetarian bistro with a food truck feel & an Asian slant – gyoza are a speciality, as well as falafel, poké, miso soup & kimchi. €€

Sushi Bar Tokyo 📍 223 C7; Strakova 2; 📞 02 5443 4982; **w** sushi-bar.sk; ⏱ 11.00–midnight daily; 🚋 1, 3, 4 to Centrum; 🚌 N31, N34, N44, N47, N53, N55, N70, N72, N80, N93, N95 to Hodžovo námestie. Japanese & Thai cuisine in this long-running favourite. Sushi pieces €2.90–7.90. €€

BEYOND THE OLD TOWN GATES, CENTRUM AND FURTHER AFIELD

Houdini 📍 223 H7; Tobrucká 4 (Marrol's Hotel); 📞 02 5778 4600; **w** restauranthoudini.sk; ⏱ noon–22.00 Mon–Sat, noon–15.00 & 18.00–22.00 Sun; 🚌 50, N33 or 🚋 1, 4 to Námestie Ľudovíta Štúra. Hearty central European food (rabbit, veal, dumplings) but also healthy options. On w/days there's a choice of 4 lunches for €19.50 for 2 courses or €22.50 for 3, but at w/ends it costs €9–12.50 for starters & €20–40 for mains. €€€€€

Irin 📍 223 B6; Rudnayovo námestie 2; **m** 09 08 667 740; **w** irinrestaurant.com; ⏱ 17.30–23.00 Tue–Fri; 🚋 9 to Kapucínska; 🚌 N31, N34, N47, N53, N55, N70, N72, N80, N93, N95 to Hodžovo námestie. A new restaurant for special occasions, serving only a 9-course tasting menu (€95), depending on availability of high-quality seasonal ingredients. You can have a flight of either wines (€50) or non-alcoholic drinks (€45), or there's a good list of largely natural, low-intervention wines. Outdoor seating in season. €€€€€

UFO 220 D8; Most SNP; 02 6252 0300; w u-f-o.sk; 10.00–23.00 daily; 80, 83, 84, 93, 94, N80, N93, N95 to Pri sade/Aupark. High-class dining at sky-high prices in the Philippe Starck-inspired interior, with one of the best views in town. Expect a stratospheric bill for the progressive Asian-Mediterranean cuisine & wine list. Check out the 'loo with the view'; you'll find yourself flashing the residents of Petržalka far down below, with only a swathe of frosted glass covering your modesty. To reach the restaurant, walk across Most SNP on the walkway below the road, then take the first set of steps down to ground level where you'll find the reception desk & lift (wheelchair-accessible). You can also visit the Watch observation deck (€9.90–11.90 adult, €6.90–9.50 student/disabled, no charge for children under 15/under 111cm); the external Skywalk & abseiling are also available for €65 pp. €€€€€

• **Veža** map, page 196; Cesta na Kamzík 14; 02 4425 6946; w veza.sk; 11.00–20.00 Tue–Sun; 44 from Hodžovo námestie to terminus at Koliba, then 25mins' walk uphill through woods. Dine in style at the highest point in Bratislava: Floor E of the TV tower (page 168). The restaurant has been renovated, but still rotates gently, so watch where you put your handbag down. A short menu of Slovak dishes & vegetarian options, with an amazing view. €€€€€

Savoy Restaurant 223 E7; Radisson Blu Carlton Hotel, Hviezdoslavovo námestie 3; 02 5939 0400; w savoyrestaurant.sk; 06.30–22.30 daily; 50, N33 or 1, 4 to Námestie Ľudovíta Štúra. Classy, international cuisine & Slovak dishes done in a lighter fashion, with grilled meats & veggies, divine desserts & informal, friendly service. In warmer months, the Savoy & adjoining Korzo bar-bistro spread their huge terrace across the southern stretches of Hviezdoslavovo námestie. €€€€–€€€€€

Au Café 220 E8; Tyršovo nábrežie, entrance on Viedenská cesta; m 09 03 902 362; w au-cafe.sk; 11.00–midnight daily; 83, 84, 93, 94, N80, N93, N95 to Pri sade/Aupark. Great setting on the Danube banks in Sad Janka Kráľa. First opened in 1827 & reopened in a modern building in 2003, it is now a 'riverside grill & lounge' offering pizza, steak & expensive Italian dishes in a room decorated in shades of grey. €€€€

Kogo 223 D7; Hviezdoslavovo námestie 21; m 09 11 757 545; w kogo.sk; 11.00–midnight daily; 50, N33 or 1, 4 to Námestie Ľudovíta Štúra. Delicious Italian fish & meat dishes in a swanky setting. Italian & Slovak fine wines. €€€€

Leberfinger 220 E8; Viedenská cesta 257; m 09 03 902 922; w leberfinger.sk; 11.00–midnight daily; 83, 84, 93, 94, N80, N93, N95 to Pri sade/Aupark. Traditional Pressburg specialities (eg: goose leg with red cabbage) in a historic building visited by Napoleon. A great venue for an afternoon chow on the summer terrace in the Sad Janka Kráľa park. Near Au Café (above), on the right bank of the Danube across from the Old Town centre. A plaque commemorates the Hungarian Jewish forced labourers held in outbuildings here in 1944–45 while digging trenches for the Nazis. €€€€

Bratislavská Flagship reštaurácia 222 F2; Námestie SNP 8; m 09 18 606 865; w bratislavskarestauracia.sk; 10.00–midnight Mon–Sat, noon–midnight Sun; 73 or 1, 4 to Centrum; N31, N34, N44, N47, N53, N55, N70, N72, N80, N93, N95 to Hodžovo námestie. This gigantic restaurant in the former Praha cinema building offers traditional Slovak dishes, with a superb selection of meaty specialities, as well as local wines & good beers from their Monastic Brewery next door. €€€–€€€€€

Mint Pradiareň 221 K4; Svätoplukova 2A; **m** 09 10 432 574; **w** mintconcept.sk/en/mints/mint-pradiaren; 07.30–22.00 Mon–Fri, 08.00–22.00 Sat, 08.00–20.00 Sun; 50, 60, N61 to Cvernovka. In a castellated former spinning mill dating from 1900 in the regenerating former industrial area, Mint aims to be a neighbourhood bistro, serving a great range of b/fast/brunch dishes, pasta, pizza, salads, & a few Asian-fusion dishes. €€€–€€€€€

Aušpic 220 C8; Viedenská cesta 24; **m** 09 19 406 403; **w** auspic.sk; 10.00–21.00 Mon, 10.00–22.00 Tue–Thu, 10.00–23.00 Fri–Sat, 11.00–21.00 Sun; 83, 84, 93, 94, N80, N93, N95 to Pri sade/Aupark. This terrace by the Danube makes a fine setting for a meal facing Bratislava Castle. Home to the Bratislava Rowing Club, it caters to locals & sporty types. Good set lunches, tasty soups. €€€–€€€€

Batoni map, page 196; Brečtanová 1/A; **m** 09 05 624 879; **w** batoni.sk; 08.00–22.00 Sun–Thu, 08.00–23.00 Fri & Sat; 44, N44 to Koliba (terminus) then walk uphill for 10mins. An attractive restaurant in a giant Swiss chalet up in the Kamzík Hills that has transitioned to serving high-quality Georgian cuisine, of all things – well worth the journey. Plenty of vegetarian options & good Georgian wine. €€€–€€€€

Brixton House 222 D4; Františkánske námestie 3; **m** 09 48 589 743; **w** brixton.sk; 10.00–midnight Mon–Thu, 10.00–02.00 Fri, 09.00–02.00 Sat, 09.00–23.00 Sun; 1, 3, 4 to Centrum. A lively, hip place that's great for brunch (to 15.00), especially if you can grab seats on the square, but less good for main meals (also sharing plates, street food etc). They have some good beers (NEIPAs & lager) but it's hardly a full range. €€€–€€€€

CarneValle 223 D7; Hviezdoslavovo námestie 20; **m** 09 03 123 164; **w** carnevalle.sk; 11.00–23.00 Mon–Sat, 11.00–22.00 Sun; 50, N33 or 1, 4 to Námestie Ľudovíta Štúra. The emphasis here is definitely on *carne*, with choice cuts of beef, veal, lamb & pork prepared to local & international recipes. Excellent-value steaks, but also pasta, risottos, fish & salads. €€€–€€€€

Kubu 220 D8; Aupark Shopping Center; **m** 09 14 346 964; **w** kubuaupark.sk; 08.30–22.00 Mon–Fri, 09.00–22.00 Sat, 10.00–22.00 Sun; 83, 84, 93, 94, N80, N93, N95 to Pri sade/Aupark. Airy, spacious restaurant ideal for a breather if shopping in Aupark, or a quick bite before a film. Homemade pasta, also pizza, risottos & salads. Welcoming décor with shelves down the middle filled with pots & bottles. Concourse level, mezzanine & suntrap terrace. €€€–€€€€

Pulitzer 222 B3; Župné námestie 7; **m** 09 40 511 179; **w** pulitzer.sk; 10.00–22.00 Mon–Fri, 11.00–22.00 Sat & Sun; 1 to Centrum; 9 to Kapucínska. Very popular restaurant with pasta, grilled meats & salads in a bistro-style bar room packed with newspapers, magazines & books. Lunch menu €9.90. €€€–€€€€

Savage Garden 220 F3; Námestie Slobody; **m** 09 17 115 116; **w** savagebistro.sk; café-bar 09.00–17.00 daily; restaurant 11.00–22.00 daily; 94, N55 or 1, 7 to Námestie Slobody. Occupying 2 separate buildings (restaurant to the west, café-bar to the east, & lots of outside seating) looking out over the huge Námestie Slobody. Good b/fasts, a set lunch 7 days a week (€8.90–11.90), pasta, superb salads, divine desserts & a large choice of 'Savage cocktails' (fresh, fruity & classic mixes; €6.90–9.90) & 'Garden lemonades' with added cucumber & mint, strawberry & basil or edible flowers (€4.90–7.90). €€€–€€€€

Werk 221 J5; Bottova 1; **m** 09 10 434 887; **w** werkbratislava.sk; 10.00–23.00 Mon–Thu, 10.00–midnight Fri, 09.00–midnight Sat,

09.00–23.00 Sun; 🚌 40, 50, 70, 78, 88, N33 to Čulenova. In a former turbine hall at the heart of the Sky Park towers, just south of the bus station, this is a stylish place serving world food small bites, & mostly pasta & salads as mains. There's a good brunch at w/ends (until 15.00). €€€–€€€€

Cozy Coza 220 C4; Kozia 21; 02 2077 3767; w cozycoza.sk; 11.00–15.00 Mon, 11.00–22.00 Tue–Thu, 11.00–23.00 Fri–Sat; 🚌 203, 207 to Kozia. An excellent Sri Lankan chef blends Slovak & Asian flavours, with curry, teriyaki & a Sri Lankan tasting menu, also good-value set lunches. €€€

Moree 220 E1; Žabotova 7; m 09 11 191 891; w moree.co; 10.00–22.00 daily; 🚌 40, 44, 61, 71, 93 or 🚊 1, 7 to Hlavná stanica. An unlikely find, in what looks like a wooden shed (actually a former pub, with a small terrace), down the steps to the east from the main railway station, this offers delightfully imaginative food, décor & service. Dish of the day €8.50. E-bike charging available. €€€

Sushi Time 221 H4; Malý trh 2/A; 02 2129 9921; w sushitime.sk; 10.30–21.00 daily; 🚌 42 to 29 Augusta. In a glass ship building, Japanese fast-food restaurant with good sushi & wok dishes. Home delivery & Wi-Fi; also 6 other branches, mainly in shopping centres. €€€

Štefanka by Pulitzer 220 E4; Palisády 59 (entrance on Hodžovo námestie); 02 5262 0847; w stefankabypulitzer.sk; 09.00–22.00 Mon–Fri, 11.00–22.00 Sat & Sun; 🚌 42, 44, 47, 83, 84, 93 to Hodžovo námestie. This historic café, opened in 1897, is named after the much-loved Princess Stephanie (1864–1945), daughter of Leopold II of Belgium; she was married to Rudolf who committed suicide at Mayerling, & lived out her days at Rusovce (page 197), with her 2nd husband, Elemér Lónyay, a minor Hungarian count. Recently refurbished by Pulitzer (opposite), it's still a traditional Habsburg-esque café with yellow walls, pine-green upholstery, polished wood & an Art Nouveau gallery. It now offers more substantial meals than before, including fish, salads, pasta, steaks, schnitzel & boar & deer goulash (€19); lunch of the day €10/14. €€–€€€

Domček Medická 221 H3; Medická Záhrada; m 09 02 431 049; w medicka.sk; 09.00–20.00 daily; 🚌 47 or 🚊 3, 4 to Americké námestie. Popular café & bistro in what could almost be the potting shed of the lovely Medical Gardens. Light lunches include quiches, baguettes, soups & salads; later in the afternoon there may only be delicious cakes & ice creams available. Also French hot chocolate & the local fave: homemade lemonade. €€

Góvinda 222 F1; Obchodná 30; 02 5296 2366; m 09 14 226 446; w govinda-bratislava.sk; 11.00–15.00 Mon–Fri; 🚊 1, 9 to Poštová. Run by the Slovak Hare Krishna community, the entirely vegetarian/vegan Govinda provides very tasty Indian meals in set menus of soup, veggies & rice (€7.50). €€

Moshi Moshi 220 D4; Panenská 24; m 09 11 125 126; moshimoshi.sk; 10.00–16.00 Mon–Fri; 🚌 44, 47 to Kozia. Different set menus of healthy food, including curries, noodles & sushi; lunch menu, such as cauliflower & potatoes, yoghurt, salad & lemonade, for €7.90. €€

Pane e Olio 222 G6; Gorkého 6; m 09 48 548 408; w paneolio.sk; 11.00–17.00 Mon, 09.00–17.00 Tue–Thu, 09.00–21.00 Fri, 11.00–21.00 Sat; 🚊 1, 4 to Jesenského. A lovely deli, with some seats in the window & outside, serving panini (€10–12), puccia, & pasta dishes (€12–17), all available to take away. The quarter-Italian owner has fantastic hot chocolate, wines, pasta & more for sale. €€

Papaya 220 F3; Námestie 1 mája 15; m 09 48 242 131; w papayavn.eu; 10.00–20.00 Mon–Sat; 🚌 42, 44, 47, 80, 94 to Kollárovo námestie. The first authentic Vietnamese street-food restaurant in Bratislava, specialising

> **SWIFT SNACKS**
>
> If you're looking for a light bite at lunchtime or want to save your appetite for a dinner to remember, here are some places which have a more fast-food vibe, yet still maintain a high quality of cuisine, service and surroundings. Food trucks have also arrived, gathering on the closed road on the south side of the Medická Záhrada gardens.
>
> **Bánh Mi Huy Vege** 222 G2; Kolárska 8; m 09 07 444 111; HuyVege; 10.00–19.00 Mon–Fri, 11.00–15.00 Sat; 1, 3, 4 to Centrum; N31, N34, N44, N47, N53, N55, N70, N72, N80, N93, N95 to Hodžovo námestie. A hole-in-the-wall place that serves Vietnamese fast food, notably vegan banh mi baguettes with tofu, vegan sushi & salad. Not much English spoken, but you can order from pictures. €€
>
> **Chutney** 221 F4; Obchodná 66; m 09 44 225 008; w chutney.sk; 11.00–22.00 Mon–Fri, noon–22.00 Sat–Sun; 1, 9 to Poštová. Indian street food & curries, including plenty of vegetarian options, in a basement room or a light & welcoming courtyard. €€
>
> **Orbis Street Food** 222 F5; Laurinská 7; m 09 11 031 322; w orbisfood.sk; noon–22.00 daily; 1, 3, 4 to Centrum; N31, N34, N44, N47, N53, N55, N70, N72, N80, N93, N95 to Hodžovo námestie. Street food from around the world draws hungry visitors in their droves with chicken wraps & burritos (€7), meat in a cone (€7) & – the big favourite – authentic, twice-cooked Belgian chips with typical sauces (€3.70–4.70). €€

in noodle soups (*pho*, €4.20–8) & wok dishes (€4.70–7.50); lunch of the day €8. €€

Soho 221 G5; Dunajská 20; m 09 48 611 449; soho.dunajska; 10.00–22.00 daily; 1, 3, 4 to Centrum. This Asian-fusion place offers interesting soup combinations (coconut & tofu, basil & banana) & lots of grilled tofu. Delicious cucumber lemonade or elderflower cordial & green teas. Sparse, modern interior décor. €€

Vegan Kiosk 221 F5; Grösslingova 11; m 09 44 476 157; w vegankiosk.sk; 11.00–21.00 Mon–Fri, 10.00–21.00 Sat, 11.00–18.00 Sun; 1, 3, 4 to Centrum. Founded in 2016, this brought vegan street food to Slovakia; there's an excellent wide-ranging menu (burgers, burritos, salad bowls) using various kinds of fake meat & cheese, & great cakes; the set lunch costs €14. €€

Olive Tree 220 E4; Vysoká 14; m 09 11 111 077; olivetreebratislava; 09.00–16.30 Mon–Fri; 1, 9 or 42, 47 to Vysoká. Popular lunch venue with lots of pizza, pasta & risottos. Daily menu €5.95 (main dish). €

CAFÉS AND TEAROOMS

Like its neighbours Vienna and Budapest, Bratislava has a long coffeehouse tradition. Some traditional cafés still exist and many Slovaks love to while away an afternoon at the patisserie (*cukráreň*). On Sunday afternoons, they used to take the tram all the way to Vienna for a coffee, and the Viennese came to Pressburg (Bratislava) for their *kaffee und kuchen*.

Roxor ♀ 220 G1; Šancová 19; **m** 09 03 757 466; **w** roxorburger.sk; ⏱ 11.00–21.00 Mon–Sat, noon–20.00 Sun; 🚌 49, 61, 63, 64, 71, N33, N55, N74 or 🚋 3, 7 to Račianske mýto. Out beyond the Technical University, Roxor serves possibly the best burgers in town (from €11.20) as well as craft beers, wine & coffee. €€

Funki Punki Palacinky ♀ 222 B4; Klariská 12; ☎ 02 2102 8881; **w** funkipunki.sk; ⏱ 11.00–22.00 daily; 🚋 9 to Kapucínska; 🚌 N31, N34, N44, N47, N53, N55, N70, N72, N80, N93, N95 to Hodžovo námestie. Sweet, savoury & vegan/gluten-/lactose-free pancakes (€2.40–3.10) with a huge choice of extra ingredients (€0.50) in a hip café setting – beer, wine & coffee available. Notice the bike hanging above the bar & the owner's humorous anti-IKEA messages. Cash only. €

＊**Soupa Bistro** ♀ 220 D5; Kozia 11; **m** 09 48 611 544; **w** soupa.sk; ⏱ 07.00–15.00 Mon–Fri; 🚌 44, 47 to Kozia. Queues start forming early for this popular little eatery. There's a b/fast bakery, then soups cost €2.90/4.50 (small/large), salads €2.90. Huge portions, although by the time the queue dies down, the broth is barely tepid. Little wooden tables, folk plates on the walls, sweet little trays, couscous, cakes & homemade lemonade. €

Spaghetti Leviathan ♀ 223 H6; Medená 18; **m** 09 10 996 630; **w** leviathan.sk; ⏱ 10.30–18.00 Mon–Fri; 🚋 1, 4 to Jesenského. 'Healthy fast food' in a very green canteen-style interior. Spaghetti with a choice of sauces arrives in 3 portion sizes: 400g (€3.90), 600g (€5.00) or 800g (€6.90). The lunch menu (soup & pasta) is a bargain; there's home delivery, too. €

Do the traditional thing and order a heart-blasting coffee topped with whipped cream (*viedenská káva*) and strudel (*štrúdĺa*) with poppyseed and curd cheese (*makovo-tvarohová*). Most places also serve cappuccinos, lattes and variations on the java jive. As in Vienna, you'll get a tiny biscuit or bit of chocolate with your brew.

If you prefer tea, Bratislava has a scattering of *čajovňa* or **tearooms**. Most are non-smoking and offer a variety of premium teas from all parts of the globe. The Pressburg croissant or bagel (*Bratislavské rožky* or *bajgle*), first recorded in 1599, is either a glazed crescent-shaped roll filled with walnuts, or more like a horseshoe with poppyseeds. Other favourite cake items include *krémeš* (huge cubes of custard cream held in place with pastry) and *šamrola* (pastries filled with cream and dusted with icing sugar).

Bratislava also has a swelling 'chocolate café' scene. The **čokoládovňa** offers a range of hot chocolate drinks, usually with imaginative, unusual taste combinations, quality, homemade chocolates with all manner of fillings, as well as all the usual teas, coffees and cakes.

With the growing bistro and café scene in Bratislava, the lines are blurred between café, bistro and bar. In many of the establishments listed here, you will be able to order a full meal, while others may specialise in coffee, tea, hot chocolate or homemade lemonade.

OLD TOWN AND CASTLE DISTRICT

Patisserie Kormuth 222 C5; Sedlárska 8; w konditoreikormuth.sk; 09.00–20.00 Sun–Thu, 09.00–21.00 Fri–Sat; 1, 3, 4 to Centrum. Undeniably a tourist trap (min spend €13), but the setting & food are both superb. The rooms are totally covered in frescoes & filled with antique furniture, porcelain & crystal; they claim to use Habsburg-era recipes & no artificial flavourings, colourings or preservatives. €€€

Habibi Café 223 D6; Panská 9; m 09 17 171 041; 13.00–midnight Sun–Thu, 13.00–01.00 Fri & Sat; 1, 3, 4 to Centrum; N31, N34, N44, N47, N53, N55, N70, N72, N80, N93, N95 to Hodžovo námestie. Cosy café with interesting meze & teas plus shisha pipes with a fruity tobacco selection; the tables on pedestrianised Panská are the place to be on warm evenings. €€

Kaffee Mayer 222 D5; Hlavné námestie 4; 02 5441 1741; w kaffeemayer.sk; 08.00–21.00 Mon–Thu, 08.00–22.00 Fri, 09.00–23.00 Sat, 09.30–22.00 Sun; 1, 3, 4 to Centrum; N31, N34, N44, N47, N53, N55, N70, N72, N80, N93, N95 to Hodžovo námestie. An old-style Viennese *kaffee und kuchen*, one of 3 biggies on Hlavné námestie. Dark & reassuring with polished wood & 37 great types of cake. €€

La Putika 222 F4; Klobučnícka 4; m 09 11 610 743; laputika cafe; 09.00–midnight Mon–Thu, 09.00–02.00 Fri, 13.00–02.00 Sat, 13.00–midnight Sun; 1, 3, 4 to Centrum; N31, N34, N44, N47, N53, N55, N70, N72, N80, N93, N95 to Hodžovo námestie. (Also at Mýtna 39; 221 G1; m 09 11 610 742; 21, 39 or 3, 7 to Račianske mýto; & at Panská 12; 223 D6; m 09 01 709 079; 1, 3, 4 to Centrum; N31, N34, N44, N47, N53, N55, N70, N72, N80, N93, N95 to Hodžovo námestie.) Mini-chain of café-bistros with a Gallic ambience, a selection of Belgian beers, wines, bar snacks & tasty lunches. Smoking allowed in some rooms & the non-smoking spaces get packed out. 'Putika' translates as a 'shebeen', 'dive', 'greasy spoon' or 'watering hole' but the cafés are much more salubrious than that. €€

Malewill Café Bistro 222 F4; Uršulínska 9; 02 5443 4440; w malewill.mailchimpsites.com; 09.00–midnight Mon–Thu, 09.00–02.00 Fri, 14.00–02.00 Sat, noon–22.00 Sun; 1, 3, 4 to Centrum; N31, N34, N44, N47, N53, N55, N70, N72, N80, N93, N95 to Hodžovo námestie. The rather spooky vaulted bar (the name comes from a post-apocalyptic novel) has 20 versions of a cup of coffee, not to mention cakes & beer (& free Wi-Fi). The plant-strewn courtyard is quite different, serving light Italian lunches (11.00–15.00 Mon–Fri). €€

Martineum Café 223 A7; Rudnayovo námestie 3; m 09 05 434 782; ; 10.00–20.00 daily; 50 or 4 to Most SNP. The beautifully restored Baroque building linked to the cathedral by a new glass bridge now houses the cathedral's information centre & a charming café serving hot & cold drinks, wine, cocktails & cakes – some vegan. €€

Mondieu 223 C7; Panská 27 m 09 05 063 507; w mondieu.sk; 08.00–22.00 Mon–Wed, 08.00–23.00 Thu–Sat, 08.30–21.00 Sun; 1, 3, 4 to Centrum. Popular chain known for its coffee, tea, hot chocolate, & smoothies, but also following the trend for excellent brunches as well as great salads & crêpes. Also at Laurinska 3 (also known as Franchise no.1) & 7; 222 E5. The branch at Hviezdoslavovo námestie 11 (223 B8) does little more than drinks. €€

◀ 1 Patisserie Kormuth is undoubtedly a tourist trap, but both its food and décor are beautiful. 2 There are always queues for delicious ice cream in summer.

LITERARY TEA HOUSES

There is a growing trend in bookish Bratislava for linking up drinking with literary pursuits. Some venues, such as **Avra Kehdabra Literárna čajovňa** (Abracadabra Literary Tea House; opposite), start off as a café, then add the books, magazines and literary evenings. Others, such as **Artforum** at Kozia 20 (page 140), are bookshops that have added comfy chairs, coffee machines and cakes to make the book-buying experience even more pleasurable. A large chunk of the giant **Martinus** bookshop (page 140) at Obchodná 26 is given over to the **Foxford** café (page 112). **Urban House** (page 100) has a selection of books, magazines and newspapers to enjoy, and there is even a hammock, where visitors can chill out with a good read. Check out the bookshops on page 140.

Schokocafé Maximilian Delikateso 222 D5; Hlavné námestie 2; 02 5441 0296; 09.00–21.00 daily; 1, 3, 4 to Centrum. This 2-level café & terrace on the main square next to Roland (page 147), has the same owner & is also a tourist trap. Go for the hot chocolate, the architecture & the view. €€

Bodega 222 F4; Nedbalova 10; 07.30–20.00 Mon–Wed, 07.30–22.00 Thu–Fri, 09.00–22.00 Sat, 10.00–20.00 Sun; 1, 3, 4 to Centrum. A good, but relatively basic, café that offers a peaceful refuge from the nearby tourist drag – b/fast pastries, cakes & sandwiches are available, including Bratislava bagels, & you can pick up free Wi-Fi from the tourist office across the road. €

Bratislavská Pekáreň a mliekareň 222 E2; Poštová 5; 07.00–17.00 Mon–Sat; 1, 9 to Poštová. The best traditional bakery in the city centre, with all kinds of delicious products including Bratislava bagels, poppy & walnut rolls & sourdough bread. There's also a cheese shop, where you may see traditional string cheese being hand-pulled. €

Kaviareň Radnička 222 E5; Stará Radnica, Primaciálne námestie 3; 02 5441 9510; 11.00–19.00 Tue–Sun; 1, 3, 4 to Centrum. Charming café under the arch leading to the City Museum in the Old Town Hall. It's a 'protected workshop' of the OZ Inklúzia organisation (w inkluzia.sk), integrating people with learning difficulties into the community. €

Lab 222 G4; Námestie SNP 25 (next to Stará Tržnica); m 09 45 449 450; w lab.cafe; 08.00–22.00 Mon–Thu, 08.00–midnight Fri–Sat, 10.00–22.00 Sun; 1, 3, 4 to Centrum; N31, N34, N44, N47, N53, N55, N70, N72, N80, N93, N95 to Hodžovo námestie. Attractive co-working space, workshop & café, with great cakes, hot chocolate, rooibos, cappuccino, beer, punch, wine &, of course, free Wi-Fi. €

Pressburg Bajgel 223 C7; Ventúrska 2 (also at Klemensova 5); m 09 04 326 623; w pressburgbajgel.sk; 08.00–19.00 daily; 50 or 4 to Most SNP. The bakery that has been making the distinctive (& yummy) Bratislava bagels since 1890 has new premises on the corner of Panska where you can sit & enjoy a drink with a bagel or some Pressburg cake full of poppy seeds & walnuts. €

BEYOND THE OLD TOWN GATES, CENTRUM AND FURTHER AFIELD

Bistro St Germain 221 G5; Rajská 7; m 09 11 331 999; w stgermain.sk; 10.00–23.00 Mon–Fri, noon–23.00 Sat & Sun; 3, 4 to Centrum or Mariánska. Wonderful Parisian-style bistro-café with gorgeous tiles, chic décor & cool jazz, fabulous lemonade concoctions, chicken-liver paté, wraps & quiches. Opposite Kino Lumière, an art-house cinema, so the ideal spot for a bite before or after a film. €€–€€€

Balans Bistro 220 F3; Jozefská 23; m 09 44 913 520; balansbistro; 11.00–15.00 Mon, 11.00–21.00 Tue–Fri, noon–21.00 Sat, noon–19.00 Sun; 31, 39, 94, N55 to Kollárovo námestie. Excellent vegan bistro with a Mexican twist, serving quesadillas & Mexican burgers, as well as quiches & other tasty meat-free burgers & hot dogs. €€

Café Opera 222 F7; Jesenského 2; m 09 05 643 735; 10.00–20.00 Sun–Mon, 10.00–22.00 Tue–Sat; 1, 4 to Jesenského. A stylish café with plenty of seating inside & out, serving b/fast plates, pastries, soups & quiche, & also natural & orange wines. €€

Fach Bistro 222 C6; Ventúrska 10; m 09 18 734 149; w fachbratislava.sk; 09.00–18.00 daily; 9 to Kapucínska. In a stylishly restored Baroque townhouse there are a bistro, bakery & juice bar, all focused on healthy high-quality offerings. The juices (10.00–17.00 Mon–Fri) boost immunity & vitamin levels, the bread is sourdough, & the bistro (b/fast 09.00–16.00 daily, full menu 11.00–17.30) has lots of vegan options & salads, as well as fruit pies, puddings, local beers, wines & lemonades. €€

Pinch Bistro 223 H6; Štefanovičova 6; m 09 49 585 018; w pinch.sk; 07.00–20.00 Mon–Fri, 09.00–20.00 Sat & Sun; 21, 61, 201, 204, 209, 210 or 1, 7 to Námestie Franza Liszta. Great b/fasts, 2 choices of lunch of the day, superb sandwiches, their famous ginger lemonade, & heavenly desserts. €€

Allakaj bakery & caffe 221 H3; Sasinkova 1; m 09 03 788 585; 07.00–19.00 Mon–Wed, 07.00–20.00 Thu–Sat, 08.00–19.00 Sun; 47 or 3, 4 to Americké námestie. Delightful family-run (since 1953) bakery & coffee shop, with tables on the pavement outside. €

Avra Kehdabra Literárna čajovňa 221 H5; Grösslingová 49; m 09 04 546 409; w literarnacajovna.sk; 11.00–19.00 Mon–Fri, noon–20.00 Sat & Sun; 3, 4 to Centrum. Abracadabra! Here's a great literary tea house, one of a growing number of bookish cafés in the city (opposite). The owner is a friendly young man who studied history & knows loads about the district. Apparently, the Danube used to flow along here (on Dunajská) & the street name, Grösslingová, comes from 'kressling', a fish that lived in the river. The area is becoming very cosmopolitan, with lots of artists & cafés. Loose leaf & imported teas are available to buy & brew at home. €

Café L'aura 223 B7; Rudnyavovo námestie 4; m 09 08 710 499; 10.00–22.00 Mon–Fri, noon–22.00 Sat–Sun; 49 or 1, 3 to Centrum; N31, N34, N44, N47, N53, N55, N70, N72, N80, N93, N95 to Hodžovo námestie. Just below St Martin's Cathedral, L'aura (which really is run by Laura) resembles an old antique shop, & on w/days (10.00–18.00) there is an 'Antik Bazar' here, when you can purchase ceramics, books & other bric-a-brac. Good coffee, tea & wine selection. Board games, too – if you're up to Scrabble in Slovak! €

Café Le Petit 220 E4; Suché mýto 19; m 09 48 446 199; 08.00–22.00 Mon–Sat, 08.00–noon Sun; 42, 44, 47, 83, 84, 93 to Hodžovo námestie. A pleasant café on the ground floor of a guesthouse, with cheap b/fasts & a daily lunch menu. There's

Eating and Drinking **CAFÉS AND TEAROOMS**

ZMRZLINA – ICE CREAM QUEUES

Bratislava is in the midst of homemade ice cream fever. Everywhere you turn in the Old Town, you'll see signs for 'ice cream artigianale' or 'gelato'. Personally, I find this multi-lingual nature a pity, because *zmrzlina* is my favourite Slovak word! I find it quite onomatopoeic, as the lip-licking 'zmmmmr' sound is just what I make after trying yet another divine, creamy creation.

Sometimes Bratislava resembles Moscow in the 1980s, with people queuing for ice cream even in the depths of winter, but when the sun shines, the line is even longer.

Imaginative flavours include Bounty, After Eight, fruit punch (*punč*), chocolate (*čoki*), nougat, coffee, strawberry (*jahoda*), apple (*jablko*), lemon (*citron*), vanilla, cappuccino and banana (*banán;* very popular). A scoop (*kopček*) costs about €2.50, and the cornet is often thrown in, too.

THE PICK OF THE BUNCH Of the other cafés listed in this chapter, Mondieu (page 107) is also known for good ice cream.

Arthur 223 E6; Rybárska brána 9; m 09 07 176 121; 10.00–23.00 daily; 1, 3, 4 to Centrum. Fine homemade ice cream.

F X Messerschmidt Café & Museum 222 F2; Námestie SNP 8; m 09 05 237 054; 08.30–22.00 daily; 1, 3, 4 to Centrum. A counter opening on to the pedestrianised street. Good coffee & cakes, too, inside or at the tables outside.

I Nonni Craft Gelato 223 E5; Laurinská 9; 11.00–20.00 daily; 1, 3, 4 to Centrum. Fabulous all-natural ice creams, on the Old Town's main tourist street.

Koun 223 D8; Paulínyho 1; m 09 48 687 795; w koun.sk; 11.00–19.00 Tue–Thu & Sun, 11.00–20.00 Fri–Sat; 50 or 1, 4 to Námestie Ľudovíta Štúra. Barbara, of the brother-&-sister team behind Koun, studied at Gelato University Carpigiani in Bologna, & they make the best ice cream in Bratislava, if not all Slovakia! Different flavours every day, such as fig & ricotta, poppyseed, raspberry sorbet, walnut cream, amaretti. No preservatives, & there's always a vegan option... Also hot waffles with ice cream (*pizzelles*) & brioche/ice cream sandwiches. Divine.

Luculus 223 C7; Hviezdoslavovo námestie 16 & 24, Panská 29 & Račianske mýto 5; m 09 17 931 068; w luculus. com; 10.00–22.00 daily (summer 09.00–midnight); 50 or 4 to Most SNP. The chilli-choc is divine & there are dairy-based & vegan options, also ice creams sweetened with stevia, & flavours such as lavender, amaretto & dragon fruit. Eat in or out, but there may be long queues either way.

Satisfy your caffeine craving at one of the many vans, bikes and trikes dotted around the city. ▶

a smoking area set apart from the eating section. €

Foxford 222 E1; Martinus, Obchodná 26; 02 3266 0368; w foxford.sk; 08.30–21.00 Mon–Fri, 10.00–20.00 Sat & Sun; 1, 9 to Poštová. A convivial café upstairs in the Martinus bookshop, part of a growing trend of literary cafés linking up with bookshops (page 108). Settle down in a comfy chair with a brew & a good book & while away an hour or 2. Snacks are limited & it's not the cheapest (with table service) but there's good jazz & a big central table for laptoppers. €

KeP's Caffetteria 222 F5; Laurinská 11 (also at Moskovská 1, Ventúrska 8, Trenčianska 56D, 29 Augusta 23, Mliekarenská 1 & Cintorínska 12); m 09 49 381 818; w kepscaffetteria.sk; 07.00–22.00 Mon–Fri, 08.00–22.00 Sat & Sun; 1, 3, 4 to Centrum. A chain of unpretentious cafés with strong Italian coffees, paninis & pizza. Some were previously branded as Vespa, & surviving Vespa branches may become KeP's. €

Next Apache 220 D4; Panenská 28; m 09 03 818 169; 09.00–22.00 Mon–Fri, 10.00–22.00 Sat & Sun; 44, 47 to Kozia. Fabulous little café-bar in the old Lutheran high-school building with low vaults & creaky wooden floors, where Ľudovít Štúr (page 208) once studied, then taught. Created by Canadian Ben Pascoe, there's a magnificent collection of secondhand books, chess & backgammon sets, & a gorgeous sunny courtyard in which to sip a beer or lemonade & read the newspapers. The name has an interesting origin & comes from Pascoe's attempts to memorise the Slovak language. It's his version of *Nech sa páči* (meaning 'there you go'), which waiters say when they bring your dinner. He also has a good way of remembering the Slovak for 'cheers' (*Na zdravie*) which is 'nice driveway'! €

BARS, PUBS AND CLUBS

The beery, leery tourist and stag pubs have died away significantly in the Old Town, although Sedlárska remains defiantly unreconstructed – the Barrock bar announced proudly that it was 'the hottest, most sexist and sexiest bar in the city' although, thankfully, it's a bit more correct. These days, the most popular bars are cultured bistro-café combos, literary tea houses (page 108) and hip bars with imaginative décor.

Slovakia is legendary as a beer lover's destination and there are now half a dozen micro-breweries in town, offering excellent brews (page 96). The Slovak wine industry is also enjoying a renaissance with many sophisticated wine bars and quality wine shops (page 143) in town, and restaurants have trained sommeliers who can advise on local vintages. Cocktails are always popular. Bratislava is also becoming a great choice for the teetotal traveller, with homemade lemonade in a wide variety of flavour combinations being the favourite choice. Half-litres of cooling soft drinks – elderflower cordial, lemonades and local juices – are always very reasonably priced.

OLD TOWN AND CASTLE DISTRICT
Cork 223 D6; Panská 4; m 09 18 834 761; w cork.sk; 09.00–midnight Sun–Thu, 09.00–02.00 Fri–Sat; 50, N33 or 1, 4 to Námestie Ľudovíta Štúra. This classy but popular wine bar has a strong list of Slovak &

international wines, plus grappas; tapas-type snacks available too. €€

Kláštorný Pivovar 222 F2; Námestie SNP 7; m 09 18 606 865; w klastornypivovar.sk; noon–22.00 Tue–Sat; 1, 3, 4 to Centrum; N31, N34, N44, N47, N53, N55, N70, N72, N80, N93, N95 to Hodžovo námestie. The Kláštorný Pivovar (Monastic Brewery) dates only from 2015, when the prior of the order of Merciful Brethren consecrated a brewery in the monastery's Baroque cellars; they're actually partially beneath the Bratislavská Flagship Reštaurácia (page 101) & supply that & the 1st Slovak Pub (page 116). In the pleasantly traditional bar you can sample their 11° pilsners & the award-winning 14° dark lager, as well as traditional pub grub such as fried fish & potato pancakes; cellar tours & tastings also available (€9–16). €€

Nervosa 220 C5; Zámocká 30; m 09 03 652 696; w nervosa.sk; 10.00–21.00 Mon & Tue, 10.00–22.00 Wed & Thu, 10.00–23.00 Fri & Sun, noon–23.00 Sat; 9 to Kapucínska; 44, N47 to Zochova. On the way up to the castle, this pleasant bar offers a range of craft beers, including Urpiner lager from Banska Bystrica, as well as coffee & pizza. €€

Sladovňa House of Beer 223 C6; Ventúrska 5; m 09 17 211 111, 09 15 880 528; w sladovna.info; 11.00–23.00 Sun–Thu, 11.00–midnight Fri & Sat; 1, 3, 4 to Centrum; N31, N34, N44, N47, N53, N55, N70, N72, N80, N93, N95 to Hodžovo námestie. Great destination for beer lovers. Try different versions of the Slovak Zlatý Bažant, along with Guinness, Czech, Belgian & German brews. Woody décor & a meaty menu – the soups are filling & good value, likewise the lunch of the day. €€

Vinopolitan 222 E2; Námestie SNP 6; m 09 05 384 151; w vinopolitan.sk; 10.30–23.00 Mon–Thu, 10.00–midnight Fri, 10.00–23.00 Sat, 14.00–22.00 Sun (closed Sun in winter); 1, 3, 4 to Centrum; N31, N34, N44, N47, N53, N55, N70, N72, N80, N93, N95 to Hodžovo námestie. Primarily a wine shop (for more quality wine shops, see page 143), but you can sample the produce (mostly imported); great coffee, too. €€

Grand Cru Wine Gallery 222 D3; Zámočnícka 8; m 09 08 656 259; ; w grandcruwinegallery.com; 17.00–22.00 Mon–Sat; 1, 9 to Poštová. Martin is extremely knowledgeable about local wines but also very unassuming; this is a lovely little back-street wine bar with very reasonable prices & outdoor seating. €

Pod Kamenným Stromom 222 C5; Sedlárska 10; 02 2072 1408; ; noon–midnight Sun–Thu, noon–02.00 Fri–Sat; 1, 3, 4 to Centrum; N31, N34, N44, N47, N53, N55, N70, N72, N80, N93, N95 to Hodžovo námestie. At the cellar bar 'Under the Stone Tree', you can find a haven of calm & culture, despite sharing the street with the stags. Good music, books, local food (especially fish) & a choice of smoking & non-smoking areas. €

U čerta 220 D6; Beblavého 2; m 09 49 103 788; 14.00–midnight Sun–Mon, 16.00–midnight Tue, 16.00–01.00 Wed–Thu, 16.00–02.00 Fri, 14.00–02.00 Sat; 44, 47, N47 to Zámocká. Those who wish to drink 'at the devil' – as 'U čerta' translates – can do so here in this dark, woody & restful bar at the start of the old red-light district. Good for a swift half on the climb up to the castle; snacks such as burgers, nachos & chicken wings are on offer. €

Viecha malých vinárov 222 F4; Nedbalova 13; m 09 05 736 956; w viecha.com; noon–midnight Mon–Fri, 09.00–01.00 Sat, 17.00–23.00 Sun; 1, 3, 4 to Centrum; N31, N34, N44, N47, N53, N55, N70, N72, N80, N93, N95 to Hodžovo námestie. At the rear of the Old Market, this lovely bar serves excellent wines from small local wineries, as well as tasty snacks. Also has 3 less-central branches, at Košická 48 (♥ 221 K4; m 09 08 134 994; ⏰ 15.00–23.00 daily), Zámocké schody 5 (♥ 220 D6; m 09 05 220 994; ⏰ 16.00–midnight Mon–Thu, 16.00–01.00 Fri, 14.00–01.00 Sat, 14.00–midnight Sun) & Kozia 23 (♥ 220 C4; m 09 03 140 157; ⏰ 16.00–22.00 Mon, 16.00–23.00 Tue–Thu, 16.00–midnight Fri–Sat). €

Viecha Modranských Vinárov ♥ 220 H2; Radlinského 24B; m 09 18 463 110; ⏰ 15.00–midnight Mon–Fri, 17.00–midnight Sat, 17.00–23.00 Sun. Just north of the Blumenthal Church, this is very similar to the Viecha malých vinárov wine bars (page 113) but focuses entirely on wines from Modra (page 199), to drink there or take away, from bulk tanks or bottles. €

Výčap U Ernőho ♥ 222 F4; Námestie SNP 30; m 09 48 360 153; 🇫 vycapuernoho; ⏰ 16.00–22.00 Mon, 16.00–midnight Tue–Thu, 16.00–01.00 Fri, 10.00–01.00 Sat, noon–22.00 Sun; 🚋 1, 3, 4 to Centrum; 🚌 N31, N34, N44, N47, N53, N55, N70, N72, N80, N93, N95 to Hodžovo námestie. Part of the wonderful revitalisation of the Old Market, & linked to the Shenk brewery in the basement (there are always 4 of their beers on tap, eg: smoked corn lager, cold-hopped red, dark oat beer & 1 guest). There's also veggie tapas, from vegan cheese to tofu/walnut sausages, or get food from food trucks out front or Foodstock next door (page 100). €

BEYOND THE OLD TOWN GATES, CENTRUM AND FURTHER AFIELD

Prazdroj ♥ 223 E8; Mostová 8; ☎ 02 5441 1108; ⏰ 11.00–midnight Mon–Tue, 11.00–01.00 Wed–Thu, 11.00–02.00 Fri, 11.00–01.00 Sat, 11.00–23.00 Sun; 🚌 50, N33 or 🚋 1, 4 to Námestie Ľudovíta Štúra. Peppermint-ice-cream walls hide a down-to-earth Czech beer hall (the first outside the Czech Republic to serve draught Pilsner Urquell). There's classic Czech food too, eg: pork or duck with dumplings. €€€

Sky Bar & Restaurant ♥ 223 C8; Hviezdoslavovo námestie 7; m 09 48 109 400; w skybar.sk; ⏰ 17.00–midnight Tue–Sat; 🚌 50, N33 or 🚋 1, 4 to Námestie Ľudovíta Štúra. On the 7th & 8th floors, the Sky Bar offers Mediterranean & Thai cuisine, tangy cocktails & a great view of the castle & St Martin's Cathedral. €€€

10 Prstov ♥ 222 F5; Gorkého 7/Laurinská 10; w 10prstov.sk; ⏰ 09.30–23.00 daily; 🚋 1, 3, 4 to Centrum; 🚌 N31, N34, N44, N47, N53, N55, N70, N72, N80, N93, N95 to Hodžovo námestie. In the gallery between Gorkého & Laurinská, the popular little 'Ten Fingers' bar serves coffee all day plus prosecco & cocktails. Friendly & good value. €€

Amfora ♥ 220 J5; Továrenska 12; m 09 08 404 506; w amfora-winebar.com; ⏰ 15.30–23.30 daily; 🚌 40, 50, 70, 78, 88, N33 to Čulenova; 🚌 21, 40, 42, 50, 60, 88, N61, N72 to Autobusová Stanica. In Zaha Hadid's last project, Sky Park, this small bar & shop specialises in natural & orange wines, with a wide knowledge of local producers in particular. You can sit outside & graze on tapas while you ponder your wine choices. €€

Beer Palace ♥ 223 F6; Gorkého 5; m 09 03 499 499; w beerpalace.sk; ⏰ 08.00–23.00 Mon–Thu, 08.00–01.00 Fri, 10.00–01.00 Sat; 🚋 1, 4 to Jesenského; 🚌 N33 to Námestie Ľudovíta Štúra. A beer lover's paradise with combinations involving draught Czech beer served with burgers & other meaty, starchy nibbles. 10 beers available in metre-long glasses. €€

Bratislavský Meštiansky Pivovar ♥ 222 D1; Drevená 8; m 09 44 512 265; w mestianskypivovar.sk; ⏰ 11.00–22.00 Sun–Mon, 11.00–midnight Tue–Sat; 🚋 1, 9 to Poštová; 🚌 N31, N34, N44, N47, N53,

> **BREWS ON WHEELS**
>
> Bratislava locals love their coffee so much, they need access to it at all times. *Káva so sebou* ('coffee to go') signs spring out of almost every café window and several young enterprises have started offering coffee, tea and hot chocolate options from well-stocked giant tricycles and vans. **The Coffee Brothers**, who brew up fresh coffee in a vintage La Pavoni machine on a tricycle, can be found by Laurinská brána, one of the gates to the Old Town (w coffeebrothers.sk; ⏲ 08.00–16.00 Mon–Thu, 08.00–13.00 Fri). **Pán Králiček** (Mr Rabbit; w pankralicek.sk) parks his trike on Poštová and creates steaming hot brews with coffee beans from Papua New Guinea in a powerful Francino machine (he now has four colleagues elsewhere in the Old Town). A lovely guy sells tea and coffee from a dinky little van on Hviezdoslavovo námestie, by Námestie Eugena Suchoňa, and brews up an excellent paper mug of Earl Grey (€1).

N55, N70, N72, N80, N93, N95 to Hodžovo námestie. Gigantic, 3-floored pub recalling the ambience of the original brewery, founded by 1477 (near where the SNP Bridge now is); originally owned by the city, it was sold in 1880 & renamed the Bratislava Burgess Brewery. They serve light & dark classic lagers (both 12°) & traditional Slovak food, notably a filling cabbage soup. It has the same owners as the Pivovarská Reštaurácia at Dunajská 21 (page 116). €€

Café Verne ♀ 223 D7; Hviezdoslavovo námestie 18; m 09 05 224 637; w cafeverne.sk; ⏲ 09.00–midnight Sun–Thu, 09.00–01.00 Fri, 10.00–01.00 Sat; 🚌 50, N33 or 🚋 1, 4 to Námestie Ľudovíta Štúra. Arty students crowd this venue with decorations based on Jules Verne's stories. 'It's like sitting in somebody's living room,' notes a Danish visitor. There is quiet music & earnest conversations, as well as good food – b/fast served until 11.00; set lunch for €7.80 then simple pasta dishes, salads & steaks. More or less around the back in an Esterházy palace at Panska 13 is the Žil Verne craft beer bar (m 09 03 454 108; ⏲ 15.00–23.00 Sun–Mon, 15.00–midnight Tue–Thu, 15.00–02.00 Fri–Sat), which has a similar but boozier vibe. €€

KGB ♀ 221 F4; Obchodná 52; m 09 07 888 123; ⏲ 11.00–midnight Mon–Wed, 14.00–midnight Thu, 11.00–02.00 Fri, 16.00–02.00 Sat; 🚋 1, 9 to Poštová; 🚌 N31, N34, N44, N47, N53, N55, N70, N72, N80, N93, N95 to Hodžovo námestie. Cellar bar with a clichéd commie theme; busts & pictures of Lenin, Stalin & Gustáv Husák, Czechoslovakia's last communist leader, although the name is actually an abbreviation for Krčma Gurmánov Bratislavy (Pub of Bratislava Gourmets). A friendly place with fairly standard Slovak beers & food. €€

Kollarko ♀ 221 F3; Kollárovo námestie 23; m 09 10 748 408; ⬜ Kollarko23; ⏲ 14.00–midnight Sun–Thu, 14.00–02.00 Fri–Sat; 🚌 42, 47, 80 or 🚋 1, 9 to Vysoká; 🚌 N53, N55, N70, N72 to Kollárovo námestie. Opened in 2018 in a converted bus stop, this is a very welcoming outlet for the JAMA & Stupavar breweries; in winter there's a heated tent, & in summer its terraces spread out into the park. €€

Mestský pivovar Alžbetka ♀ 221 F3; Mickiewiczova 1; m 09 05 534 102;

pivovaralzbetka; w pivovaralzbetka.sk/en; ⏰ 10.00–23.00 Mon, 10.00–midnight Tue–Wed, 10.00–01.00 Thu–Fri, 11.00–midnight Sat, 11.00–23.00 Sun; 🚋 1, 9 to Vysoká; 🚌 N53, N55, N70, N72 to Kollárovo námestie. This attractive Baroque building facing down Obchodná houses another of Bratislava's new micro-breweries, with a long row of tanks behind the bar. Most of their beers are bottom-fermented pilsners, but they do produce top-fermented IPA, APA, red & brown ales too. Strengths are measured by EPM (*extrakt původní mladiny*; extract of the original wort) which is similar to the Plato scale, just over double our familiar percentage of alcohol by volume (11% EPM is about 4.5% ABV). They also serve Hungarian spirits & a menu of traditional meats & more veggie-friendly world food. €€

Pivovarská Reštaurácia 📍 221 G5; Dunajská 21; m 09 48 710 888; w dunajska.mestianskypivovar.sk; ⏰ 11.00–23.00 Tue–Sat, 11.00–22.00 Sun–Mon; 🚋 3, 4 to Mariánska; 🚌 42, N72 to Špitálska. There has been a history of brewing in the street named after the Danube, which used to flow this way, between the 15th & 19th centuries. A big noisy beer hall, with much the same beer & meaty menu as at the Bratislavský Meštiansky Pivovar (page 114), but there's a spacious garden & car parking here. €€

Skupinová Terapia All Day Bar 📍 221 F3; Námestie 1 Mája 18; m 09 10 133 741; skupinovaterapiaalldaybar; ⏰ 11.00–22.00 Mon, 11.00–midnight Tue–Thu, 11.00–02.00 Fri, 16.00–01.00 Sat; 🚌 31, 42, 44,47, 80, 94, N44, N53, N55, N70, N72 to Kollárovo námestie. In the shiny modern Amazon building, the Group Therapy bar is not at all pubby in feel, with lots of comfy chairs & big glass windows, & a range of wines, rums & whiskies as well as craft beers; food (to 21.00 Mon–Thu, 22.00 Fri–Sat) includes chicken & fries & 2 lunch options (Mon–Fri) for €7.90. €€

Umelka 📍 221 G7; Dostojevského 2; m 09 04 581 295; w umelka.com; 🚌 29, 50, 70, N33 to Malá Scéna. Umelka consists of 4 venues in one 1926 building, adding the 1st letter of their description to 'umelka' ('artist'): Gumelka, upstairs, is the gallery of the Slovak Union of Visual Artists (page 174); Zumelka is a shady beer garden (*záhradná piváreň*; ⏰ 10.00–midnight Mon–Thu, 10.00–01.00 Fri, 11.00–01.00 Sat, 11.00–midnight Sun) opposite Komenského University; Pumelka is a pub (*piváreň*; ⏰ 10.00–midnight Mon–Thu, 10.00–01.00 Fri, 11.00–01.00 Sat, 11.00–midnight Sun) with a woody interior created by organic woodcarver Peter Strassner; Rumelka, at the east end of the venue, is a restaurant (⏰ 10.00–22.00 Mon, 10.00–midnight Tue–Fri, 11.00–midnight Sat, 11.00–22.00 Sun), serving world food such as tacos, chilli & burgers; & Klub Kumelká (⏰ 15.00–01.00 Mon–Sat) is a café with excellent lemonade. This is also home to Bratislava's beer bike (w partybike.sk), which a cheery group can pedal around town while drinking. €€

Veža 📍 map, page 196; Cesta na Kamzík 14; ☎ 02 4425 6946; ⏰ 11.00–20.00 Sun & Tue–Thu, 11.00–21.00 Fri–Sat; 🚌 44 from Hodžovo námestie to terminus at Koliba, then 25mins' walk uphill through woods. On Floor D of the TV tower, the bar & brasserie make a great spot for a snack & a drink in less formal surroundings, but still with the best view in town (entry €6). Gaze out in all directions across the hills &, on a clear day, you can see as far as Hungary & Austria. €€

1 Slovenská krčma (1st Slovak Pub) 📍 221 F4; Obchodná 62; ☎ 02 5292 6367; w slovakpub.sk; ⏰ 11.00–22.00 Mon–Fri, noon–22.00 Sat & Sun; 🚋 1, 9 to Poštová; 🚌 N31, N34, N44, N47, N53, N55, N70, N72, N80, N93, N95 to Hodžovo námestie. In a pink building on bustling Obchodná, this pub is made up of 11 separate rooms, some spacious, some cramped, representing various periods in Slovakia's history – such as Janošik's Room, dedicated to the Slovak Robin Hood. 1 cottage is done up like a *chata* from the Liptov region, while a less likely place to sup a beer is the Room of St Cyril & St Methodius, creators of the written Slav language. Well-executed traditional dishes (⏰ 11.00–22.00 daily) are made with fresh ingredients from the pub's own organic farm. €

17s Bar 📍 223 C7; Hviezdoslavovo námestie 17; **m** 09 08 759 429; **w** 17bar.sk; ⏰ 11.00–midnight daily; 🚌 50, N33 or 🚋 1, 4 to Námestie Ľudovíta Štúra. Long-running, always-popular bar. Famous garlic soup; also great pizza served until late & Czech beer on draught. Seating in cosy booths or out on the gorgeous, tree-lined square. Live music; cash only. €

100 Pív 📍 223 G6; Medená 33; **m** 09 48 405 409; **w** 100piv.sk; ⏰ noon–22.00 Mon–Fri, 15.00–22.00 Sat & Sun; 🚋 1, 4 to Jesenského. This friendly little beer shop & bar has a good range of local & Belgian beers & ciders, on tap & in bottles. €

✳ **Funus** 📍 220 B1; Prokopa Veľkého 1; **m** 09 03 907 327; 📘; ⏰ 10.00–22.00 daily; 🚌 147 to Kalvária. I discovered Funus quite by chance when walking up Hlboká cesta en route to the Slavín monument & was immediately wafted straight back to my student days in Brno in 1982. It turns out that this is one of Bratislava's oldest bars, with a lovely beer garden under ancient chestnut trees, & a rustic, woody restaurant (mains around €10; Mon–Fri lunch menu, posted on Facebook, €6.90/7.90). Draught beers are from the Pivovar Karpat & the Czech Svijany & Chotěboř breweries (including an unfiltered 11° pilsner). Add Horec, a shot of alcohol infused with gentian, to make your brew bitter. If I hadn't been working, I could have recreated my student days & happily stayed all afternoon! €

Hostinec Opapa; 📍 221 H3; Moskovská 16; **m** 09 40 892 019; **w** opapa.sk; ⏰ 16.00–22.00 Mon–Fri; 🚌 207, 212 or 🚋 4, 9 to Americké námestie; 🚌 N61 to Špitálska. Honest-to-goodness pub near the university that houses Bratislava's 1st micro-brewery (founded in 2009, although it changed hands in 2022). They have 14 taps including 3 regular beers (10° & 12° lagers & a 13° dark lager) as well as *medovina* (hot or cold) & *korma* (a mix of beer & mead), plus cheese & sausages. All the beer choices chalked up on the blackboard are available in 100ml taster glasses. There's a small smoking room & a large summer terrace. €

Mešuge Craft Beer Pub 📍 221 F4; Vysoká 15; **m** 09 44 737 688; 📘; ⏰ 11.00–23.00 Sun–Tue, 11.00–midnight Wed–Thu, 11.00–01.00 Fri–Sat; 🚋 1, 9 to Poštová; 🚌 N31, N34, N44, N47, N53, N55, N70, N72, N80, N93, N95 to Hodžovo námestie. This cellar bar, done up like a High Tatra mountain cabin, has 9 taps serving their own Pressburg beers, including semi-dark, wheat, porter, EPA & IPA styles; tasting flight available. Traditional snacks include cheese from a dairy that's been making sheep's cheese since 1797. The lunch of the day (€8) is posted on Facebook daily. €

Pink Whale 📍 220 C7; Nábrežie Arm Gen L Svobodu; **m** 09 11 177 172; 📘; ⏰ 18.00–23.00 Wed–Thu, 18.00–01.00 Fri, 17.00–01.00 Sat, 17.00–23.00 Sun; 🚌 29, 31, 39, N31, N33, N34 or 🚋 4 to Vodná veža. Alternative arts centre & club on a boat moored just upstream from the Most SNP Bridge. Rustic, woody décor & lots of plants. Serves bottled beers & shots, or whatever the young people are drinking this week. €

Pivovar Hops 📍 220 D8; Vilová 4; **m** 09 03 200 691; **w** pivovarhops.sk; ⏰ 15.00–22.00 Sun–Thu, 15.00–23.00 Fri–Sat; 🚌 80, N93 or train to ŽST Petržalka. If you want a proper pub on the south side of the Danube, this is your best option – they brew a good range of beers, all available in small tasting glasses, & there's good, solid pub grub, too. €

Viecha Drevená Dedina 220 E1; Žilinska 47; **m** 09 08 704 663; **w** drevenadedina.sk; 08.30–21.30 Mon–Fri, 08.00–14.00 Sat; 21, 40, 44, 49, 61, 63, 71, N33, N44, N74 to Karpatská. At the back of a local veg market (page 139), this crusty old beer yard (you can't really call it a garden) provides a glimpse into local, working-class drinking habits. There's a lunch of the day (€7), or try a deep-fried savoury doughnut (*langoš*) first to soak up the alcohol. €

Adventures in Britain

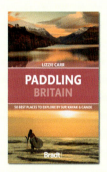
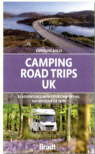
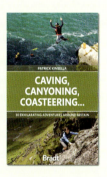
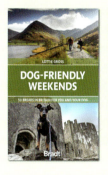

TRAVEL TAKEN SERIOUSLY

bradtguides.com/shop

 BradtGuides   @BradtGuides 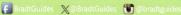 @bradtguides

Entertainment, Nightlife, Sport and Shopping

In the spring and summer and even early autumn, Bratislava's Old Town comes alive in the late afternoon as the pavement cafés fill with people enjoying an aperitif or chilled beer in the sunshine before heading off to a restaurant, show or another bar. The pretty, tree-lined Hviezdoslavovo námestie is crowded with people dressed up in their glad rags, gathering before a performance at the historic Slovak National Theatre, the newer SND building (opened in 2007 by the Danube) or the gorgeous Reduta concert hall. Even if your mission is to drink Bratislava dry, you should consider a night at the opera. You will never again have such a great opportunity to see world-class singers in a gorgeous setting for the price of a couple of pints in London.

Pick up a copy of *Kam do Mesta*, the pocket-sized monthly listings guide, or see w kamdomesta.sk or inba.sk. They're both in Slovak but fairly decipherable. You can book most events online at w navstevnik.sk (you'll probably need to print your ticket or save it to your phone).

THEATRE

Bratislava has a strong theatrical tradition, and while most performances will be in Slovak and out of reach for many visitors' ears, the Slovak National Theatre is a must for opera or ballet and venues such as the Puppet Theatre and the more alternative Stoka may have shows that appeal. Musicals, showing at the Nová scéna and sometimes at the beautiful Aréna, go down well in any language.

Aréna 221 F8; Viedenská cesta 10; 02 6720 2557; w divadloarena.sk; 3 or 50 to Sad Janka Kráľa. In Sad Janka Kráľa next to the Old Bridge. The oldest theatre in Bratislava, showing exciting, contemporary plays. Built in 1828 as an open-air summer theatre (hence the name), it was replaced by a permanent building in 1899. Ticket office 14.00–18.00 Mon–Fri & before performances; shows at 19.00.

Astorka Korzo '90 (Playhouse) 222 E3; Námestie SNP 33; 02 5443 2093; w astorka.sk; 1, 3, 4 to Centrum. A small group giving well-regarded dramatic performances. Ticket office ⏲ 16.00–19.00 Mon & Wed, 18.00–19.00 Tue, Thu & Sat, 17.00–19.00 Fri & before performances; shows at 19.00 Mon–Sat.

Malá scéna STU 📍 221 H6; Dostojevského rad 7; ☎ 02 2042 0020; w malascena.sk; 🚋 1, 3, 4 to Šafárikovo námestie; 🚌 29, 50, 70, 78 to Malá scéna. Small theatrical company formed in 1991. Ticket office ⏲ 10.00–18.00 Mon–Sat & before performances; shows at 19.00.

Mestské Divadlo P O Hviezdoslava 📍 222 G5; Laurinská 19; ☎ 02 5910 3134; w dpoh.sk; 🚋 1, 3, 4 to Centrum. Popular theatre in the heart of the Old Town. Ticket office ⏲ 14.00–19.00 Mon–Fri & before performances; shows usually at 19.00, but some at 17.00 or 20.00, plus matinees.

Nová scéna 📍 221 F3; Živnostenská 1; ☎ 02 2048 8530; w nova-scena.sk; 🚌 98 or 🚋 1 to Vysoká; 🚌 31, 39, 42, 47, 94 to Kollárovo námestie. A venue for musicals, & very popular in the last decade. Ticket office ⏲ 08.00–14.00 Mon–Fri; shows at 19.00.

Puppet Theatre – Bratislavské Bábkové Divadlo 📍 221 G5; Dunajská 36; ☎ 02 5292 3668; w babkovedivadlo.sk/en; 🚋 1, 3, 4 to Centrum. Performances for children & adults with a rich & varied repertoire. Shows usually at 10.00 & 14.00.

Slovak National Theatre – The New Building 📍 221 H6; Nová budova SND; Pribinova 17; ☎ 02 2047 2299; w snd.sk; 🚌 40, 78, 90 to Nové SND; 🚌 50 to Malá Scéna or Landererova; ticket office: ☎ 02 2047 2298; ⏲ 08.00–19.00 Mon–Fri, 08.00–noon, 14.00–19.00 & 1hr before performance Sat, 14.00–19.00 & 1hr before performance Sun. The historic home of the Slovak National Theatre was constructed in 1884–86 by Fellner & Helmer & closed for long-term refurbishment in 2021. The New Building opened in 2007, comprising 2 large theatres, a smaller recital hall, rehearsal rooms & 200 offices; the acoustics are simply stunning. It hosts drama, opera & ballet, with tickets costing from €19 up to

GENERAL TICKET SELLERS

Eventim ☎ 02 5263 2425; w eventim.sk. Sells tickets for classical concerts as well as international rock bands (Marilyn Manson, Simply Red, etc), big-show productions & events at the big sports arenas. Ticket outlets at Dr Horák CD Shop (Medená 19), Martinus Bookshop (page 140), Artforum (page 140), NTC (page 135), Eurovea Galleria (page 143) & Avion Shopping Park (page 143).

Hummel Music 📍 222 F4; Hse of J N Hummel, Klobučnícka 2; ☎ 02 5443 3888; w divyd.sk; ⏲ 10.00–17.00 Mon–Fri, 11.00–17.00 Sat. Sells tickets for classical & rock concerts, sporting events & shows, as with Eventim & Ticketportal.

Návštevník w navstevnik.sk. The information & booking site of the Ministry of Culture; bookings on the National Theatre & Philharmonic websites are automatically transferred here, but it handles many other cultural events too.

Ticketportal Radlinského 27; ☎ 02 5293 3323; w ticketportal.sk. Tickets for such diverse events as Abba Slovakia, the European Figure Skating Championships, Disney on Ice & top rock bands. Offices can be found in the shopping malls Aupark, Avion, VIVO! and Eurovea Galleria (all page 143), and Artforum (page 140) & in the tourist offices of Satur & Hydrotour.

€80 for a prime perch. English-speaking reservations from Žaneta Domaracká (Pribinova 17; 02 2047 2293). The season runs Sep–Jun with a summer break in Jul & Aug.

Stoka Theatre 221 F1; Karpatská 2; **w** stoka.sk; 40, 44, 49, 61, 63, 64, 71 to Karpatská. In the former YMCA (page 126), this is Bratislava's main alternative theatre.

Tanečný Divadlo (Tánc-szinhaus) 223 E8; Mostová 8; 02 2047 4104; **w** sdt.sk; 50 or 1, 4 to Námestie Ľudovíta Štura. Opposite the Reduta concert hall, this is Bratislava's dance theatre.

Teatro Colorato 222 D4; Františkánske námestie 2; **m** 09 05 827 465, 09 05 827 465; **w** colorato.sk/en; 1, 3, 4 to Centrum. A new company of recently trained actors, presenting lively colourful shows.

Teátro Wüstenrot – Bratislavské Hudobné Divadlo 220 G1; Dom kultúry Ružinov, Ružinovská 28; 02 5022 8530; **w** gedur.sk; 78 or 9 to Súmračná. The Bratislava Musical Theatre stages musicals, children's shows & visiting performers. Ticket office noon–18.00 Mon–Fri & to 19.00 on performance days.

MUSIC

CLASSICAL MUSIC Given Bratislava's rich musical heritage – composers Dohnányi and Hummel were born here, and such luminaries as Liszt, Mendelssohn, Mozart, Beethoven, Bartók and Haydn also visited and performed in the city – you'd be mad to miss a classical music production while in the presence of such greats. The great coloratura soprano Edita Gruberová was born in Bratislava in 1946 and announced her retirement from the stage in 2019; Lucia Popp (actually Poppová; 1939–93), another of the 20th century's leading operatic sopranos, was born in a village in the Bratislava region.

The buildings of the Slovak National Theatre and the Reduta are beautiful historic monuments and the opera productions rival those in Budapest and Vienna for a much more reasonable price. Those who can only dream of attending a performance at Covent Garden or New York's Met can take in several shows of comparable quality and enjoyment in Bratislava and still have change left to buy dinner afterwards. Visit the elegant Primate's and Mirbach palaces to hear chamber music concerts or piano recitals in an atmospheric setting. You can also catch many excellent choirs free of charge if you pop into churches such as the Lutheran church in the Old Town. The bizarre inverted pyramid building of Slovak Radio has amazing acoustics. There are several fine festivals of classical music and jazz; for more information, see page 28.

◄ **1** The 200-year-old Aréna is Bratislava's oldest theatre. **2** Children and adults alike will enjoy performances at the Puppet Theatre. **3 & 4** The historic home of the Slovak National Theatre is one of the city's iconic landmarks. The stunning New Building hosts drama, opera and ballet to complement the Historical Building's repertoire.

MUSICAL HERITAGE

Many of the musical greats have connections with Bratislava; either living here for a period of time, studying at one of the prestigious academies or giving a concert performance at one of several beautiful music halls.

JOSEPH HAYDN (1732–1809) In the 1760s and 1770s Haydn came often to Bratislava with his employer, Prince Nikolaus Esterházy, and in 1766 conducted the premiere of his opera *La Canterina* at the then Esterházy Palace.

WOLFGANG AMADEUS MOZART (1756–91) Mozart, aged six, gave a concert (accompanied by his father) for local aristocracy at a Pálffy residence in 1762. His *Requiem* was performed in St Martin's Cathedral in 1834.

LUDWIG VAN BEETHOVEN (1770–1827) Beethoven visited Bratislava in 1796 and gave a concert at Count Keglevich's Baroque palace (Keglevičov palác, at Panská 27). He also gave piano lessons to Anna Louise Barbara Keglevich, also called Babetta (1780–1813), daughter of Carl Keglevich and Catherine Zichy, and dedicated his Sonata no.4 in E flat major, op.7 and Piano Concerto no.1 in C major, op.15 to her. Naturally there's talk of romance between them, but it certainly seems that she must have been a very fine pianist herself.

JOHANN NEPOMUK HUMMEL (1778–1837) Hummel was born at Klobučnícka 2 222 F4, which is now a museum dedicated to his life and work (page 164). A pupil of Mozart and a friend of Beethoven and Schubert, Hummel became the first great virtuoso of the newly invented piano, known for his staggering improvisations. He succeeded Haydn

Bratislava Castle Concert Hall 220 C6; 02 5441 1444; w bratislava-hrad.sk; 44, 47 to Hrad. Listen to music in the stunning, historical setting of the castle chapel.
Klarisky Concert Hall 222 B5; Farská 4; 02 5441 1508; 9 to Kapucínska. The 14th-century Poor Clares Church & Convent sometimes serves as a concert hall with great acoustics.
Mirbach Palace 222 D4; Františkánske námestie 11; 02 5443 1556; w gmb.sk; 1, 3, 4 to Centrum. Concerts every Sun at 10.30.

Mirror Hall of the Primate's Palace 222 E5; Primaciálne námestie; 02 5935 6204; 10.00–17.00 Tue–Sun; 1, 3, 4 to Centrum. Concerts in an elegant setting.
Moyzes Concert Hall 221 G7; Gondova 2, access from Vajanského nábrežie 12; 02 5443 3351; 50, 95 or 1, 4 to Námestie Ľudovíta Štúra. Concerts in a beautiful Art Nouveau hall, part of Comenius University.
Music Centre Slovakia 222 C4; Hudobné Centrum, Michalská 10; 02 2047

as Prince Esterházy's concert master in 1804; the trumpet concerto that he wrote to celebrate his appointment is, alas, his only work that gets performed nowadays.

FRANZ LISZT (1811–86) In 1820, nine-year-old Liszt gave a concert in the garden pavilion of the Leopold De Pauli Palace (page 146) and started on his triumphal career. Always grateful to the city that gave him his break, he gave many more concerts here, notably in the cathedral and the City Theatre. In 1911, a bust of Liszt was unveiled on Domplatz, now Rudnayavo námestie.

ANTON GRIGORIEVICH RUBINSTEIN (1829–94) The great Russian pianist and composer Rubinstein was considered a rival to Liszt. In 1847, he lived and worked in the building that now hosts the French Institute.

ERNŐ DOHNÁNYI (1877–1960) The Hungarian composer/pianist was born in Bratislava and studied at the Catholic School at the Convent of Clare Nuns on Klariská ulica.

BÉLA BARTÓK (1881–1945) Hungarian Bartók went to school here from 1892 to 1899 and then worked from 1894 to 1908 at the monastery near the Sv Ladislav church. There's a bust of Bartók nearby at Špitálska 7 221 F4, where his head emerges from pink stone.

ZOLTÁN KODÁLY (1882–1967) The Hungarian composer Kodály's father was stationmaster at Galánta, east of Bratislava, when he was a child, and his *Dances of Galanta* (1933) was based on the region's Hungarian and Gypsy folk music.

0111; w hc.sk; 1, 3, 4 to Centrum. In the courtyard & upstairs, this agency has a database & list of musical events in Bratislava: classical, jazz & blues concerts, festivals & music courses.
Reduta 223 E8; Námestie Eugena Suchoňa 1; 02 2047 5233; reservations: 02 2047 5218; w ilharmonia.sk; ticket office: 09.00–14.00 Mon, 13.00–19.00 Tue–Fri, & 1hr before the concert at the venue; 50 or 1, 4 to Námestie Ľudovíta Štura. This stunning (but relatively small) concert hall is the setting for daily concerts by the **Slovak Philharmonic** (Slovenska filharmonia), one of the best orchestras in central Europe, & also by the Conservatoire students. Tickets €15–40. Check whether your ticket is in Block A (left) or B (right) as the same seat numbers appear on each side.
Slovak Radio Concert Hall 221 F2; Mýtna 1; 02 3250 5111; w sosr.rtvs.sk; 94 to Námestie Slobody. The Slovak Radio

Symphony Orchestra, founded in 1929, is the country's oldest orchestra & plays here roughly once a month except in summer (also live on the radio, of course). The hall's acoustics are wonderful.

FOLK MUSIC Many restaurants in Bratislava have folk-music performances to accompany the food, and Bratislava's districts are dotted with culture houses where you can watch or take part in a 'dance house' (*tanečný dom*), a combination of folk-dance lesson and performance. See ☐ Tanečný dom for an explanation and details of upcoming events.

SĽUK (Slovenský ľudový umelecký kolektív) ♀ map, page 196; Balkánska 31/66, Rusovce; ☎ 02 2047 8111; w sluk.sk; 🚌 91 from Most SNP or 90 from Nové SND to the Gerulata stop. Actually on Madarská, next to the Rusovce castle, this is a theatre for folk ensembles performing Slovak music & dance. Folk traditions from all over the country are represented in unique arrangements.

LIVE MUSIC BARS AND CLUBS Live rock music is still very popular in Bratislava, and reggae goes down well, too. Bratislavans are mad about jazz and there are many places to hear live concerts in a funky setting, often with food and drink to accompany the cool tunes.

A4 – Nultý Priestor ♀ 221 F1; Karpatská 2; w a4.sk; 🚌 40, 44, 49, 61, 63, 64, 71, N33, N44, N74 to Karpatská. The old YMCA building is now known as Nultý Priestor or 'Zero Space' & provides a space for non-commercial groups & individuals to put on shows of theatre, dance, music, cinema & creative art. Workshops & discussion groups are also held here. Venues in the building include the Randal rock 'n' roll music pub (w randalclub.eu; ⊕ 16.00–02.00 daily) in the basement; the Hopkirk Club (⊕ 16.00–02.00 Mon–Thu, 16.00–04.00 Fri & Sat, 16.00–midnight Sun), playing electro music – I'd be amazed if anyone actually got the reference to the 1969 British TV series *Randall & Hopkirk (Deceased)*; the Majestic Music Club (w majestic.sk; ⊕ 16.00–04.00 daily); a concert hall (⊕ 16.00–02.00 daily), with young local bands; & a bar & café.
Bon Bon Jazz Bar ♀ 220 D2; Štefániková 31; ☐ bonbonjazz; ⊕ 09.00–22.00 Mon–Fri; 🚌 42, 83, 84, 93, N31, N34, N80, N93, N95 to Pod Stanicou. A pleasant all-day café-bar, with free Wi-Fi, & live jazz on w/end evenings.
Café Studio Club ♀ 222 F5; Laurinska 11; m 09 05 435 661; ☐ Cafe-Studio-Club; ⊕ 10.00–midnight Mon–Thu, 10.00–03.00 Fri & Sat; 🚋 1, 3, 4 to Centrum; 🚌 N31, N34, N44, N47, N53, N55, N70, N72, N80, N93, N95 to Hodžovo námestie. A good place for live jazz (it was a well-known recording studio in the 1970s & 1980s), with artists such as the favourite local saxophonist, Peter Cardarelli. Discos every Sat from 22.00.
Jazztikot ♀ 222 D4; Biela 5; m 09 48 327 333, 09 15 178 895; w jazztikot.sk; ⊕ 10.00–

---

1 & 2 The Reduta hosts daily concerts by the Slovak Philharmonic, one of the best orchestras of central Europe. **3** Many great composers, including Mozart, had connections with Bratislava. ▶

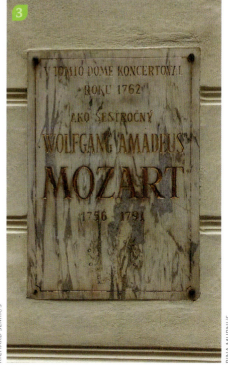

midnight Tue–Sat; 🚋 9 to Kapucínska. Jazz café with free entry & live music at 19.30 most nights; closed late Jul to late Aug.
KC Dunaj 📍 222 E3; Kamenné Námestie 1A; **m** 09 48 599 891, 09 04 330 049; **w** kcdunaj.sk; ⏱ 16.00–midnight Sun–Thu, 16.00–03.00 Fri–Sat; 🚋 1, 3, 4 to Centrum; 🚌 N31, N34, N44, N47, N53, N55, N70, N72, N80, N93, N95 to Hodžovo námestie. KC Dunaj stands for 'Kultúrne Centrum Dunaj' & there is a photo gallery, video gallery, bar, yoga room, workshops, concert venues & more, all recently installed in the brutalist Prior building.

GIG VENUES Bratislava has some massive halls and attracts a mix of international bands and world stars and the more modest local singers. Musicals and big spectaculars are also popular. You will also find a 'Twilight Zone' aspect to live music in Bratislava, as bands and singers you thought had long since given up touring, such as the late Demis Roussos and Big Brother and the Holding Company (once Janis Joplin's backing band). However, more recent visitors such as Sting, Massive Attack, Limp Bizkit, Garbage, AC/DC and FFS (Franz Ferdinand & Sparks) have given the city a hipper reputation on the touring scene. For tickets to the venues listed below, see page 121.

Babylon 📍 222 G3; Kolarska 3; ☎ 02 2072 6609; **w** babylonatelier.sk; 🚋 1, 3, 4 to Centrum; 🚌 N31, N34, N44, N47, N53, N55, N70, N72, N80, N93, N95 to Hodžovo námestie. Concerts, theatrical performances & films, all in a huge former cinema.
Incheba 📍 220 C8; Viedenská cesta 3–7; ☎ 02 6727 1111; **w** incheba.sk; 🚌 80, 83, 84, 88, 93, 94, N80, N93, N95 to Aupark/Pri sade. Large conference centre with a hall where the biggest acts perform.
Gopass Aréna 📍 221 G1; Trnavská cesta 29; ☎ 02 4437 2127; **m** 09 02 805 111; 🚌 39, 53, 60, 61, 63, 98, N53 to Bajkalská. Large basketball stadium (also known as ŠH Pasienky & Hant Aréna), home to BK Inter Bratislava. Concerts & sporting events are held here.
Peugeot Arena – National Tennis Centre 📍 221 G1; Príkopova 6; ☎ 02 4920 9888; **w** ntc.sk; 🚌 N53 or 🚋 4 to Česká. The National Tennis Centre is also used as a concert hall when big names visit on tour. It names itself after sponsors – it was previously named after the Dutch insurance company Aegon.
Stará tržnica 📍 222 F4; Námestie SNP 25; **w** staratrznica.sk; 🚋 1, 3, 4 to Centrum; 🚌 N31, N34, N44, N47, N53, N55, N70, N72, N80, N93, N95 to Hodžovo námestie. The Old Market, built in 1910, has been revived mainly as a centre of foodie culture, but various events & concerts are also staged here.

NIGHTCLUBS AND DISCOS

When the lights go down, Bratislava becomes party central, at least on Friday and Saturday nights. There are many places where the beautiful people go to swing their hips.

Aldea Club 📍 222 D4; Františkánske námestie 3; ⏱ 23.00–03.00 Fri–Sat; 🚋 1, 3, 4 to Centrum; 🚌 N31, N34, N44, N47, N53, N55, N70, N72, N80, N93, N95 to Hodžovo námestie.

A new nightclub with electronic music on Fri & themed party nights on Sat.

Barrock 222 C5; Sedlárska 1; m 09 14 346 968; w barrock.sk; 18.00–04.00 Wed–Sat; 1, 3, 4 to Centrum; N31, N34, N44, N47, N53, N55, N70, N72, N80, N93, N95 to Hodžovo námestie. Fairly unavoidable, conveniently located on the stag parties' favourite street. It used to proclaim itself as 'the hottest, most sexist & sexiest bar' in Bratislava, but is now a bit more corporate.

Bohéma Bar 221 F5; Kamenné Námestie 1; w bohema.sk, 16.00–midnight Sun–Thu, 16.00–03.00 Fri–Sat. On the ground floor of the former Prior shopping centre, this is a dark, nightclubby lounge but with big glass windows.

Nu Spirit Bar 223 H7; Medená 16; m 09 05 865 566; w nuspirit.sk; 10.00–midnight Wed–Thu, 20.00–03.00 Fri–Sat; 50, N33 or 1, 4 to Námestie Ľudovíta Štúra. A cellar bar with an easy-going attitude & top local DJs playing cool tunes.

Radosť 222 F1; Obchodná 48; m 09 48 086 016; radost.music.club; 23.00–04.00 Thu, 23.00–08.00 Fri–Sat; 1, 9 to Poštová; N31, N34, N44, N47, N53, N55, N70, N72, N80, N93, N95 to Hodžovo námestie. A chill-out bar attracting a hip young crowd with DJs every night.

Šafko Klub 221 G6; Šafárikovo námestie 7; m 09 50 470 419; safkoklub; 20.00–02.00 Fri & Sat; 1, 3, 4 to Šafárikovo námestie; N33 to Námestie Ľudovíta Štúra. With 3 stages & 2 bars, this new club offers a wide range of music & drinks.

The Club 223 B8; Rybné námestie 1; m 09 10 777 789; w theclubbratislava.com; 22.00–05.00 Fri–Sat; 50, N33 or 1, 4 to Námestie Ľudovíta Štúra. Stylish dance club with DJs; also jazz gigs.

Trafo 223 C7; Ventúrska 1; m 09 07 704 849; w trafo.sk; 21.00–04.00 Thu–Sat; 1, 3, 4 to Centrum; N31, N34, N44, N47, N53, N55, N70, N72, N80, N93, N95 to Hodžovo námestie. A flashy nightclub, part of the Medusa Group, responsible for a chain of posh Bratislava restaurants. Party until the wee hours with house, techno, chill-out, funk, pop, nu-jazz, hip-hop & drum 'n' bass.

CASINOS

Banco Casino 220 E4; Crowne Plaza Hotel, Hodžovo námestie 2; 02 5262 4378; w bancocasino.sk; 24/7; 1, 9 to Poštová; 202, 203, 207, 208, 212, N31, N34, N44, N47, N53, N55, N70, N72, N80, N93, N95 to Hodžovo námestie. 61 slot machines, 12 roulette, blackjack, poker & Texas Hold'em poker tables.

Casino Victory Aupark 220 D8; Aupark Shopping Center, Einsteinova 18; m 09 03 677 388; w senator-aupark.sk; 24/7; 80, 83, 84, 88, 93, 94, N80, N93, N95 to Aupark/Pri sade. 4 roulette tables, 50 slot machines.

Olympic Casino Carlton 223 D8; Radisson Blu Carlton Hotel, Hviezdoslavovo námestie 3; m 09 17 314 807; w olympic-casino.com; 24/7; 50, N33 or 1, 4 to Námestie Ľudovíta Štúra. Car & cash campaigns, popular poker tournaments, 61 slot machines & 12 roulette, blackjack, Oasis Poker & THP tables.

Olympic Casino Eurovea 221 H7; Pribinova 8; m 09 07 750 327; w olympic-casino.com; bar & slots 09.00–04.00 daily, live games 17.00–04.00 daily; 28, 50, 70, N33 to Malá scéna; 50, 88, 90 to Landererova; 28, 40, 78, 90 to Nové SND;. 11 gaming tables & 45 slot machines inc AlfaStreet electronic roulette. Lounge bar.

LGBTQIA+ BRATISLAVA

The LGBTQIA+ scene in Bratislava is quiet and discreet. There are a few options for a big night out for gay men, but nothing for gay women, except for private parties. Drag shows are called *travestie* nights. Check out w bratislava. gayguide.net, w inakost.sk and w lesba.sk for links, although there is not a lot in English.

Apollon 220 D4; Panenská 24; m 09 48 900 093; apollongayclub/?hl=en ; 20.00–03.00 Tue–Thu, 20.00–05.00 Fri–Sat; 44, 47, N47 to Kozia. Slovakia's oldest gay club is tucked into a vaulted cellar with 2 bars & a friendly atmosphere. Karaoke on Mon & Tue, Film Club at 20.00 on Thu, Dance Club on Wed, Fri & Sat. Men only on Sun.
Tepláreň Café 220 C5; Zámocká 30; m 09 05 135 218; w queerslovakia.sk/ teplaren-en; teplaren; 15.00–midnight Mon–Thu, 15.00–01.00 Fri & Sat, winter from 17.00; 9 to Kapucínska; 80, 83, 84, 93, 94, N31, N34, N80, N93, N95 to Zochova. A relaxed non-smoking café-bar for coffee, lemonade, wine & other drinks. They occasionally host dance parties, sometimes on a boat in the Danube or at Šafko Klub (page 129).

CINEMA

You can catch all the latest Hollywood blockbusters at gigantic multiplexes, many of which are in the original language with subtitles in Slovak and/or Czech. Comedies and children's movies are usually dubbed. If you want to see a film, look out for the codes ST (with Slovak subtitles), ČT (with Czech subtitles) and be wary of films with SD (Slovak dubbing) or ČD (Czech dubbing). ČV means it's the Czech version, SV the Slovak version. When looking for a film make sure it is *na tento týždeň*, meaning 'showing this week'.

Cinema City Aupark (multiplex) 220 D8; Einsteinova 20; 02 6820 2222; w cinemacity.sk/aupark; 13.30–22.00 Mon–Fri, 10.30–22.00 Sat & Sun; 80, 83, 84, 88, 93, 94, N80, N93, N95 to Aupark/Pri sade. 4DX (including smells…).
Cinema City Eurovea (multiplex) 221 H7; Pribinova 8; 02 6820 2222; w cinemacity.sk/eurovea; 13.30–22.00 Mon–Fri, 10.30–22.00 Sat & Sun; 28, 50, 70 to Malá scéna; 50, 88, 90 to Landererova; 28, 40, 78, 90 to Nové SND.
Cinema City VIVO! (multiplex) 221 G1; Vajnorská 100, VIVO!; 02 6820 2222; w cinemacity.sk/cinemas/vivo; 13.30–22.00 Mon–Fri, 10.30–22.00 Sat & Sun; 50, 51, 98 or 4 to Miestny úrad Nové Mesto.
Kino Film Europe 220 D2; Štefánikova 25; 09 11 420 264; w kino.filmeurope. sk; films mostly at 15.00, 17.00 & 19.00, occasionally at 11.00; 42, 83, 84, 93, N31, N34, N80, N93, N95 to Pod stanicou. Great cinema, showing the best of European film, in the Pisztory Palace cultural centre, opposite the Grassalkovich Palace.
Kino Lumière 221 G4; Špitalská 4; m 09 08 748 723; w kino-lumiere.sk; 17.30–23.00 Mon–Fri, 11.00–23.00 Sat & Sun; 1, 3, 4 to Centrum; N61 to Špitálska.

CULTURAL INSTITUTES

These institutes offer language courses, advice on travel to the country concerned and many cultural events, such as exhibitions, book readings and cultural evenings.

Austrian Cultural Forum 220 E4; Hodžovo námestie 1/A; 02 5930 1500; w rakuskekulturneforum.sk; 09.00–16.00 Mon–Fri; 42, 44, 47, 83, 84, 93 to Hodžovo námestie. Exhibitions, concerts, theatre performances, lectures & literary readings.

British Council 223 C6; Panská 17; 02 5910 2400; w britishcouncil.sk/en; 09.00–19.00 Mon & Wed, 09.00–17.00 Tue, Thu & Fri, reduced in Jul/Aug; 1, 3, 4 to Centrum. English-language classes & courses. Gatto Matto café (11.00–22.00 Sun–Thu, 11.00–23.00 Fri–Sat; €) in the courtyard.

Goethe Institut 220 D4; Panenská 33; 02 5920 4311; w goethe.de/slovensko; 08.00–20.00 Mon–Fri, 08.00–13.00 Sat; 44, 47 to Kozia. Language classes & cultural events.

Hungarian Institute in Bratislava 220 E3; Štefánikova 1; 02 5244 2961; w culture.hu/sk/bratislava; 09.00–16.00 Mon–Thu; 42, 44, 47, 83, 84, 93 to Hodžovo námestie. Language classes & cultural events.

Institut Français in Slovakia 222 D5; Sedlárska 7; 02 5934 7739; w institutfrancais.sk; 09.00–20.30 Mon–Thu, 09.00–19.00 Fri, 09.00–13.00 Sat; 1, 3, 4 to Centrum. Art exhibitions, language classes, films, médiathéque & cultural evenings.

Italian Institute 222 A4; Kapucínska 7; 02 5930 7111; w iicbratislava.esteri.it; library 10.00–12.30 & 14.00–18.00 Mon–Wed, 10.00–12.30 & 14.00–16.00 Thu; 9 to Kapucínska. Language classes & exhibitions.

Polish Institute 222 F3; Námestie SNP 27; 02 5443 2013; w instytutpolski.pl/bratislava; 10.00–17.00 Mon–Thu, 09.00–15.00 Fri; 1, 3, 4 to Centrum. Language classes, library, theatre, film, music & exhibitions.

Opposite the wonderful Bistro St Germain (page 109), so a great destination for a meal & a movie. The city's best art-house cinema, host to the Bratislava International Film Festival (w iffbratislava.sk).

Kino Mladosť 223 C7; Hviezdoslavovo námestie 17; 02 5443 5003; w kinomladost.sk; showings 14.00–20.15 daily; 50, N33 or 1, 4 to Námestie Ľudovíta Štúra. Art-house cinema showing dramas, documentaries & European cinema.

Kino Nostalgia Nivy 221 J4; Súťažná 18; 02 5556 9091; w nostalgia.sk; 18.00–22.00 daily; 21, 25, 40, 78, N33 to Malý trh. Art-house film club showing European films, in Bratislava's oldest housing estate, known as '500 apartments' (500 Bytov). The Nostalgia Café & Restaurant (10.00–22.00 Mon–Fri, 11.00–22.00 Sat & Sun; €€) is dog-friendly & non-smoking, offering pizza, pasta, Slovak wine & Czech beer.

SPORTS

WATCHING SPORTS Bars in Bratislava show a lot of sports, particularly during the colder months when guests sit indoors instead of sunning themselves on the pavement terraces. Ice hockey is extremely popular and a Slovan Bratislava match will take priority over Barcelona, AC Milan or Chelsea games.

The Dubliner Irish Pub 222 C5; Sedlárska 6; m 09 08 792 794; w irish-pub.sk; 10.00–01.00 Sun–Wed, 10.00–03.00 Thu–Sat; 1, 3, 4 to Centrum; N31, N34, N44, N47, N53, N55, N70, N72, N80, N93, N95 to Hodžovo námestie. Long-running expat, stag & tourist favourite; a comforting venue where you don't have to dress up to drink Guinness. Opened in 1996, the pub offers a taste of Ireland with a long dark bar & a log fire in winter. Shows ice hockey, cricket, boxing, rugby, football & some American sports from 10.00 every day on Sky Sports & Setanta. Guinness is €5.80 & Zlatý Bažant 12° €3.20 for a half-litre. €€

The Red Lion 222 C4; Michalská 5; m 09 08 367 352; redlionbratislava; 16.00–01.00 Mon–Wed, 16.00–04.00 Thu & Fri, 13.00–04.00 Sat, 13.00–midnight Sun; 1, 3, 4 to Centrum; N31, N34, N44, N47, N53, N55, N70, N72, N80, N93, N95 to Hodžovo námestie. On the main tourist drag, this is another stag-friendly pub that shows plenty of live sport, with karaoke downstairs later on. Local & British beers (just €1 at happy hour) & panini. €€

ACTIVE SPORTS Slovaks have branched out a lot from the 'traditional' sports, such as ice hockey, football and hiking, to embrace enthusiastically cycling, golf and tennis – the sort of recreational activities that were previously considered expensive, Western sports. Fitness clubs are also extremely popular, and while Slovakia is landlocked, there are still plenty of places to practise your backstroke. Newer 'extreme' sports, such as climbing and white-water rafting, are also well catered for in the Bratislava region.

Cycling and mountain biking Cycling is incredibly popular in Slovakia. The 5,400km network (w cykloportal.sk/cyklotrasy-na-mape) of well-signposted cycle routes passes through some of the most gorgeous countryside in Europe, with a web of well-marked trails in all hilly areas. Europe's longest cycling route, EuroVelo 6 (w en.eurovelo.com/ev6), from the Atlantic to the Black Sea, passes through Vienna, Bratislava and on to Štúrovo. Cyclists can then continue their journey by taking the restored bridge across the Danube into Hungary. Similarly, EV13 (w en.eurovelo.com/ev13), the Iron Curtain route, runs south along the Morava Valley to Devín and Bratislava and into Hungary (while EuroVelo 9, from the Baltic to the Adriatic, follows a parallel route just across the border in Austria).

There are various popular local routes near Bratislava; one follows the Danube east to Komárno, another swerves its way up the Small Carpathian Wine Route, and others run along the south bank of the Danube from Petržalka, west to the quaint town of Hainburg in Austria, and east to Danubiana (page

162) and into Hungary. A good route from Bratislava to Devín would be far more popular than these, but unfortunately the main road by the Danube is narrow and busy and cannot be widened owing to being in a protected area – alternatives are to cycle through the forest from Karlova Ves (8km), or to take a train to Devínska Nová Ves and then follow the excellent cycleway south along the Morava Valley to Devín (4.5km). This forms part of the EuroVelo 13 route, and is also lined with information boards describing the ecology of the Morava floodplain. A tributary of the Danube, the Morava marks the border between Slovakia and Austria north of Devín.

The 955m-long **Bridge of Freedom** crosses the Morava River between Devínska Nová Ves and Schlosshof in Austria. Financed via the Cross Border Cooperation Programme Slovak Republic–Austria 2007–13, this cycle bridge connects not only the Slovak and Austrian cycle routes, but also the hiking networks.

The Koliba Bikepark (w bikeparkkoliba.sk) offers downhill mountain-bike tracks, covering over 15km in all, for a range of abilities; return uphill by the Chair Lift (page 181) – bikers pay €5.50 for one ride or €10 for three.

Cycle hire

Bike Bratislava 220 E4; Panenská 25; m 09 48 884 997; w bikebratislava.sk; daily (by reservation only); 42, 44, 47, 83, 84, 93 to Hodžovo námestie. Friendly company offering bikes, tandems, road racers, mountain bikes, children's bikes, scooters, advice & guides. Mountain-bike hire starts at €20 for 2hrs.

Rekola w rekola.sk. A Czech bike-sharing scheme that's recently arrived in Bratislava. Download the app & either pay for rides separately (€1.25 for half an hour) or subscribe (€2.49 per month) to have 4 free 30min rides per month.

Slovnaft Bajk w slovnaftbajk.sk/en; 24/7. The city's bike-sharing system works from scores of docking stations across the city; register online & a PIN will be sent as an SMS to your phone. A charge of €9 for 2 days or €12/month gives unlimited rides (up to 30/60mins each) for 12hrs & then €0.15/6mins. The bikes are heavy but sturdy & reliable. Cycles can also be rented from many hostels & hotels.

Cycling maps The regional government publishes the free *Cyklomapa Podunajsko-Malé Karpaty* (Danube Region-Small Carpathians Cyclemap; 1:60,000), covering the area from Devín to beyond Modra and the Danubiana art gallery; available from the tourist office, it's ideal for touring the Small Carpathian Wine Route. You can also buy the VKÚ map (1:50,000) *Dunajská Cyklistická Cestá*, which divides the entire length of the Bratislava–Štúrovo (bridge to Hungary) route into 16 sections with details in English, Slovak, German and Hungarian. It can be ordered from the Martinus Bookshop (w martinus.sk) or bought in Bratislava from the shop itself (page 140).

Golf The Black and White Golf Resort combines two locations (Bernolákovo and Malacky) to create 55 greens and four courses with varying degrees of difficulty. Black and White also offers 'footgolf' – a 1980s blend of the two sports.

Black River Golf Resort Bratislava
map, page 196; Kaštieľ 5, Bernolákovo; 02 4599 4221; m 09 10 899 877; w golf.sk; 622 & 630; S60, S65 trains to Bernolákovo. Situated 16km northeast from Bratislava towards Chorvátsky Grob, this was Slovakia's 1st golf course, with 9- & 18-hole courses.

Grafobal Group Golf Resort Skalica
220 D1; Potočná 40/260, 909 01 Skalica; 034 774 9627; m 09 10 925 121; w golfskalica.sk; 1hr drive from Bratislava on route E65, 90km north of the capital. A beautiful 18-hole course.

White Eurovalley Golf Resort 220 D1; Eurovalley Golf Park Club, Továrenská ulica, Malacky; m 09 11 243 101; w golf.sk. Black River's sister golf course is in Malacky, 40km north of Bratislava on route E65 towards Brno, Czech Republic. Malacky is reached by regular buses from Bratislava's main bus station & also by S20 suburban trains.

Hiking and running Slovakia is an appealing destination for the adventure traveller as the Carpathian and Tatra mountain ranges provide good terrain for walking and trekking. There are also some great walks along the banks of the Danube and up in the Small Carpathian Hills above Kamzík (page 184) and Devín (page 163). Between the Apollo and Lanfranconi bridges is a certified running track (with kilometre markers) along both sides of the Danube.

Ice hockey This is one of the most popular sports in the country. However, the national team has slumped from fourth to ninth in the world rankings in recent years, and the once world-beating **HC Slovan Bratislava** (w hcslovan.sk) are now near the bottom of the Russian-dominated Kontinental Hockey League. The home ice is at the Ondrej Nepela Arena, still generally known as the Winter Stadium (Zimný Štadión), which holds 10,000. The ice is also open to the public (16.00–18.00 Wed, 09.00–noon & 14.00–17.00 Sat & Sun).

TIPOS Aréna (Štadión Ondreja Nepelu) 221 G1; Odbojárov 9; w nepela-arena.eu; 47, 60, 61, 63 to Zimný Štadión/TIPOS Aréna. Behind VIVO! in the Pasienky district of sports arenas, pools & playing fields.

Tennis Slovakia's first tennis courts were built in Bratislava in the 1880s, where the game became popular with the elite classes. The first official tennis tournament was played in 1910. Miloslav Mečíř won gold at the Seoul Olympics in 1988 and has since played a big part in popularising tennis in Slovakia; now they regularly have ten or more players, both men and women, in the world top 100 rankings. The leading Slovak player is Dominika Cibulková (number 32 in the WTA rankings in April 2019), who has won eight WTA singles titles, while the most successful male player is Martin Kližan, 49th in the ATP rankings at the time of writing.

Peugeot Arena – National Tennis Centre 221 G1; Príkopova 6; 02 4920 9888; w ntc.sk; ⏱ 07.00–22.00 Mon–Fri, 07.00–21.00 Sat & Sun; N53 or 4 to Česká. Bratislava locals are justifiably very proud of this modern sports hall. 6 tennis courts in a hall with a sliding roof. Tennis, squash, badminton & fitness. Also a concert hall (page 128).

Other activities
Beach sports
Tyršák Beach 221 F8; Tyršovo nábrežie, between the Aréna theatre & Stary Most on the south bank of the Danube; m 09 02 752 175; w tyrsak.sk; ⏱ 09.00–23.00 daily; 50 or 3 to Sad Janka Kráľa. All summer long, Bratislava has its very own beach on the parkland right bank of the Danube. Imported sand for beach volleyball, beach tennis, concerts, little stalls selling healthy snacks,

THE STATE OF SLOVAK SOCCER

The top 12 Slovak soccer clubs play in the **Slovak Super Liga**, which, at the time of writing, was known as the Niké Liga owing to a sponsorship deal. The title has gone to teams from Bratislava a dozen times since the division of Czechoslovakia in 1993, but recently two of those three title winners have folded and now languish in the lower leagues.

Top club **ŠK Slovan Bratislava** (w en.skslovan.com) have been champions of the top-flight league ten times since 2003, most recently in the 2023–24 season. They play in the newly rebuilt National Stadium at Tehelné pole (capacity 22,500; 98 or 4 to Nová doba). Marek Hamšík, who won 138 international caps, more than any other Slovak player, actually only played here for one season in 2004 before moving to Italy – he was captain of Napoli from 2014 to 2019 and the club's all-time top scorer – and retired in 2023, moving into coaching.

FK Inter Bratislava (w fkinterbratislava.sk), champions in the 1999–2000 and 2000–01 seasons, fell to the third flight after their financial collapse but were promoted to the second division in 2017. They play at the Stadium FK Stupava, a little way north of Bratislava.

The third team, **FC Petržalka** (w fcpetrzalka.sk), was founded in 1898 as the Pozsonyi Torna Egyesület and has had 18 names since. Having won the title in 2004–05 and 2007–08, famously beating Celtic 5–0 in the Champions League in 2005, Petržalka collapsed when the owners sold the stadium for development in 2008. The club was dissolved and reformed in 2014, starting in the bottom (fifth) division and has now fought its way back up to the second division. Their replacement stadium, the 3,000-capacity Stadium FC Petržalka, opened in 2012 at M Curie-Sklodovskej 1 (84, 98, 99 to Ovsištské námestie).

trampolines, children's zone & chill-out zone. There are hammocks, chairs & umbrellas, & there's often live music on w/ends. You can't swim in the Danube, but you can swim at the pool near the bar, or participate in a group yoga class.

Bowling

BNC – Bowlingové národné centrum (National Bowling Centre) 221 G1; Turbínová 1; 02 4911 5110; w bnc-sk.sk; 14.00–midnight Mon–Wed, 14.00–01.00 Thu, 13.00–01.00 Fri, noon–01.00 Sat, noon–22.00 Sun; 60, 61, 96 to Slovinská. 16 modern, professional lanes. In the Nové Mesto district.

Climbing and ropes courses

Lanoland 221 G1; Koliba–Kamzík; m 09 18 507 669; w lanoland.sk; Jul & Aug 13.00–19.00 Tue–Fri, 11.00–19.00 Sat & Sun; Apr–Jun, Sep & Oct 11.00–19.00 Sat & Sun; adult/child/student €13/10/10 per hr; 44 to Koliba terminus then walk uphill for 20mins. Up in the hills near the Bobovka (bobsleigh track), you'll find Lanoland; a system of ropes with many different levels & courses, & 2 zip lines that's popular with locals, children & team-building events.
Vertigo 221 K1; Trenčianska 47; m 09 48 223 173; w lezeckecentrum.sk; 15.00–22.00 Mon, 07.00–22.00 Tue–Thu, 09.00–22.00 Fri, 09.00–21.00 Sat & Sun; €8–10; 49, 66, N61 to Ružová dolina. Indoor gym with climbing ropes & bouldering for all levels.

Escape room

BrainTeaseLava 220 D5; Zámocká 36; 02 2102 5536; w brainteaselava.sk/en; 09.30–22.00 daily; 9 to Kapucínska; 80, 83, 84, 93, 94, N31, N34, N80, N93, N95 to Zochova. Use all your skills & ingenuity to escape from a locked room (€59 for 2–5 players; 70mins), compete in the City Game with a backpack of special items (€59 for 2–5 players; 2–3hrs; 2–3km walking), or identify a murderer at the Mystery Dinner (€15, plus meal from €13).

Fitness and wellness centres

Most of the 5- & 4-star hotels (page 81) have their own fitness/wellness centres (many are part of the Zion Spa chain; w zionspa.sk), open to the general public for a fee.

Golem Club 220 D8; Aupark Shopping Center, Einsteinova 18; w golemclub.sk; 06.00–22.00 Mon–Fri, 08.00–22.00 Sat & Sun; 80, 83, 84, 88, 93, 94, N80, N93, N95 to Aupark/Pri sade. The latest equipment & classes (aerobics, kick-box, Tae-Bo, Zumba, Piloxing, spinning); also 3 squash courts. There are more Golem Clubs at Eurovea, Avion & Central malls with the same opening times.

Horse racing

Závodisko Bratislava race track map, page 196; Starohájska 29; 02 5241 1504; w zavodisko.sk; 83 to Hrobákova. Bratislava's horse-racing track is in the south of Petržalka.

Summer bobsleigh run

Bobová dráha Lanová 8; m 09 18 683 202; w bobodraha.sk; summer 10.00–18.00 Fri–Sun; 1 ride €3, 3 rides €8.50. A popular destination with kids is the bob track on Kamzík Hill (page 184). The track is 360m long, with 10 bends in the woods & a tunnel before emerging into a beautiful meadow. Rides are pretty speedy & descend 40m in altitude.

Swimming pools and spas

Aquathermal Senec See page 198.
Hotel Nivy See page 85. In the Ružinov district by the Štrkovec Lake (Štrkovecké jazero), Hotel Nivy's main attraction is its 25m

pool & wellness centre (⏱ 10.00–22.00 daily; adults €6/first 1hr 25mins & €1.50/additional 30mins, child under 120cm height €3.50/1hr 25mins, then €1/additional 30mins, sauna €7). The wellness centre has 5 kinds of sauna, 3 whirlpools & a chill-out area, making this a great destination for a rainy afternoon.
Piešťany Spa See page 202.
Plaváreň Pasienky (pool) 📍 221 G1; Junácka 4; ☎ 02 4437 3477; w starz.sk; ⏱ noon–22.00 Mon, 06.00–22.00 Tue–Fri, 08.00–22.00 Sat–Sun; adult/child €4/2; 🚌 50, 51, 58 or 🚌 4 to Miestny úrad Nové Mesto. 2 pools: 50m adult pool & 25m children's pool.
Zlaté Piesky 📍 map, page 196; Senecká cesta; ⏱ 09.00–19.00 daily; 🚌 4 to terminus. Swim outside in summer in the large, soft-water lake, with a water slide & beach volleyball. Alongside is Wakelake (w wakelake.sk), with wakeboarding & flyboarding (with jetpacks strapped to your feet...) in the daytime (⏱ 09.00–dusk daily) & DJ parties at night.

Watersports
Areál Divoká Voda (Whitewater Resort) 📍 map, page 196; Areál vodnych športov, Čunovo; ☎ 02 6252 8002; m 09 05 313 429; w divokavoda.sk; ⏱ mid-Mar–mid-Nov 08.00–20.00, summer to 21.00; 🚌 90 from Nové SND to Areál vodných športov. Many different kinds of watersports can be tried here, & if you want to stay longer, there's a hotel & campsite (pages 85 & 87). Watersports include rafting, kayaking, hydrospeed, jet skiing, surfing, wakeboard, aquaroller; also on offer are paintball, beach volleyball, beach football, horse & pony riding, among others. There are some of the best manmade channels in Europe for white-water rafting, with 6 levels of difficulty; they're used by Olympic sportsmen & top Slovak slalom teams.

SHOPPING

Bratislava is well on its way to becoming a top destination for shopaholics. The Old Town centre is crammed with stores selling luxury goods: china, crystal, ceramics, jewellery and fine wines, while the range of shops in the giant malls dotted around the outskirts, coupled with the favourable opening hours and good public transport, make the whole experience highly enjoyable. As the Old Town centre is car- and bus-free, it makes a stroll around the shops much less frantic and stressful than a dash along Oxford Street or the Champs Élysées.

Swanky **designer shops** line up along Michalská and Ventúrska and top-range fashion and accessories stores such as Pierre Cardin, Ralph Lauren, Tommy Hilfiger, Coccinelle and Frey Wille mingle with exciting local designers. Obchodná ('Shopping' street), now open only to trams, is a major shopping drag with endless teeny jeans shops and music stores interspersed with welcome break stops in the many pubs, cafés and bars en route. An alley between Obchodná and Jedlikova houses an Asian bazaar, if you need very cheap clothes or sunglasses. There's a huge IKEA out towards the airport and Tesco has gigantic superstores in the same area and in Petržalka (though they are no longer open 24 hours). There's also a busy Tesco Express in the basement of the Prior shopping centre on Kamenné námestie, right in the

> **MARKET VALUES**
>
> If all those dumplings are getting you down and you hanker for some fresh fruit, check out one of the city's markets:
>
> **Centrálne trhovisko** 221 K1; Miletičova 54 (Košická); m 09 03 158 710; 06.00–20.00 Mon–Fri, 06.00–16.00 Sat; 49, 61, 63, 64, 71 or 4, 9 to Trnavské mýto. Also known as Miletiča, this is Bratislava's oldest vegetable market, where you can find fresh fruit & veg, as well as lots of snacking opportunities. Some of the best *langoše* can be found here too.
>
> **Stará tržnica** 222 F4; Námestie SNP 25; m 09 05 877 088; w staratrznica.sk; 09.00–15.00 Sat; 1, 3, 4 to Centrum. The splendid 1910 market hall has been beautifully refurbished, but fresh fruit & veg are now only on sale on Sat, together with lots of goodies from local producers & a flea market & community kitchen (run by a rotating roster of immigrant groups). Books (mostly secondhand) & music are for sale upstairs. There's also the Street Food Park (Tue–Fri once a month). This is usually held on the square in front of the market, but in winter they squeeze the food trucks inside. Good toilets & Wi-Fi. Also used as a concert venue (page 128).
>
> **Trh na Žilinskej** 220 E1; Žilinska 5; TrhoviskoZilinska; 05.30–16.00 Tue–Fri, 05.30–14.00 Sat; 40, 44, 49, 61, 63, 64, 71 to Karpatská. For a glimpse at how locals get their greens, try this lovely little local market selling flowers & fresh fruit & veg. Hungarian grannies sell organic veg from their gardens, & look for one granddad's geometric displays of pears from his orchard. Also snack on *langoše* at the back, near the Viecha Drevená Dedina pub (page 118).

heart of town. The main local chain of convenience stores is Delia (w edelia.sk), and Billa and Lidl are fairly widespread food stores. Yeme (222 H4; w yeme.sk) is an upmarket equivalent of Waitrose or Booths in the UK that's fantastic for buying tasty presents.

If that isn't enough, take a tram or a cheap taxi (around €10) out to one of the city's mammoth **malls**. The Nivy centre at the new bus station (page 50) is closest to the centre and just beyond it is the giant Eurovea Galleria mall (page 143) with a vast range of shops, restaurants, cafés and cinemas, plus a lovely riverside promenade to relax on. Aupark is within walking distance of the Old Town centre, a short hop across Most SNP, hidden behind the greenery of Sad Janka Kráľa, at the beginning

---

◀ **1** The beautifully refurbished Stará tržnica hosts a wide range of activities. **2** Bars and cafés spill out on to the pedestrianised streets of the Old Town, offering refreshment to shoppers. **3** Painted Easter eggs make a great souvenir. **4** There are a couple of delightful antique shops in the Old Town, notably Stanley Art. **5** Eurovea Galleria – the place to go in central Europe for shopaholics.

of the Petržalka suburb. Aupark also has a range of facilities, numerous restaurants and cafés, a bookshop and multiplex cinema, spa and the like. VIVO! is out towards Zlaté Piesky and contains everything under the sun, plus restaurants, cafés, a cinema, bowling alley and other leisure facilities; Avion is, as you might guess, a bit further out towards the airport, and has a similar range of shops and facilities. Finally, the new Bory Mall is out to the northwest in Lamač, on the highway to Brno.

There are some fascinating **speciality shops** in Bratislava, selling anything from antiques (*starožitnosti*) and quality wine to rare books. Jewellery fans might pick up a bargain necklace and there are some excellent outlets for fine art, ceramics, crystal, interior design and woodcrafts. There are many shops selling **folk arts and crafts**. In the warmer months, and during the Christmas season, there are dozens of little stalls out on Františkánske námestie (by the Town Hall) and on Hviezdoslavovo námestie with all manner of gift items, folk products, crafts, badges, fridge magnets, T-shirts, bottles of mysterious drinks and little handmade wooden toys; you are sure to find something for everybody back home.

ANTIQUES AND MAPS

Stanley Art 222 C5; Ventúrska 14; 02 5441 1525; 10.00–13.00 & 14.00–18.00 Mon–Fri, 10.00–13.00 Sat; 1, 3, 4 to Centrum. Toby jugs, china tea sets, pewter jugs & silver trinkets.

Steiner Antikvariat 222 C5; Ventúrska 20; 02 5443 3778; w antikvariatsteiner. sk; 13.00–18.00 Mon–Fri; 1, 3, 4 to Centrum. Founded in 1847, this holds maps, ex-libris plates, secondhand books & etchings. Wonderful shop for browsing & fantasising about finding a treasure map.

BOOKS, MAGAZINES AND PAPERS

Adka Books 223 C6; Zelená 6; m 09 11 853 366; 10.00–18.00 Mon–Fri; 1, 3, 4 to Centrum. This little place has some books in English but is mainly a comics specialist.

Artforum 220 D4; Kozia 20; 02 5441 1898; w artforum.sk; 09.00–20.00 Mon–Fri, 09.00–14.00 Sat; 44, 47 to Kozia. Bookshop with cards, magazines, English books, DVDs & a small, friendly café with trendy juices, good coffee & cakes to accompany quiet literary contemplation.

Eurobooks 223 G6; Jesenského 5–9; 02 5441 7959; w eurobooks.sk; 10.00–17.00 Mon–Fri; 1, 4 to Jesenského. Excellent selection of foreign-language books & Bradt guides.

Knihy LIC (Slovak Literary Centre) 222 F3; Námestie SNP 12; 02 2047 3519; w litcentrum.sk; 08.00–19.00 Mon–Fri, 09.00–13.00 Sat; 1, 3, 4 to Centrum. In the Kunsthalle, this is the place for contemporary Slovak literature, as well as books on Bratislava & Slovakia.

Martinus 222 E1; Obchodná 26; 02 3266 0366; w martinus.sk; 08.30–21.00 Mon–Fri, 10.00–20.00 Sat & Sun; 9 to Poštová. Giant bookshop (around 100,000 titles, including lots in English) with a comprehensive internet service & the Foxford café (page 112) providing brews & snacks. Also at the Nivy shopping centre (09.00–21.00 daily).

Megabooks 222 F5; Laurinská 9; m 09 17 286 925; w megabooks.sk/ bratislava; 10.00–19.00 Mon–Fri, 10.00–17.00 Sat; 1, 3, 4 to Centrum. Huge range of books in English, both

fiction & non-fiction. Many interesting books on Bratislava & Slovakia.
Panta Rhei 220 E4; Vysoká 2/A; 0800 333 000; w pantarhei.sk; 08.00–20.00 daily; 1, 9 to Poštová. Huge bookshop (under the AC Hotel) with an emphasis on internet sales; good for maps & guidebooks, lots in English. Also in the Aupark, Avion & VIVO! shopping centres (all 09.00–21.00 daily).
Press Shop 222 C5; Sedlárska 2; 09.00–18.00 Mon–Fri, 10.00–18.00 Sat; 1, 3, 4 to Centrum. By far the best place for foreign newspapers & magazines.

FASHION For a list of places to discover Slovak fashion and design, including shops, galleries & boutiques, visit w map.slovakfashioncouncil.sk/en.

Buffet 222 G4; Laurinská 19; w buffetclothing.com; 11.00–19.00 Mon–Fri, noon–18.00 Sat–Sun; 1, 3, 4 to Centrum. Small batches of designer clothing made from leftovers of quality Italian textiles.
Ethno Sumba 222 B4; Klariská 14; m 09 50 462 467; w ethnosumba.sk; 10.30–18.30 Mon–Sat, 11.00–18.00 Sun; 9 to Kapucínska. Hippie/new-age/Asian clothing (& fat Buddhas).
In Vivo 222 C4; Laurinská 5; 09 15 713 626; w invivo.sk; 10.00–19.00 daily; 1, 3, 4 to Centrum. Bags, purses, ceramics, jewellery, cushions by local artists & designers.
Kompot 222 G4; Panenská 30; m 09 48 630 852; w kompot.sk; 11.00–18.00 Mon–Fri; 1, 3, 4 to Centrum. Designer shop with CDs, DVDs, books & prints, shoes, children's clothes & the hippest T-shirts in town. If you buy a T-shirt, & have sturdy luggage, they'll parcel it up in a kompot – a large jam jar, used by Slovak grannies to store jam or fruit compote.
Slávica Design Shop 222 G5; Laurinská 19; m 09 17 968 736; w slavicadesign.sk;
11.00–20.00 daily; 1, 3, 4 to Centrum. A small design shop selling high-quality clothes, jewellery, bags & ceramics by young local designers.
Slowatch 222 G4; Laurinská 19; m 09 08 704 256; w slowatch.sk; 11.00–19.00 Mon–Fri, 13.00–19.00 Sat; 1, 3, 4 to Centrum. Uber-cool clothes shop, with hip T-shirts, sneakers & bike accessories.
SlowConcept Store 223 G8; Medena 17; m 09 07 600 671; w slow.sk; 11.00–19.00 Mon–Fri, 11.00–16.00 Sat; 50, N33 or 1, 4 to Námestie Ľudovíta Štúra. Sustainable, fair fashion, beauty products & gifts; also organic coffee!
Twigi 222 B4; Klariská 7; 02 5443 3806; twigi; 11.00–18.00 Mon–Sat; 9 to Kapucínska. Attractive little shop crammed with clothes, souvenirs & cards.

FOLK ART AND CRAFTS

Crystal Katka 223 B7; Panská 24; 02 5443 1264; w crystalkatka.sk; 10.00–18.00 Mon–Fri, 09.00–17.00 Sat; 1, 3, 4 to Centrum. Handmade, hand-cut crystal goods in a beautiful 15th-century setting.
Shop in the Museum 222 D4; Biela 6; m 09 05 349 049; 10.00–18.00 Tue–Sat; 1, 3, 4 to Centrum. The fascinating Museum of Trade (free) displays old advertising signs, ancient silver cash registers & authentic furniture from old Pressburg in the 'oldest shop in town'. It is also a functioning store where you can buy folk crafts & food items such as *bryndza* cheese, honey wine, Devín redcurrant wine, painted eggs & traditional bread rolls.
Úľuv Gallery & Shop 222 G3; Námestie SNP 12; 02 5292 3802; w uluv.sk; 10.30–18.00 Mon–Fri; 1, 3, 4 to Centrum; & Obchodná 64; 221 F4; noon–18.00 Mon–Fri; 1, 9 to Vysoká. Úľuv, the Centre for Folk Art Production, has 2 shops in Bratislava with a great selection of goods & gifts.

CHRISTMAS MARKET

Bratislava is the third capital making up the triangle of great Austro-Hungarian cities (Budapest–Vienna–Bratislava), and although all three have wonderfully atmospheric and traditional Christmas fairs, Bratislava's is possibly the most inviting. With its beautifully renovated and totally pedestrianised Old Town centre, it's perfect for tottering around after one too many mulled wines (to keep out the cold, of course) without fear of being mown down by a Škoda, careening across the icy roads.

The Bratislava Christmas market takes place from 20 November to 22 December in the twin main squares of the Old Town – Františkánske námestie and Hlavné námestie right in front of the City History Museum – and also on the graceful tree-lined square of Hviezdoslavovo námestie a few steps away. In December, the squares are packed with wooden booths offering Christmas gifts, ornaments and a wide variety of festive food and drink. Dishes to try include *lokše* (potato pancakes) available with a choice of fillings, grilled meats such as *cigánská pečienka* (Gypsy cutlet), *langoše* (deep-fried doughnuts) or *chlieb s masťou* (fresh bread smeared with lard and sprinkled with chopped onions), ideal for accompanying the mulled wine or the special Christmas punch drink. In 2005, the city commissioned the construction of new stalls inspired by the architecture of old Bratislava. Traders offer wooden toys, blown-glass ornaments, hand-painted pottery, Slovak folk art, beeswax candles and handmade gifts. Musical performances take place on a stage set up in front of the City History Museum and here you can also sample the special Slovak Christmas cabbage soup (*kapustnica*), a delicious warming dish enhanced with homemade sausage, whipped cream, dried mushrooms and plums.

The Christmas market is a highlight of the cultural year.

SHOPPING CENTRES

Aupark Shopping Center 220 D8; Einsteinova 18; w aupark-bratislava.sk; 10.00–21.00 daily; 80, 83, 84, 88, 93, 94, N80, N93, N95 to Aupark. Large mall south of the Danube with cinema, bowling alley, food court & hundreds of shops. Also post office (10.00–20.00 Mon–Fri, 09.00–20.00 Sat & Sun), ATMs & Wi-Fi (free but with a tedious sign-up).

Avion Shopping Park 221 K1; Ivánska cesta 16; w avion.sk; 10.00–21.00 daily; 61, 63, 96 to Avion Shopping Park. The city's largest shopping complex, near the airport, with a huge IKEA store, C&A, H&M, Kaufland & much more.

Bory Mall map, page 196; 02 6920 4849; w borymall.sk; 10.00–21.00 Mon–Fri, 09.00–21.00 Sat–Sun; 21 to OC Bory. Bratislava's newest mall, just off the E65 highway to Brno; shops, restaurants & an IMAX cinema.

Central 221 G1; Metodova 6; 02 3211 5121; w central.sk; 10.00–21.00 daily; 49, 61, 63, 64, 71 or 4, 9 to Trnavské mýto. Stores, fast-food outlets, post office & fitness centre. In Ružinov, 20mins by tram east from the city centre.

Eurovea Galleria 221 H7; Pribinova 8; 02 2091 5000; w eurovea.sk/en; 10.00–21.00 daily, food court to 22.00; 28, 50, 70 to Malá scéna; 50, 88, 90 to Landererova; 28, 40, 78, 90 to Nové SND. With 60,000m^2 of prime retail, leisure & entertainment zones, this is central Europe's leading retail therapy destination. Opposite the New SND building near the Apollo Bridge, with restaurants on the Danube embankment.

Galeria Petržalka map, page 196; Panónska cesta 25; 02 5262 3349; w petrzalka.ocgaleria.sk; 09.00–21.00 daily; 59, 93, 98, 99 to Lúky II; 91, 191 to OC Lúky. Anchored by a huge Tesco Extra (06.00–22.00 daily), as well as H&M, Panta Rhei bookshop, food court, etc. Across the main road the Danubia Centre consists mainly of a Kaufland & Lidl.

Nivy m 09 05 593 845; w nivy.com/en; 10.00–21.00 Mon–Fri, 09.00–21.00 Sat–Sun; 21, 42, 50, 60, 70, 88 to Autobusová stanica. At the new bus station, with Yeme & Lidl supermarkets, a Martinus bookshop, food court, & garden, playgrounds & a barbecue area on the Green Roof (no cinema).

River Park 220 A6; Nábrežie arm gen L Svobodu; w riverpark.sk; 10.00–22.00 daily; 29, 31, 37, 39 or 4 to Chatam Sófer; 9 to Kráľovské údolie. Luxury apartments, restaurants & shops, & the Grand Hotel River Park (page 81).

Shopping Palace Bratislava 221 G1; Cesta na Senec 2/A; w shoppingpalace.sk; 09.00–21.00 daily; 4 to Shopping Palace (just short of the Zlaté Piesky terminal). Shopping complex with clothes shops, electronics stores, cafés & banks.

VIVO! 221 G1; Vajnorská 100; w vivo-shopping.com/en/bratislava; 09.00–21.00 daily; 50, 51, 98 or 4 to Miestny úrad Nové Mesto. Shops, cinema, gym & hypermarket.

SOUVENIRS

Fanatik Fanswear 222 E5; Laurinská 6; 02 5296 2523; w fanatik.sk; 10.00–20.00 daily; 1, 3, 4 to Centrum. Sporting memorabilia, Slovak ice-hockey shirts, baseball caps, scarves & also folk crafts.

WINE SHOPS The website w vinoteka-vinaren.sk has links to many vineyards, wine shops & wine bars throughout Slovakia.

Billa 222 F2; Námestie SNP 7; 07.00–22.00 Mon–Sat, 08.00–21.00 Sun; 3, 4 to Centrum. Convenient central supermarket with a good selection of wines & spirits

MILAN RASTISLAV ŠTEFÁNIK – TO BELIEVE, TO LOVE AND TO WORK

Between the two halves of the Eurovea shopping complex (page 143) in east Bratislava by the Apollo Bridge stands an impressive statue of Milan Rastislav Štefánik. The huge 7.4m bronze sculpture was rebuilt in 2009 on the 90th anniversary of Štefánik's tragic death in an air crash by Bohumil Kafka, whose original work was created in 1938. Behind Štefánik, who gazes out across the Danube, is a high obelisk on which a lion holds the Czechoslovak coat of arms. You can also see a replica of Štefánik's biplane hanging from the rafters in Bratislava Airport, which bears his name.

Milan Rastislav Štefánik, born in 1880 in Košariská in Trenčin County, was a Slovak politician, diplomat, astronomer and great hero to the Slovaks during difficult times. In 1900, he went to the Charles University in Prague to study astronomy, physics, optics, mathematics and philosophy. The philosophy lectures were taught by Tomáš Masaryk (the future first president of Czechoslovakia), who inspired Štefánik with the idea of Czech and Slovak co-operation. In 1904, Štefánik went to Paris to work at the famous Observatoire de Paris-Meudon, whose director, Pierre Janssen (one of the co-founders of astrophysics), noticed Štefánik's talent. At the outbreak of World War I in 1914, Štefánik realised that a defeat for Austria–Hungary (and Germany) would mean the opportunity for the Slovaks and Czechs to gain independence. Despite ill health, he insisted on fighting in the French air force, and was sent as a pilot to Serbia in 1915 and flew on 30 missions.

(less good for beers). Also at Mostová 2 (⏰ 07.00–21.00 Mon–Sat, 08.00–21.00 Sun) & elsewhere.

Bottleshop 📍 221 F6; Tallerova 2; m 09 11 766 777; w bottleshop.sk; ⏰ 09.00–22.00 Mon–Fri, 10.00–22.00 Sat; 🚌 50 or 🚋 1, 3, 4 to Šafárikovo námestie. Excellent range of imported liqueurs, as well as cigars, chocolate, etc; also at Krížna 26 📍 221 J2.

Bottle Store 📍 223 E8; Mostová 6; m 09 45 999 000; ⏰ 10.00–19.00 Mon–Thu, 10.00–20.00 Fri, noon–19.00 Sat; 🚌 50, N33 or 🚋 1, 4 to Námestie Ľudovíta Štúra. Imported wines & brandies, absinthe & more.

Národný Salón Vín 📍 222 E5; Apponyi Palace, Radničná 1; m 09 18 664 992; w salonvin.sk/en; ⏰ 10.00–18.00 Tue–Fri, 11.00–18.00 Sat–Sun; 🚋 1, 3, 4 to Centrum. The Apponyi Palace (page 160) hosts the Slovak National Collection of Wine with wine tastings (€9 for 2 wines, €18 for 4, €36 for 8, €36 for 100min free tasting, €55 for 6 premium wines), bottles for sale & links to 40 wineries in Slovakia.

Pálffy 📍 222 E3; Námestie SNP 33; ⏰ 10.00–18.00 Tue–Fri; 🚋 1, 3, 4 to Centrum. Quality wines & spirits as well as food hampers.

St Nicolaus Distillery Shop & Lounge 📍 221 G4; Rajská 7; ☎ 02 2086 9300; w nicolaus.sk/en; ⏰ 09.00–19.00 Mon–Fri; 🚋 3, 4 to Mariánska. At the outlet for Slovakia's leading spirits, founded in 1867, you

On returning to Paris, Štefánik met Edvard Beneš and also contacted his former professor Masaryk. In 1916, the three men founded the Czechoslovak National Council, the government of Czecho-Slovak resistance abroad which would lead to the creation of Czechoslovakia in 1918. In 1916, Štefánik and the resistance gathered Czechoslovak troops to fight against Austria–Hungary and Germany. Because of Štefánik's personal diplomatic skills, the Allies recognised the Czechoslovak National Council as a de facto government, and the Czechoslovak Legion troops as allied forces, in 1918. In January 1919, after the war ended, Štefánik went from Russia to France and Italy, where he organised the evacuation of Czechoslovak troops from Siberia. His diplomatic skills were also required to solve arguments between the French and Italian missions in Czechoslovakia.

On 4 May 1919, Štefánik wanted to return to Slovakia to see his family, and so flew from Italy in an Italian military plane. It tried to land in Bratislava, which was under threat by communist Hungarian troops led by Béla Kun, but crashed near Ivánka pri Dunaji. Štefánik died along with two Italian officers. The reason for the plane crash is disputed to this day. The official explanation at that time was that the plane was shot down 'accidentally', because its Italian tricolour was mistaken for the similar Hungarian flag. Štefánik's sudden death, combined with his recent quarrels with Beneš, contributed to suspicion among Slovaks towards the Czechs during the First Republic of Czechoslovakia. Štefánik's personal motto was: *To Believe, To Love and To Work*.

can taste & buy their vodka, Jubilejná-brand fruit spirit drinks & the bitter herbal liqueur Demänovka. They also import sherry, London gin & New World wines.

Wine Gallery Trunk 222 C3; Hurbanovo námestie 8; m 09 48 677 706 w trunk.sk; 11.00–23.00 Mon–Thu, 11.00–01.00 Fri, 16.00–midnight Sat; 1, 9 to Poštová; N31, N34, N44, N47, N53, N55, N70, N72, N80, N93, N95 to Hodžovo námestie. Large selection of wines with bottles lining the walls & tables & chairs so you can sit down & have a taster or 2.

Wine Not? 222 D5; Hlávne námestie 3; m 09 11 472 099; w winenot.sk; noon– midnight Sun–Thu, noon–02.00 Fri & Sat; 1, 3, 4 to Centrum; N31, N34, N44, N47, N53, N55, N70, N72, N80, N93, N95 to Hodžovo námestie. Wine bar & shop right on the central square. A wide choice of wines (displayed on an iPad, but staff are well informed).

8

Walking Tours

Bratislava is such an easy city to explore on foot, but with its irregular shape and winding alleyways, a tour has to double back on itself. See map, page 224, for routes described.

WALK ONE – OLD TOWN *Estimated time: 2 hours*

A good place to start is **Michael's Gate** (Michalská veža; page 155). This is also point zero, where you can see the global distances to cities all around the world under the tower. Climb up five flights and you'll be rewarded with a great view of the 'little big city' as it now calls itself. It's a magnificent panorama with the castle on one side, contrasting with the bizarre sight of a spaceship landing on the bridge.

Back down again on the right is **Baštová**, the narrowest alley in town and, in medieval times, home to the city hangman. For a quick detour, turn right and nip up Klariská and Farská to see the elegant church and convent of the **Poor Clares** (Kostol klarisiek; page 180); behind it, Kapitulska is lined with largely disused religious buildings, and has to be the quietest street in the Old Town. The streets of **Michalská** and **Ventúrska** are a continuation of each other and a good introduction to the town, lined with swanky shops and historic buildings. The largest building on Michalská is the former Hungarian Chamber built in 1756, home to sessions of the Diet in the 19th century and now the university library.

At the point where Michalská and Ventúrska meet you'll see a big rock with *'Korzo'* written on it. This signals the start of the *korzo* or promenade, a custom that continues to this day as families stroll down towards the river in the evening. For a small town, Bratislava is packed with palaces; nearby, at number 15, is the **Leopold De Pauli Palace** (Palác Leopolda de Pauliho), where Franz Liszt (aged nine) gave a concert in the garden pavilion (page 125). Just opposite is a palace owned by Leopold Pálffy (Ventúrska 10) where Mozart performed for the local aristocracy in 1762, aged six, accompanied by his father. It was the only concert he gave in the then Hungary. Further on at Ventúrska 9, the **Zichy Palace** (Zichyho palác) was built from 1770 to 1780 on the site of three medieval town houses.

The **Universitas Istropolitana**, further along at Ventúrska 3, was founded in 1465 by Matthias Corvinus, King of Hungary, and at the time was the only university in Slovakia or Hungary. At Panská 27, the **Keglevich Palace** (Keglevičov palác) was the scene of a concert by Beethoven (page 124).

Head next for **St Martin's Cathedral** (Dóm svätého Martina; page 158), scene of the coronation of 11 Hungarian kings and eight royal spouses. Look out for a gold model of the crown of Szent István, Hungary's first monarch, on top of the spire.

A walkway leading north from the cathedral between the highway and the old city walls is lined with detailed information panels on the local Jewish community. Just to the south, in Rudnayovo námestie, a **statue in molten metal** with a Star of David on the top commemorates the synagogue that stood here but was demolished to make way for the construction of the Most SNP (then called Nový most – New Bridge) in 1971 – see page 159 for more. Panská ('Street of the Lords'), now a busy pedestrianised shopping street, is the main east–west route across the Old Town – follow it past the official **Pálffy Palace** (Pálffyho palác), which holds one of Bratislava's best galleries (page 171). Further on, you'll trip over a man's head poking out of a manhole – this is **Čumil**, one of the favourites of all the humorous works of art dotted around town. There are debates as to who he represents – whether a partisan or just a guy who likes to look up skirts. Turning left, you'll soon be on **Hlavné námestie** (page 186), site of some fine patisseries and perhaps a good place to relax for a while.

One of **Napoleon's soldiers** can still be found on the square, leaning over the back of a bench, smiling smugly at the city he once tried to destroy. Follow the soldier's gaze and you arrive at the square's centrepiece, the **Roland Fountain** (Rolandova fontána). Roland was a knight who was known as the protector of Bratislava and its citizens, yet the man on the top of the fountain is actually Maximilián II, the first Hungarian king to be crowned in Bratislava. In 1572, after the town was ravaged by fire, Maximilián had the fountain built to provide water in case of future fires. According to a local legend, at midnight on New Year's Eve Maximilián turns and salutes to all four directions – however, only female virgins can see this.

The red-roofed building with a yellow tower on the east side of the square is the 15th-century **Old Town Hall** (Stará radnica; page 157). A cannonball, fired into the city by Napoleon's army, is embedded in the wall – it's one of ten dotted across the Old Town as memorials to the siege of 1809. The barn-like **Jesuit church** (Jezuitský kostol) next door was built by the Lutherans in 1638 and on the king's wish it couldn't have a tower.

Walk through the Old Town Hall courtyard to Primaciálne námestie where the **Primate's Palace** (Primaciálny palác; page 158) is an explosion of pink and there's a black cardinal's hat on the tympanum. You can walk through the three courtyards, and it's also worth going inside to see the hall of mirrors. The **House of J N Hummel** (Hummelov dom; page 164) just up the road celebrates the life of composer Johan Nepomuk Hummel.

From there it's a left, right, left southwards through narrow streets and you'll find yourself on **Hviezdoslavovo námestie** (page 186), a tongue-twisting square lined with trees and dominated by a statue to **Pavol Országh Hviezdoslav**, the 'father of Slovak poetry'. On the left is the neo-Renaissance Historical Building of the **Slovak National Theatre** (page 121), home to the opera. Over the square is the **Reduta**, home to the Slovak Philharmonic (page 125). The huge Buckingham-Palace-like building dominating the square is the **Radisson Blu Carlton Hotel** and there's a good restaurant inside (page 101). Walk down between the Reduta and the Carlton, passing the bizarre statue to patriot **Ľudovít Štúr** with figures suspended halfway up a pillar, and you're out by the Danube.

To the right is the Esterházy Palace, now the **Slovak National Gallery** (page 178); cross the road to the embankment, where you'll see a cute little waiting room for the ferry to Petržalka, built in 1931, and disused since 2003. It has been used as an arty café, known as Propellor, but is currently empty. Turning left, you'll pass the minimalist Tomb of the Unknown Soldier and a **statue of a soldier** in a trenchcoat holding a machine gun – a Bulgarian war memorial with the message 'Those who fall in the battle for freedom never die'. Carry on towards the **Slovak National Museum** (Slovenské národné múzeum; page 170), where a statue of the first Czechoslovak president Tomáš Garrigue Masaryk stands tall. It used to be guarded by a statue of a proud lion, commemorating the creation of the Czechoslovak Republic on 28 October 1918 'from two brother nations'; however, this was removed to stand guard over the Eurovea Galleria mall (page 143).

From here, to reach the Blue Church it's best to cross over the main road, Vajanského nábrežie, by the Slovak National Museum and walk up Kúpeľňa. Take the first right on to Medená and follow the road along to the busy Štúrova thoroughfare. Cross the road and walk along Grösslingova which will lead you to the **Blue Church**, passing some interesting Art Nouveau buildings en route. Ödön Lechner, 'father' of modern Hungarian architecture, designed the church and also the high school at Grösslingova 18, with its light brown and beige colours; during term time you can pop inside and check out the grand staircase in custard and cream, but watch out for the officious school porter. There are also several doorways with Socialist Realist reliefs of enthusiastic workers. At the first turning right on to Bezručova, an amazing image will come into view: the incredible, almost

---

1 Grassalkovich Palace is the residence of Slovakia's president. **2** The Roland Fountain, centrepiece of Bratislava's main square, Hlavné námestie. **3** Nearby, the *Napoleonic Soldier* recalls the siege of 1809. **4** Global distances to cities around the world are marked at 'point zero', under Michael's Tower. ▶

edible **Blue Church** (Modrý kostolík; page 152), an Art Nouveau building dedicated to St Elizabeth, which looks like it's covered in blue icing.

If you head east on Dobrovičova, just south of the Blue Church, you'll see the towers of **Sky Park** ahead of you – designed by Zaha Hadid Architects but with little of the late starchitect's inspiration, the centrepiece is actually a red-brick former heating plant (1942) by Dušan Jurkovič, father of modern Slovak architecture. This whole area is known as the New Downtown, once an area of docks and factories that is now sprouting statement towers (the Nivy Centre and the new bus station to the north, and the two wings of the Eurovea Centre to the south).

WALK TWO – CASTLE AND BEYOND Estimated time: 3 hours

This is slightly more complicated than Walk 1 as you may want a couple of tram tickets (€1.20 – available from little yellow machines by most tram stops). Cross under or over **Staromestská**, the busy main road which slices through the city and cuts off the Old Town from the castle, to begin at the **House of the Good Shepherd** (Dom u dobrého pastiera; page 192), a tall yellow Rococo whimsy which houses the **Clock Museum** (Múzeum hodín; page 161). This area is the old Jewish quarter, although little remains of it. Walk up the steep **Beblavého**, which in the past was the city's red-light street and which author Patrick Leigh Fermor, on his walking journey to Istanbul, found strangely fascinating. It's a steep climb up to **Bratislava Castle** (Bratislavsky hrad; page 153), dubbed the 'upside-down bedstead', but it's worth it for the view and the museum inside. There is also a good restaurant (Reštaurácia Hradná; page 98) in which to recuperate. The view is mixed – you can see the **UFO café** (page 101) perched above the bridge, but over the river the sprawling housing district of **Petržalka** (page 192) fits the stereotypical 'eastern European tower block' image.

The long concrete monolith that you'll see over the river is **Incheba** (page 128), a massive convention and exhibition site, and the 20-storey construction is **Aupark Tower**, a giant office block above a huge shopping centre. Over the river and to the right are the woods of Austria. At night, the castle is illuminated and looks magical in its position of dominance overlooking the Danube.

Either return the same way and go a short way west on the Danube embankment, or take the narrow flight of steps down from Mudroňova, just west of the castle. You'll come to a strange, foreboding black block, the memorial to **Chatam Sófer**, the scholar and rabbi Moshe Schreiber. If you wish to visit, call (see page 179 for contact details) to arrange an appointment. Walk a little way upstream to the **River Park area**, containing shops, restaurants and the Grand Hotel River Park.

At the Chatam Sófer tram stop, you can catch the number 9 tram which will take you on a spooky ghost-train ride under the castle. It's good to get off at the first stop (Kapucínska) after the tunnel, as there are some pretty churches to visit. Walk in the same direction as the tram, along to **Hurbanovo námestie**, and you'll come to the **Holy Trinity Church** (Kostol svätého Jána z Mathy; page 180), one of the finest examples of Baroque architecture in Bratislava. Walk up Suché mýto (Dry toll) and you'll reach **Hodžovo námestie** and a view of the **Grassalkovich Palace** (Grassalkovičov palác; page 155), a fine Rococo building constructed in 1760, now home to the president. Behind is a spacious park where Slovaks enjoy the sun in their lunch hours. Further north is **Námestie Slobody** (page 187), home to what was supposedly the largest post office in the world, although it's now mostly ministry offices. At the northern side of the square is the magnificent Baroque **Archbishop's Summer Palace** (Letný arcibiskunský palác; page 152), built in the second half of the 18th century by Viennese royal architect F A Hillebrandt. A little further along the street is the bizarre vision of Slovak Radio's **inverted pyramid** (page 193).

From here, cross the road and walk down Starohorská to Americké námestie. Across this square and a little to the right is the **Medical Garden** (page 184), a lovely park enjoyed by office workers on their lunch break. In the far corner, you can find a statue to the great Hungarian poet, Sándor Petőfi (born Alexander Petrovics to second generation Slovaks). If you are hungry, there is a lovely bistro, Domček Medická (page 103), offering soups, salads, quiches, great homemade lemonade and hot chocolate.

From Americké námestie, you might want to jump on the number 3 or 4 tram for two stops to Centrum. Take a short stroll down Štúrova, turn right on to Gorkého and head for Hviezdoslavovo námestie. Wander the length of this beautiful tree-lined square, treating yourself to a delicious ice cream at Luculus or Koun (page 110). At the far end of the square is the Most SNP bridge.

If you have any energy left, I suggest walking over the Danube on **Most SNP** and taking the lift up to the **UFO café** for a drink, a meal and a spectacular view (page 101), before walking back downstream in the **Sad Janka Kráľa** (page 185), a lovely green space, and returning to the northern side by the Starý Most.

9

Museums and Sightseeing

Although entry fees are included below, many sights can be visited for free with a Bratislava City Card. See page 71 for more information.

MAJOR SIGHTS

ARCHBISHOP'S SUMMER PALACE (Letný arcibiskupský palác) 220 E2; Námestie Slobody 1; 94 to Námestie Slobody

Today, the Archbishop's Summer Palace houses the Slovak Republic Government Office, and the restored palace and English garden are inaccessible to the public. The palace was built in about 1614, as a Renaissance summer seat for the archbishops of Esztergom (in Hungary) as Esztergom had been occupied by the Ottoman Empire in 1543, meaning they had to base themselves in Bratislava. The Baroque sculptor Georg Rafael Donner (page 158) had a studio in the palace garden for almost ten years. In 1940–41, Slovak architect Emil Belluš removed all buildings from the garden and added the two wings of the palace, creating the building we see today. Belluš secured the project after his previous work on the nearby Grassalkovich Palace (page 155). Today, most of the original statues have been lost: the St John statue now stands in the courtyard of the Primate's Palace, and the other statues are in Kittsee, Austria. In the palace interior, only two original pieces remain: a fresco on the ceiling of the palace's 18th-century chapel and an altar.

BLUE CHURCH (Modrý kostolík) 221 G6; Bezručova 2; 02 5273 3571; w modrykostol. fara.sk; ⏱ 07.00–07.30 & 17.30–19.00 Mon–Sat, 07.30–noon & 17.30–19.00 Sun; 50 or 1, 3, 4 to Šafárikovo námestie

The Blue Church's full title is the Church of St Elizabeth (Kostol sv Alžbety). According to legend, Elizabeth, the daughter of Endre II of Hungary, was born in Bratislava in 1207 and was the city's only well-known saint (page 155). It was decided that a church be built in her honour and permission was asked from the Hungarian archbishop Vászáry. The Hungarian architect and 'father of Hungarian Art Nouveau' Ödön Lechner was commissioned to design a church in 1907, on the 700th anniversary of Elizabeth's birth, while Antal Durvay was in charge of the construction work. Lechner used concrete for the church and covered the exterior with plaster painted in several shades of blue, decorated with ceramic floral tiles in darker blue and tiny mirrors. He knew the legend of St Elizabeth (page 155) well and used her rose motif many times in the decoration. Budapest painter Gyula Tury decorated the altar showing Elizabeth giving alms to the poor outside Wartburg Castle. The church was consecrated on 11 October 1913.

Note that the church's opening hours are awkward and unreliable, especially in winter; you can at least look through the glass doors and it should be open for half an hour before the daily 18.00 service. The parish house (to the south) and high school (to the north) are also worth a look.

BRATISLAVA CASTLE (Bratislavský hrad) 220 C6; Námestie Alexandra Dubčeka 1; 02 2048 3110; **w** snm.sk/en; 10.00–18.00 Wed–Mon; adult/concession/child €14/7/3; 44, 47 to Hrad

In *A Time of Gifts*, Patrick Leigh Fermor wrote that 'the symmetry of the huge gaunt castle and the height of its corner towers gave it the look of an upside-down table' (although he saw it before it was restored and painted white as today). Also described somewhat cruelly as an 'upside-down bedstead', the present Bratislava Castle was constructed in 1430 by King Sigismund of Luxembourg. There had been previous fortifications on the hill, rising 85m above the Danube, built first by Celts then Romans then in the 9th century by the Slavs. The conquering Magyars also built fortifications on the hill and there was extensive construction work in the 13th century. King Sigismund reconstructed the castle and added outer defence walls, some 11m thick, and the Habsburgs used the castle as protection against the Turks, the Hungarian Crown Jewels being kept there from 1552. Its trademark four corner towers were added between 1635 and 1649 when the Hungarian Viceroy Pál Pálffy called in Giovanni Battista Carlone to help with a redesign.

Maria Theresa called it 'her castle' and converted it into a grand palace in 1761, when the interior was redesigned in a lavish Rococo style and a number of annexes were added to the north and west. It became the residence of her favourite daughter Maria Cristina and her husband, Archduke Albert of Saxony-Teschen, who was Governor of Hungary from 1765 to 1781 (the story goes that she was the only one of Maria Theresa's daughters allowed to marry for love, the others being married off for diplomatic purposes). He was a great art collector but unfortunately his paintings didn't remain here but instead became the basis of the fabulous Albertina Museum in Vienna.

In any case, Maria Theresa's successors did not share her love for Bratislava and the castle, and it fell into disrepair: it was used for a while as a seminary and a barracks, and in 1811 it burnt down in a devastating fire and remained in ruin for 140 years, almost being demolished in the 1940s, until restoration work began in 1953. Today it houses exhibitions for the Slovak

National Museum (page 167) as well as state rooms of the Slovak National Council. Most recently, the Winter Riding Hall and the Baroque gardens on the castle's north side have been restored to their 1780 condition (though with a new underground car park beneath).

The hilltop castle, with its huge courtyard (free access), is an imposing and atmospheric building and the tree-studded grounds (⏲ 08.00–22.00

THE UNMISSABLES

Bratislava packs a vast selection of cultural and leisure attractions into one pocket-sized capital, with a huge choice of museums, galleries, churches and historic monuments. The city is also one of the greenest in Europe and there are numerous parks and sporting facilities to try out. If your time in Bratislava is limited, here are a few suggestions for the places you shouldn't miss to get a real feel for the vibrant Slovak capital.

BLUE CHURCH (Modrý kostolík) 221 G6. St Elizabeth's Church is a stunning example of Art Nouveau architecture and, with its light blue 'icing' and decorative elements, is considered the most beautiful church in Bratislava (page 152).

BRATISLAVA CASTLE (Bratislavský hrad) 220 C6. Bratislava's iconic castle has dominated the city skyline since the 11th century and houses a fascinating museum of Slovak history (page 153).

DEVÍN CASTLE (Hrad Devín) map, page 196. Perched strategically on a rocky outcrop at the confluence of the Danube and Morava rivers, this is one of the oldest castles in the country and has played an important role in Slovakia's history (page 195).

ST MARTIN'S CATHEDRAL (Dóm sv Martina) 223 B7. Bratislava's mini cathedral is the most important church in the country and the location of the coronation of 19 Hungarian monarchs (page 158).

SLOVAK NATIONAL THEATRE – HISTORICAL BUILDING (Slovenské národné divadlo – Historická budova) 221 F6. A beautiful historical setting for world-class opera or exciting modern theatre, but currently closed for refurbishment (page 121).

UFO 220 D8. The UFO hovers 80m above the Most SNP and offers an unparalleled view of the city. The bridge and UFO were built in 1967–72 and declared 'Building of the Century' in Slovakia in 2001 (page 159).

> **THE LEGEND OF ST ELIZABETH**
>
> St Elizabeth was famed for looking after and feeding the poor and needy. Her husband, Prince Louis of Thuringia, supported her, but rumours were spread that she was taking treasure to pay for food. Once, he stopped her and asked to look under her apron to see if she was carrying roses, as she claimed. When he lifted the apron the bread had been miraculously changed to roses.
>
> Widowed at the age of 20, she founded a hospital at Marburg and dedicated herself to caring for the sick and poor; she died at 24 and was canonised just four years later.

daily, summer until midnight) offer a lovely place for a stroll or a picnic with a view over the Old Town and Petržalka. There's a fine restaurant within the castle area too, the Reštaurácia Hradná (page 98) with a great terrace overlooking the city and the Danube.

GRASSALKOVICH PALACE (Grassalkovičov palác) 220 E3; Hodžovo námestie 1; 42, 44, 47, 83, 84, 93, 94 to Hodžovo námestie

Built in 1760–65 as a summer residence for Count Anton Grassalkovitch, president of the Hungarian Royal Chamber, by architect Andreas Mayerhoffer, the Baroque palace stands in an open space north of the Old Town with a French-style garden behind. Grassalkovitch was an influential advisor to Empress Maria Theresa, and the palace was a meeting place for the Hungarian aristocracy. Today, it serves as the residence for the President of Slovakia and is not open to the public; however, the garden (page 182) can be visited for free (08.00–18.00 Mon–Fri). Visitors can also watch the changing of the guard in front of the palace (on the hour, every hour, but the main change is at 13.00).

MICHAEL'S GATE (Michalská brána) 222 C3; Michalská 22; 02 5443 3044; w muzeum.bratislava.sk; 1, 9 to Poštová

Construction of the town fortifications began in the 13th century; by the end of the 14th century, the system had three gates (page 182): Michalská, Laurinská and Vydrická brána. Rybárska brána was added later. During the 15th century, the town's outer line of defence had five outer gates: Kozia brána, the gate at Suché mýto (Dry toll-gate), Schöndorfská, Špitálska and Dunajská gates. As military technology developed, the inner lines of the fortification system were extended by cannon bastions: Mäsiarska (Butchers'), Obuvnícka (Shoemakers'), Pekárska (Bakers') and Prašňa Bašta (Powder Bastion).

Michael's Gate with its tower is the best-preserved part of the town's fortification system. The original 14th-century prism-like tower was

enlarged by an octagonal extension in 1511–17. The fortification in front of the gate was closed off over a moat; if you pass over St Michael's Bridge, you can see the remaining moat below. During the coronation of 19 Hungarian kings and queens (1563–1830) in Bratislava, the ruler would enter through Vydrická brána, be crowned in St Martin's Cathedral and then the procession would move through the town, leaving by Michael's Gate, where the new king would pledge his royal oath to the hands of the archbishop.

MIRBACH PALACE (Mirbachov palác) 222 D4; Františkánske námestie 11; 1, 3, 4 to Centrum
A Rococo palace built by a rich brewer, Martin Spech, during 1768–70. Its last owner, Emil Mirbach, donated the palace to the city, with a proviso that a gallery was established there – see page 171.

OLD TOWN HALL (Stará radnica) 222 D5; Hlavné námestie; 02 5910 0847; w muzeum.bratislava.sk; 1, 3, 4 to Centrum
Right in the heart of Hlavné námestie is the Old Town Hall with its distinctive yellow tower and red roof. It was developed in the 14th century from a group of houses belonging to the mayors of the city to form the unusual conglomeration of styles and colours known as the 'House with the Tower'. The rib-vaulted late Gothic passage leads to a beautiful courtyard with Renaissance arcades. Following a fire in 1733, the tower was restored in the Baroque style. It has a cannonball embedded in the wall as a memento of the Napoleonic siege. Inside, the 14th-century Gothic chapel was restored in 1969, and can be visited as it forms part of the City History Museum (page 161). Looking up at the right of the entrance from the main square you will see an unusual portrait of the 'Man in Black' painted directly on to the façade. Legend states that it is an illustration left by the devil portraying a devious councillor who tried to defraud a widow out of her property. On the entrance wall, to the left, is a cubit (77.7cm), a measuring tool created from a thin iron rod with notches with which visitors to the market could check their purchases to see that they measured up.

PÁLFFY PALACE (Pálffyho palác) 223 C7; Panská 19–21; 1, 3, 4 to Centrum
The Pálffy family had two palaces in the Old Town. The first was built at Ventúrska 10 for Leopold Pálffy (where Mozart gave a concert; page 124); the second, on Panská, was built in the 1850s for Ján Pálffy, then *župan* (governor) of Bratislava. This is the official Pálffy Palace and its beige walls now house one of Bratislava's best galleries (page 171).

◀ **1** The distinctive yellow clock tower of the Old Town Hall. **2** The Archbishop's Summer Palace. **3** Michael's Gate with its tower is the best-preserved part of the Old Town's fortification system. **4** The stunning Gothic interior of St Martin's Cathedral – Slovakia's most important church.

PRIMATE'S PALACE (Primaciálny palác) 222 E5; Primaciálne námestie 3; 1, 3, 4 to Centrum

The powder-pink Neoclassical palace was built between 1777 and 1781 by Melchior Hefele for Cardinal József Batthyányi, Archbishop of Esztergom and Primate of Hungary, who used it as his winter palace; today, the entry hall and courtyards are open to all. The tympanum above the façade features a mosaic based on a fresco by Franz Anton Maulpertsch and right on the top is a 150kg cast-iron black cardinal's hat. The palace has a set of tapestries from Mortlake, London. The Hall of Mirrors was the scene of the signing of the 'Peace of Pressburg' treaty between Napoleon and Emperor Francis II on 26 December 1805 after the French victory at the Battle of Austerlitz; the Holy Roman Empire was soon dissolved, leaving Francis II as merely Emperor of Austria. See page 177 for details on the tapestries and the gallery that's also found here.

REDUTA 223 E8; Medená 3; 02 2047 5214; w filharmonia.sk; 50, N33 or 1, 4 to Námestie Ľudovíta Štúra

Built as a concert hall, cinema and ballroom in 1915 in eclectic style to designs by Budapest architects Marcel Komor and Dezső Jakab and renovated in 2009–12, this is home to the Slovak Philharmonic (page 125).

ST MARTIN'S CATHEDRAL (Dóm sv Martina) 223 B7; 02 5443 3430 (parsonage); w dom.fara.sk; 09.00–11.30 & 13.00–18.00 Mon–Sat, 13.30–16.00 Sun, daily services; 50 or 4 to Most SNP; 9 to Kapucínska

Construction of this triple-naved church lasted from 1311 to 1452. Between 1563 and 1830 it was the coronation church for the kings of Hungary and witnessed the crowning of 11 kings and eight royal spouses. The tower is 85m tall, topped with a 150kg gilded model of the crown of Szent István (St Stephen), the first king of Hungary (from AD1000). The late Gothic vaulting is by Hans Puchspaum under direct influence of master masons from Vienna. In 1728 the Archbishop of Esztergom, Emeric Esterházy, invited a famous Austrian sculptor, Georg Rafael Donner, to Bratislava to establish a workshop and he stayed 11 years creating many masterpieces for the city. From 1732 to 1734 he built the chapel of St John the Almsgiver (or Merciful), in the north aisle with the kneeling figure of the archbishop, and in 1734 he created a new high altar featuring a huge equestrian statue of *St Martin and the Beggar*, which now stands in the southeast corner of the nave – the figure of St Martin was supposedly modelled on the archbishop and the beggar on Donner himself. The first complete performance of Beethoven's *Missa Solemnis* took place here in 1830, and Franz Liszt conducted his *Coronation Mass* here in 1884.

From April to mid-November you can visit the Treasury (09.00–11.30 & 13.00–18.00 Mon–Sat, 13.00–16.30 Sun; €4.50); there are various fine religious objects on display, but you also get the view from the organ gallery at the west end.

SLAVÍN MONUMENT 220 C2; 147 (Mon–Fri) to Slavín; 44, 47 to Búdková

In a well-to-do part of town (home to ambassadors and the like), just northwest of the centre, Slavín Hill is crowned with a monumental Soviet war memorial (chief architect Ján Svetlík, 1960) to the 6,845 Red Army soldiers who lost their lives in the battle for Bratislava (spring 1945) and are buried here in six mass graves and 317 individual graves. A 37m-tall column by Tibor Bártfay (creator of the Peace/World globe statue in front of Grassalkovich Palace; page 155) has a 7m soldier raising a flag and crushing a swastika; a gold star on the top was created by the Slovak Alexander Trizuljak. Around the base of the monument are the names of Slovak towns and the dates they were 'liberated' by the Red Army. At one side there is a peace garden of eight white poles, instigated by Alexander Dubček.

From here, there is a great view of the city and it seems huge with many more skyscrapers and tower blocks than other cities in the region. It's easy to find the monument as Slavín is visible from all parts of town – just head off uphill through a district of villas with interesting architectural styles.

SLOVAK NATIONAL THEATRE – HISTORICAL BUILDING SND (Slovenské národné divadlo – Historická budova SND) 223 F6; Hviezdoslavovo námestie; 50, N33 or 1, 4 to Námestie Ľudovíta Štúra

The Slovak National Theatre was constructed in place of the original Theatre of Estates during 1884–86 on the basis of designs by Viennese architects Fellner and Helmer. Since 1920, it has been the home of the Slovak National Theatre, but is currently closed for refurbishment. In front is the Ganymede Fountain, created in 1888 by Viktor Tilgner.

SLOVAK NATIONAL THEATRE – NEW BUILDING SND (Slovenské národné divadlo – Nová budova SND) 220 H6; Pribinova 17 (ticket office entrance from Olejkárska ulica); 29, 50, N33 to Malá scéna; 40, 78, 90 to Nové SND

The new building of the Slovak National Theatre opened with a gala performance on 14 April 2007. The building faces the Eurovea (page 143) complex of shops, offices and leisure facilities to the east of the city centre by the Apollo Bridge over the Danube. This house of drama, opera and ballet was designed by architects Peter Bauer, Martin Kusý and Pavol Paňák during the Socialist regime. Construction started in 1986 but took 21 years to complete, owing to the financial and political wrangles that came with the change of the entire regime. The modern, white building comprises travertine rock from the Spiš region in eastern Slovakia and curved walls have mirrored glass surfaces facing a large modern fountain. For tickets and information, see page 121.

UFO AND MOST SNP 220 D8; Most SNP; 50, 80, 83, 84, 88, 93, 94 to Aupark/Pri sade or walk over the SNP Bridge

Built in 1972, Most Slovenského národného povstania (Bridge of the Slovak National Uprising), commonly referred to as Most SNP or the UFO Bridge,

> **LITTLE CORONATION CROWNS**
>
> Walking around the Old Town, particularly in the cobbled back streets near St Martin's Cathedral, you will see little brass crowns fixed into the pavement at intervals of several metres. These commemorate the coronation procession and allow everyone the opportunity to follow in the footsteps of kings and queens. The procession started at St Martin's Cathedral and led along Kapitulská, one of the oldest thoroughfares in the city, dating from 1204, towards Františkánske námestie before heading out of the Old Town at Michael's Gate. The last weekend in June sees the Coronation Days festival (page 31), when Bratislava turns back the clock and thousands join in the celebrations, shouting 'Vivat rex!' ('Long live the king!'), drinking wine from the fountain and feasting on an ox-roast.

and named Nový most (New Bridge) from 1993 to 2012, is a four-lane road bridge over the Danube with a lower level on either side for pedestrians and cyclists. Until 2000 it was the world's longest cable-stayed bridge that has one pylon and one cable-stayed span. The asymmetrical structure has a main span length of 303m, and the unique attraction is the flying-saucer-shaped object housing a restaurant, bar and lookout platform above. The UFO restaurant, previously called Bystrica, perches on top of the bridge's 84.6m sloping pylon. The viewing platform above the restaurant offers stunning views over the Danube, the Old Town and the Petržalka district. The east pillar has a lift, while the west pillar houses an emergency staircase with 430 steps. See pages 101 and 189 for more information.

MUSEUMS

Bratislava is packed with museums and there is a great variety of themes, from wine to cars, from dungeons to clocks. Everyone will find something to entertain them on a rainy Wednesday afternoon. Museums in Bratislava are almost always open from 10.00 to 17.00 and closed on Monday. Unless otherwise specified, labels are in Slovak and English.

APPONYI PALACE MUSEUM OF VITICULTURE AND PERIOD ROOMS
MUSEUM (Vinohradícke múzeum) 222 E5; Radničná ulica 3; 02 5910 0856; w muzeumbratislava.sk/en/apponyi-palace; 10.00–17.00 Tue–Sun; combined ticket with the City History Museum €8/4; 1, 3, 4 to Centrum

Count Apponyi of Oponice had the palace built in Rococo style in 1761–62, but in 1867 it was taken over as an annexe to the City Hall. Since 1932 the building has served as part of the Bratislava City Museum, detailing the history of winemaking in Slovakia for over 2,000 years in a well-presented exhibition in the basement. Upstairs, the Period Rooms are fairly lacking in atmosphere, but the first floor still has its original wooden wall panelling, and is furnished as a nobleman's house from the end of the 18th century. The second-floor rooms are examples of town house interiors from the end of the 1700s up until the end of the 19th century, with a striking Empire bed.

ARCHAEOLOGICAL MUSEUM (Archeologické múzeum) 220 B7; Žižkova 12; 02 5920 7275; 10.00–17.00 Tue–Sun; adult/concession €3/1.50 (1 ticket for all 3 museums on Žižkova); 4 to Vodná veža

In a charming 16th-century Renaissance building (rebuilt in the 18th century) in the ancient fishing district, now a tiny island of historic houses and a small church separated from the Danube and city centre by hectic main roads and the Vydrica construction site, this museum features artefacts from prehistoric times until the late Middle Ages. There's one joint ticket and a shared entrance at Žižkova 16 for three museums: Archaeological, Carpathian German Culture and Hungarian Culture (all page 166), and there's also a room on the history of this area, Podhradie (known as Zuckermandel to the Germans). There are permanent exhibitions on the early history of Slovakia with a vast collection of earthenware jugs, bowls and other household items, and Egyptian, Roman and Bronze Age artefacts from the collection of the Lutheran High School, unfortunately with no information about when or where they were made or found. In the courtyard gallery, the Lapidarium shows stone artefacts from late Roman times onwards, notably a Celtic pottery kiln and a Great Moravian glass furnace. The museum also has temporary exhibits.

CITY HISTORY MUSEUM (Múzeum mesta Bratislavy) In the Old Town Hall 222 D5; Primalciálne námestie 3; 02 5910 0847; w muzeumbratislava.sk/en/old-town-hall; 10.00–18.00 Tue–Sun; combined ticket with the Apponyi Palace Viticulture Museum €8/4; 1, 3, 4 to Centrum

Fascinating insights into the history of Bratislava in a seemingly endless series of rooms. The museum documents the history of the building itself and the life of the locals from the Neolithic period until 1940, with details of everyday life gracefully presented. You can also go up the tower for views over the town, and finish in the basement to see a surprisingly good display of replica torture devices, as well as medieval ice pits and dungeons.

CLOCK MUSEUM (Múzeum hodín) 220 D6; Židovská 3, Dom U Dobrého Pastiera (House of the Good Shepherd); 02 5441 1940; w muzeumbratislava.sk/en/house-good-shepherd; Apr–Oct only 11.00–18.00 Thu–Sun; adult/child €3/1.50; 50 or 4 to Most SNP; 9 to Kapucínska

Clocks and watches made in Bratislava during the 17th–20th centuries are showcased in a Rococo building that dates from 1762 (page 192). The

> **QUIRKY SIGHTS**
>
> Once you have seen all the famous and historical sights and sites in Bratislava, you may want to branch out and explore the unusual and quirky destinations.
>
> **ATELIER BKPŠ** 221 G1; Nobelova 34; 02 4341 2698; w bkps.sk; the inside is a working office but the exterior can be viewed 24/7; 51 to Nobelova or walk from ŽST Vinohrady (3, 7 & trains)
> The former water reservoir tower, built in 1906 in the industrial Dimitrovka district, was reconstructed in 2008 by a group of architects, Kusý-Paňák, who have their studios on the top.
>
> **BUNKER BS-1 ŠTÉRKOVIŠTÉ** Between the Danube & the Austrian border
> This bunker in the forest by the Danube gives a taste of the Cold War tensions, and can be visited on a bicycle tour with Authentic Slovakia (page 62). See also the Military Museum in the bunker BS-8 Hřbitov in Petržalka (page 166) and the website w bunker.bs8.sk/zoznam-bunkrov, which has a list of all 15 bunkers that can be found in the Bratislava area.
>
> **DEVÍNSKA KOBYLA MILITARY BASE** The highest peak in the Devín Carpathians (514m) is the site of an abandoned military radar base from the 1980s, although the surrounding area has been a nature reserve since 1965. It looks towards the Königswarte Hill in Austria, where a watchtower was used by American intelligence. To hike up from Devín head up Hadia cesta then follow blue then red stripes to reach Devínska Kobyla in under an hour. A striking modern viewing tower was built here in 2020; there can be a chilly breeze up above the trees, but the views to the Neusiedlersee

museum has a fascinating collection of 17th-century portable sundials, wrist watches and alarm clocks; on the top floor there are some amusing 19th-century picture clocks, with trompe l'oeil church clock faces.

DANUBIANA MEULENSTEEN MODERN ART MUSEUM map, page 196; Vodné dielo, Čunovo; 02 6252 8501; w danubiana.sk; 10.00–18.00 Tue–Sun; adult/concession €10/5; 90 hourly from Nové SND (there's no ticket machine at Nové SND or at the Danubiana – buy tickets at Landererova, just a couple of mins' walk from Nové SND)
An interesting and unusual modern art museum on an artificial island in the Danube. Resembling one of the passing barges, it's the brainchild of Vincent Polakovič, who decided to create the museum after an alleged encounter with the ghost of his hero, Vincent van Gogh. Opened in 2000 and extended in 2019, there's a wide range of modern Slovak artists on display, as well as what

in Austria and deep into Slovakia make it worthwhile. Descending east to Stará Dúbravka you can follow red stripes or the traffic-free road, then take tram 4 into the city. It's also accessible with Authentic Slovakia tours (page 62).

FUNUS 220 B1; Prokopa Veľkého 1; m 09 03 907 327; w krcma-funus.webnode.sk; 10.00–22.00 daily; 44, 63, 83, 84 to Hroboňova; 147 (Mon–Fri) to Kalvária
Workmen drinking cheap beer in the shade of a 100-year-old chestnut tree takes me right back to Czechoslovakia in the 1980s (page 117).

NOVÁ CVERNOVKA 221 K1; (New Thread Factory) Račianska 78; w novacvernovka.eu; N55 or 3, 7 to Námestie Biely kríž; train to Predmestie or Vinohrady
This former chemistry school hosts concerts and theatrical performances as well as a co-working space.

SLOVAK RADIO INVERTED PYRAMID 221 F2; Mýtna 1; 31, 39, 94, N55 to Námestie Slobody
A bizarre upside-down pyramid that looks like it has crash-landed into the Earth from outer space (page 193). The 80m-high concert hall for Slovak Radio took from 1967 to 1983 to construct and has been listed on the *Daily Telegraph*'s list of the 30 ugliest buildings in the world as well as being applauded by architects.

VIECHA DREVENÁ DEDINA 220 E1; Žilinska 47, at the back of the little fruit, vegetable & flower market; 21, 40, 44, 49, 61, 63, 64, 71, 74, N33 to Karpatská
Old guys drinking spritzers and eating *langoše* in a back-to-the-seventies ambience. The name translates as 'the old wooden village' (page 118).

is claimed to be Naum Gabo's most famous work (*Constructed Head No.2*; 1916) and, more surprisingly, a piece by Czech tennis star Martina Navrátilová (with Juraj Králik). There are always temporary shows by interesting contemporary artists, while the sculpture garden features larger works by international names such as Jim Dine, Hans van de Bovenkamp, Richard Hudson and El Lissitzky.

F X MESSERSCHMIDT CAFÉ AND MUSEUM 222 F2; Námestie SNP 8; 08.30–20.00 daily; free; 1, 3, 4 to Centrum
The Museum of 17 November (essentially a room at the back of the café, with nine panels of photographs that have lengthy explanations) displays the struggles of the Velvet Revolution, which began on 17 November 1989 (page 10), from student protests to political events to significant personalities such as Slovak Alexander Dubček and Czech Václav Havel.

Franz Xaver Messerschmidt (1736–83) was a talented sculptor, who is best known for his series of 12 'character' heads, on display at the Slovak National Gallery (page 178); born in Bavaria, he spent the last seven years of his life in Bratislava. The only original work by him in Bratislava is the bust of a Capuchin monk in the Mirbach Palace – the others are plaster and bronze casts. The café is more like a Habsburg-era coffeehouse with paintings of Messerschmidt's heads on the wooden wall panelling, grimacing white ceramic busts and also heads on the coffee cups – it is a rather incongruous bedfellow of the revolutionaries, but somehow it works.

HUMMEL MUSEUM (Múzeum Hummela) 222 F4; Klobučnícka 2; 02 5443 3888; w muzeumbratislava.sk/en/memorial-house-j-n-hummel; 10.00–18.00 Tue–Fri, 11.00–18.00 Sat & Sun; adult/concession €3/2; 1, 3, 4 to Centrum

The museum is in the little peach-coloured cottage (across the courtyard from the entrance) where pianist and composer Hummel (page 124) was born. There's interesting biographical information, the piano given to Hummel by Erard in London and, of course, lovely music playing. There is a shop selling CDs, too, and an agency for tickets to performances in Bratislava (page 121).

JEWISH COMMUNITY MUSEUM (Bratislavská synagóga) 222 G1; Heydukova 11–13; 02 5441 6949; w synagogue.sk; late Jun–late Sep 10.00–16.00 Fri & Sun; adult/child €6/3; 1, 3, 4 to Centrum

This museum of the history and culture of Bratislava's Jewish community is housed in the disused women's gallery of the city's last remaining synagogue, built in Cubist style in 1923–26. It includes key items from the Judaica collection of Bratislava as well as other objects donated by members of the community; there's also a Holocaust memorial wall.

MICHAEL'S GATE 222 C3; Michalská 22; 02 5443 3044; w muzeumbratislava.sk/en/michaels-tower; 10.00–18.00 Wed–Mon; adult/child €6/4, joint tickets from the Museum of Pharmacy (page 167); 1, 3, 4 to Centrum

Formerly housing a large collection of weapons and armour, the city's last surviving gate tower was restored in 2021–22 and offers a great view of the city from the top. There's a temporary exhibition on the refurbishment, but an interactive exhibition on the city's fortifications should open soon. The original Gothic tower was extended upwards in the 18th century to reach a height of 51m and crowned with a copper sculpture of St Michael killing the dragon, producing one of the most iconic images of Bratislava.

1 Three of the five original rooms are on display at the old Pharmacy at the Red Crayfish.
2 The House of the Good Shepherd houses the city's Clock Museum. **3** The Mirbach Palace boasts a splendid interior and an art gallery to match. **4** There's more than just Škoda cars in the Museum of Transport. ▶

MILITARY MUSEUM – BUNKER BS-8 AND CEMETERY (Vojenské Múzeum – Bunker BS-8 Hřbitov) 220 D8; Kopčianska ulica; m 09 02 961 164; w bunker.bs8.sk; 15.00–18.00 daily; voluntary donation (€5); 80 to Nesto

The Military Museum is in a bunker in western Petržalka-Kopčany, immediately next to a World War I cemetery marked by tall poplar trees – turn off Kopčianksa ulica following signs for Cintorín (cemetery). The bunker was built in 1938 and used in the Cold War as it sits almost on the Iron Curtain – you can still see the border crossing point, although the actual border is at the road just to the west. The museum includes many original items from the Czechoslovak army, such as weapons and radios. The website has a list of 15 bunkers in Petržalka, including BS-1 Štérkovišté, which you can visit on a bike ride with Authentic Slovakia tours (page 62).

MUSEUM OF ANCIENT GERULATA (Múzeum Antická Gerulata) Gerulatská 69, Rusovce; 02 6285 9332; w muzeumbratislava.sk/en/ancient-gerulata; Apr & Oct 10.00–17.00 Thu–Sun, May–Sep 10.00–18.00 Tue–Sun; adult/child €4/2; 91, 191 from Most SNP heading towards Čunovo (every 20mins); 90 from Nové SND towards Danubiana (hourly), to Gerulata

Archaeologists uncovered the foundations of a Roman military camp dating from AD100–400 at Rusovce (map, page 196; page 197), and the roof tiles, bricks, sculptures, tombstones and daily household items made of bronze and iron are on display here. This became Bratislava's first UNESCO World Heritage Site in 2021 (as part of the multi-national Limes Romanus site) and the exhibition has been updated.

MUSEUM OF CARPATHIAN GERMAN CULTURE (Múzeum kultúry karpatských Nemcov) 220 B7; Žižkova 14; 02 5441 5570; w snm.sk/en; 10.00–17.00 Tue–Sun; adult/concession €4/2 (1 ticket for 3 museums on Žižkova); 4 to Vodná veža

Showcases the craftsmanship of ethnic Germans in Slovakia over 900 years, with displays of enamel, glass, porcelain and jewellery, as well as fascinating details from World War II. Information in Slovak and German only.

MUSEUM OF HUNGARIAN CULTURE IN SLOVAKIA (Múzeum Kultúry Madarov na Slovensku) 220 B7; Žižkova 18; 02 2049 1258; Mar–Oct 10.00–17.00 Tue–Sun, Nov–Apr 10.00–16.00 Tue–Sun; adult/concession €4/2 (1 ticket for 3 museums on Žižkova); 4 to Vodná veža

In the old fishing district (page 161), this museum features details of the lives of the 456,000 Hungarians (as of the 2021 census) living in Slovakia, with photos and ethnographic artefacts. As Slovakia was a significant part of Hungary for the best part of 1,000 years (page 6), the two countries are inextricably linked, despite linguistic differences and ethnic tensions. The exhibition stresses the pressures on the Hungarian community in the 20th century, when its numbers fell from 651,000 in 1921 to 355,000 in 1950 – it then recovered to 527,000 in 2001.

MUSEUM OF JEWISH CULTURE (Slovenská cesta židovského kultúrneho dedičstva)
220 D6; Židovská 17; 02 2049 0101; **w** slovak-jewish-heritage.org/mblava.htm; 11.00–17.00 Sun–Fri; adult/concession €6/3; 9 to Kapucínska

Housed in the late Renaissance 17th-century Zsigray Mansion on the side of Castle Hill by the tram tunnel, this moving museum features the history and culture of Jews living in the territory of Slovakia since the times of the Great Moravian Empire. It shows the everyday life of the Jewish community, and includes displays on festivals, synagogue furnishings, important Jews in Slovakia's history, as well as a section on the Holocaust – mostly very harrowing, but there's also mention of Rudolf Vrba and Alfréd Wetzler, who actually escaped from Auschwitz in 1944 and wrote a detailed and very important report on the details of what was happening there.

MUSEUM OF PHARMACY AT THE RED CRAYFISH (Múzeum farmácie-Lekáreň u červeného raka) 222 C3; Michalská 28; 02 5413 1214; **w** muzeumbratislava.sk/en/red-crayfish-pharmacy; 10.00–18.00 Wed–Mon; adult/concession €6/4, ticket includes Michael's Gate (page 164); 1, 3, 4 to Centrum

Pharmacists were practising in Bratislava as early as the 14th century and the old Lekáreň Červeny Rak (Pharmacy at the Red Crayfish) was here by the mid 18th century. It opened as a museum in 1961, with 300 items gathered from 1890 in a Baroque house, but since 2006 the exhibition space has been greatly reduced. The museum features three of the pharmacy's original five rooms, complete with historical furniture, pharmacy equipment and Baroque–Classicist paintings and wall decorations. There is also an original edition of works by Paracelsus from 1574.

MUSEUM OF TRANSPORT (Múzeum dopravy) 220 D1; Šancová ulica 1/A; 02 5244 4163; **w** muzeumdopravy.com; 10.00–17.00 Tue–Sun; adult/concession €8/4; 42, 44, 49, 63, 64, 83, 84, 93 or 1, 7 to Pod Stanicou

More than 80 cars and 35 motorbikes make this a fun afternoon visit, and there are also displays on the history of road and rail transport. There are lots of Škodas, of course, plus Velorex three-wheelers, a 1913 Buick, a 1923 Harley Davidson, a 1942 BMW military motorbike and sidecar – and even a 1972 Ford Cortina! There are also some steam locomotives and wagons at the rear. It's housed in Bratislava's original railway station (1848), just west of the current one; there's not a lot of information, and what there is is only in Slovak.

SLOVAK NATIONAL HISTORY MUSEUM (Historické Múzeum) 220 C6; Bratislava Castle, Mudroňova 1; 02 2048 3110; **w** snm.sk/en; 10.00–18.00 Wed–Mon; €14/7, tour in English €25 per group; 44, 47 to Hrad

This museum is a fascinating display of Slovakia's history, documenting the development of society in Slovakia from the Middle Ages until the present day. Aristocratic and commoner interiors from the 16th to 20th centuries are displayed. The huge museum, surrounding the castle's cavernous

SOCIALIST RELICS

Although Bratislava has eagerly embraced the joys of the free market economy, and swanky westernised hotels, bars, restaurants and cafés cater for the high-fashion-clad beautiful youth, there are still many places where you can find remnants of the past regime, when Czechoslovakia was part of the Eastern Bloc behind Churchill's Iron Curtain. Here are some places to check out the Socialist relics:

AUTHENTIC SLOVAKIA TOUR Two brothers, Branislav and Peter Chrenka, take visitors on a 'Post Socialist City Tour' in a vintage, 1970s Škoda 110 around off-the-beaten-track remnants of Bratislava's communist past. Alternatively, pedal away on a guided cycle ride to the watchtowers and bunkers of the former Iron Curtain border. See page 62.

FEBRUÁRKA HOUSING ESTATE (Račianske mýto) Constructed in 1956, this estate used the new technique of pouring concrete to create detached blocks of apartments with shops on the ground floor.

HOTEL KYJEV (Rajská 2) The 65m-tall tower block was built in 1973 and offered 15 floors of accommodation to visiting dignitaries from fellow Eastern Bloc countries. The hotel no longer functions, but the building remains while the city decides its fate.

KAMZÍK TV TOWER The 200m-tall tower, which looks like a drop earring, dominates the skyline in the hills north of the city centre. Built in 1975, it is home to the revolving Veža restaurant and café (pages 101 and 116).

MLADÁ GARDA HOSTEL AND DORMITORY (Račianska 103) Built in 1953 in Socialist Realist style, this workers' dorm has a clock tower and reliefs of students and good citizens.

MOST SNP The New Bridge, now called the SNP Bridge, was completed in 1972. The construction necessitated the demolition of 226 old buildings, such as the Neolog synagogue, which was bulldozed in 1968; the rest of the Jewish district, including all the buildings along the east side of Židovská, was razed to build the access highway, Staromestská, which passes less than 5m from the cathedral.

courtyard, contains almost 250,000 objects from the field of national history, arts, sculpture, painting, culture, traditional and artistic crafts, numismatics, ethnography, warfare, economy, and the history of Slovaks living abroad. Several collections of the museum are the largest in Slovakia:

NÁMESTIE SLOBODY On the exterior of both sides of the Slovak Technical University (on the southwest side of the square), there's a series of concrete reliefs of bucolic farm labourers, engineers and scientists; see also the striking cantilevered lecture halls across the road to the east.

PETRŽALKA The most densely populated area in central Europe; these concrete tower blocks were constructed between 1973 and 1976, but have been revived since independence (page 192).

POST OFFICE BUILDING (Námestie Slobody, northeast side of square) Built in 1951, this is now home to offices, but with an original paternoster cyclic lift endlessly moving in the hall.

PRIOR STORE (Kamenné námestie) Two connected buildings: a triangular one dating from 1964–68 and the other from 1972–78, attached to the Hotel Kyjev. Plans to redevelop the square have been scaled back, and there are moves to have the whole area declared a national monument.

SLAVÍN MONUMENT A memorial by Ján Svetlík (1960) to the 6,850 Soviet soldiers who died in the battle for Bratislava and a statue of a soldier raising a flag by Alexander Trizuljak are found on this grassy lookout point above the city. See page 159.

SLOVAK NATIONAL GALLERY (Rázusovo nábrezie 2) A modern extension (1969–77) was added to the original barracks building, but it looks more like a multi-storey car park, notwithstanding the recent renovations. See page 178.

SLOVAK RADIO (Mýtna 1) The inverted pyramid building of Slovenský rozhlas that appears to defy gravity was built in 1967–83. See page 193.

UFO The alien spaceship hovers 85m above Most SNP on a two-legged pylon leaning towards Petržalka and supported by steel cables. See page 189.

URŠULÍNSKA This street has two reliefs in plaster on the side of the city hall: one of architects planning and the other of workers toiling.

numismatics, the historical and traditional textile, glass and ceramics, military history, crafts, historical press, sacral and folk objects and fine arts. Temporary exhibitions cover a wide variety of subjects from Ľudovít Štúr, the great reformer of Slovak society, to World War I and its effects on

Slovakia, to contemporary textile art to Great Moravia and the beginnings of Christianity in the country. The tours are interesting and give an insight into Slovak history.

You can go up to a viewing gallery in the 13th-century Crown Tower and also visit the chapel, three virtually unfurnished State Rooms and the Winter Riding School. There's a separate entrance in the main gateway to the Treasury (€4/2), with fine examples of gold and silverwork, as well as a replica of the royal crown of Hungary. A small café is on the third floor, and there are shops both near it and beneath the entry ramp and ticket office.

SLOVAK NATIONAL MUSEUM/NATURAL SCIENCE MUSEUM (Prírodovedné Múzeum) 223 H9; Vajanského nábrežie 2; 02 2046 9122; w snm.sk/en; 09.00–17.00 Tue–Sun; adult/concession €6/3; 50 or 1, 4 to Námestie Ľudovíta Štúra

This branch of the national museum covers the diversity and development of living and non-living nature in all its variety, especially in Slovakia. The second floor is a permanent exhibit of Slovakia's flora and fauna, with animals presented in naturalistic settings and clever optical illusions of painted backdrops to give a sense of space. There are models of a dinosaur, a mammoth and a great sturgeon (like a small whale), and dinosaur tracks from the Tatra Mountains. The third floor covers global biodiversity, including tundra, coasts, coral reefs, desert and rainforest.

Finally, the ground floor is a temporary exhibition space showing fascinating displays on ethnography, biodiversity, and minerals – it continues into the café at the back. With its collections (approximately 2.4 million objects) it ranks among the most significant European natural history museums.

GALLERIES

Bratislava is packed with an ever-changing roster of galleries and exhibition spaces, where you can see everything from folk crafts to hip contemporary artworks.

19 GALLERY 221 H5; Lazaretská 19; w galeria19.sk; 14.00–19.00 Mon–Fri; free; 42 to 29 Augusta; 40, 50 to Čulenova

Interesting shows of contemporary art and design with a wide variety of works, from textiles to small sculptures and paintings.

A4 SPACE FOR CONTEMPORARY CULTURE (A4 Priestor súčanej kultúry) 220 F1; Karpatská 2; w a4.sk; 18.00–midnight daily; free; 21, 40, 44, 61, 63, 64, 71 to Karpatská

A4 is a great space for art exhibitions, discussions, concerts, theatre, dance, cinema and workshops (page 126). The space is open every evening and there is always something interesting to see, with artist residencies every year.

ABC (ART BOOKS COFFEE) 222 B4; Baštová 6B; m 09 05 325 618; w artbookscoffee.sk; 14.00–18.00 Mon–Fri; free; 9 to Kapucínska
Art, art books and good coffee, with exhibitions and an emphasis on 'young art'.

BIBIANA 223 B8; Panská 41; 02 5443 4986; w bibiana.sk; 10.00–18.00 Tue–Sun; adult/child €2/1 exhibition, €2/1 theatre, €2/1 workshops; 1, 3, 4 to Centrum
Founded in 1987, Bibiana is an international house of art for children with all kinds of events: art, theatre, performance, exhibitions and books.

BOŘEK ŠÍPEK GALLERY 223 E9; Námestie Ľudovíta Štúra 2; m 09 19 311 037; w palaceoffice.sk/sala-dessewffy; 09.00–16.00 Mon–Fri; free; 50 or 1, 4 to Námestie Ľudovíta Štúra
Next to the Slovak National Gallery, the Dessewffy Palace has been transformed into a modern office block, with only its façade surviving. In the atrium is a gallery with a stylish display of bowls, vases and other glass pieces by the Czech designer and architect Bořek Šípek, a sort of small-scale European Dale Chihuly. There's also furniture and works by other artists for sale.

BRATISLAVA CITY GALLERY, MIRBACH PALACE (Galéria Mesta Bratislavy, Mirbachov Palác) 222 D4; Františkánske námestie 11; 02 5443 1556; w gmb.sk; 11.00–18.00 Tue & Thu–Sun, 13.00–20.00 Wed; adult/concession €8/free, €10 joint with Pálffy Palace; 1, 3, 4 to Centrum
A fascinating gallery where the interior is as interesting as the exhibits. There are interesting temporary shows on the ground and second floors, while two wood-panelled rooms on the first floor are lined with 290 religious prints and scenes of aristocratic life created in 1704–80. These are followed by rooms of pretty average religious paintings and statues, mostly anonymous, and some copies of heads by F X Messerschmidt (page 164).

BRATISLAVA CITY GALLERY, PÁLFFY PALACE (Galéria Mesta Bratislavy, Pálffyho Palác) 223 C7; Panská 19; 02 5443 3627; w gmb.sk; 11.00–18.00 Tue & Thu–Sun, 13.00–20.00 Wed; adult/concession €8/free, €10 joint with Mirbach Palace; 1, 3, 4 to Centrum
Like the Mirbach, the Pálffy Palace's interior is a match for the exhibits. The cellars house the remains of a Celtic mint and modern works including optical art by Milan Dobeš; on the first floor you'll find Gothic art (from the 13th to 16th centuries) and more contemporary art, and on the second floor is the city's collection of art from 1800 to 1950 (with lots of influence from Picasso). There's also an amazing permanent exhibit by Slovak artist Matej Krén called *Pasáž* (2004) where visitors walk along a visual gangplank through a seemingly endless library of bookshelves. Not for those with vertigo; unsettling yet fascinating. See page 157.

CENTRAL EUROPEAN HOUSE OF PHOTOGRAPHY 222 B5; Prepostská 4; 02 5441 8214; **w** sedf.sk/en; 13.00–18.00 Tue–Sun; €3; 1, 3, 4 to Centrum; 9 to Kapucínska

Above the lively Studňa Café are two floors of temporary exhibitions, with photographic history displays in sliding drawers.

CIT GALLERY 222 G1; Heydukova 15; **m** 09 05 203 444; **w** galeriacit.sk; 13.00–18.00 Mon–Fri; free; 1, 3, 4 to Centrum

Private gallery created to allow local visual artists to show and sell their work. A lot of abstract and modern paintings.

DESIGN STUDIO ÚĽUV (Dizajn štúdio úľuv) 221 G6; Dobrovičova 13; **w** uluv.sk; noon–19.00 Tue, Wed & Fri; free; 50 to Malá scéna

A good place to see updated traditional work by Slovak craftsmen and women. See also page 178.

DOT.GALLERY 221 H5; Lazaretská 13; **w** dotgallery.sk; 08.00–20.00 Mon–Fri, noon–19.00 Sat; free; 205 to Ulica; 42 to 29 Augusta; 50, 210 to Twin City

This rather tunnel-like space promotes younger, less well-known artists and also houses a stylish espresso bar.

F7 222 D5; Františkánske námestie 7; **w** kulturastaremesto.sk; 15.00–19.00 Tue–Sat; free; 1, 3, 4 to Centrum

A small, city-run gallery that shows both professional and amateur local artists, with shows changing every few weeks.

FLATGALLERY 222 C4; Baštová 1; **m** 09 04 820 576; Flatgallery; 11.00–21.00 daily; free; 1, 3, 4 to Centrum

Contemporary Slovak artists show their work at this central gallery in three spacious rooms of the artists' own flat. Painting, graphics, watercolours and videos are all displayed in a convivial setting.

GAGARINKA GALLERY 221 K5; Gagarinova 10A; **w** galeria.gagarinka.sk; 16.00–18.00 Wed–Fri, 13.00–18.00 Sat & Sun; free; 201, 202 to Brodná

Interesting exhibitions by contemporary local artists and designers. There's also a Tennis Museum (**w** tenisovemuzeum.sk/sk) here, with a display of wooden racquets and a Slovak Hall of Fame.

---

1 The powder-pink Primate's Palace is one of Bratislava's most spectacular buildings. Once home to the archbishop, it now houses the mayor's office. **2** The sculpture garden of the Danubiana modern art museum features large works by international artists. **3** Reopened in 2023 after lengthy refurbishment, the Slovak National Gallery houses a wide range of art in a rather controversial building. **4** Behind its façade, the spiral interior of the Nedbalka Gallery is reminiscent of New York's Guggenheim Museum. ▶

GALÉRIA ČIN ČIN 220 C5; Podjavorinskej 4a; m 09 05 206 298; w galeriacincin.sk; 14.00–18.30 Mon–Fri; free; 80, 83, 84, 93, 94 to Zochova; 44, 47 to Kozia

The name 'Čin Čin' is inspired by a sparrow poem by the writer Ľudmila Podjavorinská (after whom the street is named). This gallery shows eight or nine exhibitions a year as well as a permanent display of jewellery by local artists.

GALÉRIA UAT 221 F4; Mariánska 8, also at UAT2 at Mariánska 7 & UAT3 at Mariánska 16; m 09 04 116 683; w uat.sk/en/galleries; 13.00–18.00 Mon–Fri; free; 3, 4 to Mariánska

The SŠUPAT private art school uses its galleries both to engage with the public and also as a setting for teaching.

GALLERY OF THE SLOVAK UNION OF VISUAL ARTS (Galéria Umelka) 221 G7; Dostojevského rad 2; 02 5296 2402; w svu.sk; noon–18.00 Tue–Sun; free; 50 or 1, 3, 4 to Šafárikovo námestie

The home of the Slovak Union of Visual Arts (Slovenská výtvarná únia) is an excellent place for exhibiting: one bright roomy hall and a smaller one, both with adventurous works and installations. Also known as Umelka, it's above the pub of the same name (page 116).

GANDY GALLERY 221 G6; Sienkiewiczova 4; w gandy-gallery.com; 14.00–18.30 Wed–Fri, closed Aug; free; 50 or 1, 3, 4 to Šafárikovo námestie

Nadine Gandy moved from France to Prague in 1992 and then to Bratislava in 2005, building her reputation as a driving force behind art in 'the New Europe'. She calls her exhibition space (in an attractive Art Nouveau building) a 'laboratory' as it's a meeting point for artists. Inspiring and interesting work.

KUNSTHALLE BRATISLAVA/DOM UMENIA 222 G3; Námestie SNP 12; 02 2047 1504; w kunsthallebratislava.sk; noon–19.00 Wed–Mon; free; 1, 3, 4 to Centrum

Superb space for exhibitions, talks and international artists, plus a library. The city government had other plans for the striking modernist building (1958–65), but it seems to be off the hook for now.

MEDIUM GALLERY 223 C7; Hviezdoslavovo námestie 18; w vsvu.sk/en/medium-gallery; noon–19.00 Tue & Thu, 10.00–17.00 Wed & Fri–Sun; free; 50 or 1, 3, 4 to Námestie Ľudovíta Štúra

My personal favourite of Bratislava's galleries, in another Pálffy Palace. One or two shows a month, often of graphic designs, typefaces and fonts. Exhibition space for the students of the VŠVU – Academy of Fine Art and Design.

NEDBALKA GALLERY 222 F4; Nedbalova 17; 02 5441 0287; w nedbalka.sk; 13.00–19.00 Tue–Sun; adult/concession €8/4; 1, 3, 4 to Centrum

Stunning gallery on five floors surrounding a circular atrium (a great setting for chamber music concerts). Take the lift to the fourth floor and work your way down with the gallery guide on a digital tablet, starting c1900 and finishing with the optical art of Milan Dobeš; there are temporary shows on the ground floor, and you get a free tea or coffee in the café.

PHOTOPORT 220 D8; Rovniankova 4; m 09 03 374 603; w photoport.sk; 15.00–18.00 Wed–Thu; free; 83, 95, 96 to Romanova

Note the limited opening hours before heading to this gallery for photography and new media in Petržalka – although it'll be very close to tram 3 when the extension opens.

ART NOUVEAU IN BRATISLAVA

There are several examples of Art Nouveau (or Jugendstil) in this very Baroque city – look for the word *secesný* or *secession* on plaques.

BLUE CHURCH (Modrý kostolík) 221 G6; Bezručova 2. A masterpiece by Ödön Lechner, the 'father of Hungarian Art Nouveau', in 1910–13 (page 152).

HIGH SCHOOL 221 G5. Around the corner from the Blue Church at Grösslingova 18, also designed by Ödön Lechner in 1906–08.

MAGYAR BANK 222 D5; Hlavné námestie 5. Designed by Ödön Lechner in 1904 and built in 1908 by R Körösym, this became a popular café but was damaged by fire in 2018 and is still closed.

STAINED-GLASS ATRIUM CEILING 222 E3; in the post office at Námestie SNP 34. The Wachtler Palace was built in 1778 but its original appearance is known only from photographs. The city bought and demolished it in 1908 to make way for the building that is now the Old Post Office. Designed by architect Gyula Partos from Budapest, it was completed in 1912. The ceiling is a gentle arch of glass with beautiful floral motifs in blues, greens and reds.

TOWNHOUSE AT ŠAFÁRIKOVO NÁMESTIE 4 221 G6. On the corner of the block, the townhouse was built in 1904 by Jozef Schiller and is painted in two shades of light green. There is another townhouse (1904) in two shades of pink at the north end of the block.

TULIP HOUSE 221 F6; Štúrova 10. Now the Hotel & Residence Roset, this was built in 1903 by Komor and Jakab with stucco flowers in columns climbing up the walls.

PRIMATE'S PALACE 222 E5; Primaciálne námestie 1; 02 5935 6204; 10.00–17.00 Tue–Sun; adult/concession €3/2; 1, 3, 4 to Centrum

Behind a powder-pink wedding-cake exterior, you can enjoy a row of five rather unatmospheric state rooms, a view down into the perfect oval of the Baroque chapel, and the Hall of Mirrors, where in 1805 the Treaty of Pressburg between France and Austria was signed. When the building was being converted to the city hall, a set of six 17th-century tapestries of Hero and Leander from Mortlake in London was discovered behind the panelling, and turned out to be worth more than the city had paid for the entire building; the tapestries have retained their original colours, but it's still not known how they came to be here. Otherwise, there are lots of third-division portraits (and an English portrait of c1820 vaguely in the style of Sir Thomas Lawrence, one of the finest English portraitists) and a great lack of captions. See page 158.

PRO ART GALLERY 222 H5; Štúrova 1, also at Rázusovo nábrežie 6 & Dunajská 27; m 09 44 727 007; w proartgallery.sk; all 11.00–17.00 Mon–Fri; 1, 3, 4 to Centrum

A pretty successful group of galleries supporting local artists – there's nothing too radical, and it's all relatively affordable.

ROMAN FECIK GALLERY 222 D3; Zámočnícka 8; 02 5441 4346; m 09 18 430 102; w romanfecikgallery.sk; by appointment; free; 1, 9 to Poštová

A non-profit body that aims to develop a culture of collecting, with an art library as well as a gallery; their collection includes notable Slovak artists such as Jozef Jankovič, Rudolf Sikora and Milan Dobeš.

SATELIT 221 F4; Kollárovo námestie 10; w scd.sk; 14.00–18.00 Wed–Sun; free; 1, 9 to Vysoká; 42, 47, 80, 94 to Kollárovo námestie

Satelit is one of the recent success stories of the independent art scene in Bratislava: a former army barracks at the far end of Obchodná has been transformed into the exhibition space of the Slovak Design Centre. The ground floor is essentially a design showroom, used for ever-changing exhibitions ranging from Tuli bags through fashion to public transport. Everyone is welcome – not just design fans – to catch up on the latest trends in creation and production, and there is always something new, interesting or challenging to see. In the attic (no lift) is the new Slovak Design Museum, covering the last century both by theme (eg: consumer products, books, posters) and by material (ceramics, glass, etc). In addition to supporting local talent it also produces a magazine, *Designum*, which can be purchased here.

◄ Adorned with beautiful floral motifs in blues, greens and reds, the stained-glass ceiling of the Old Post Office is a fine example of the Art Nouveau style; delightfully, it's still in use as the city centre's main post office.

SLOVAK NATIONAL GALLERY (SNG Esterházyho palác) 223 D9; Rázusovo nábrežie 1; 02 2047 6100; w sng.sk/en; 10.00–18.00 Tue, Wed & Fri–Sun, noon–20.00 Thu; adult/concession €9/5; 50 or 1, 4 to Námestie Ľudovíta Štúra

The neo-Renaissance Esterházy Palace, built in the 1870s, has been home to the Slovak National Gallery since the 1950s; alongside it are the Baroque Water Barracks (1759–63) with in front of it a strange and very controversial bridge wing added in the 1970s which many people would like to see demolished. This closed for refurbishment in 2001 and finally reopened in 2023 (though not all galleries were open in 2024). It is also home to a small café (€) and bookshop on the ground floor.

There's a wealth of sacred art, mostly Gothic paintings and wood carvings, of which the best are by Master Paul of Levoča (perhaps a student of the German Veit Stoss) – but the most unique exhibit is the 12 'character heads' by Franz Xaver Messerschmidt, a German sculptor who died in Bratislava in 1783. He gave them evocative titles, such as 'suppressed laughter', 'top secret' and 'the most expressive smell'; for those without a title you can play a guessing game. Modern art consists of a few prints by Manet, Picasso and Braque, a couple of tiny Rodins and lots of derivative art by followers of Matisse, Dufy and Cézanne. The bridge houses good temporary exhibitions and contemporary art by names such as Július Koller, Peter Bartoš and Marko Blažo.

STEINHAUSER GALLERY 222 E5; Laurinská 3 (1st Fl); m 09 02 685 333; w steinhauser-gallery.com; 13.00–19.00 Wed–Sat; free; 1, 3, 4 to Centrum

New in 2023, this upmarket gallery puts on solo and shared exhibitions by leading Slovak and international artists.

TRANZIT.SK 220 F1; Beskydská 12; w sk.tranzit.org; 14.30–18.30 Tue–Fri; free; 21, 40, 44, 61, 63, 64, 71 to Karpatská

Just east of the main railway station on the corner of Karpatská, this is the local branch of a network of contemporary art associations across central Europe which aims to put local traditions into a regional context and to link art and society.

ÚĽUV GALLERY 221 F4; Obchodná 64; w uluv.sk; noon–18.00 Tue–Fri, 10.00–14.00 Sat; free; 1, 9 to Vysoká

A great place to see traditional crafts and folk designs such as hand-woven tablecloths, china pots, bowls and jugs, carved wooden objects, little toys, spoons and bowls, jewellery made from metals or ceramics, and painted eggs usually decorated in folk patterns of flowers, birds and swirls for Easter. The waistcoats embroidered with colourful folk designs are exquisite. There's a shop on the ground floor so you can purchase little gifts to take home, and the gallery above. You can even order a custom-designed folk costume for yourself.

UMRIAN GALLERY 222 B4; Baštová 6; **m** 09 07 853 562; **w** umrian.gallery; 13.00–19.00 Mon–Fri; free; 9 to Kapucínska
Founded in 2010 (as SODA), Umrian puts on four or five shows a year of exciting new work from young and emerging artists from Slovakia and the Czech Republic, as well as showing at Frieze and other international art fairs.

CHURCHES AND RELIGIOUS BUILDINGS

Bratislava is dotted with churches, especially in the Old Town centre (see page 158 for the cathedral). You'll usually have to view the interior through a locked grille unless there's a service on (but the Calvinist church on Námestie SNP is always shut). These are often great places to catch a concert of classical or religious music, performed by young Slovak musicians.

BROTHERS OF MERCY CHURCH (Kostol milosrdných bratov) 222 F2; Námestie SNP; mass 08.00 & 18.00 Mon–Fri, 08.00 Sat, 09.30 Sun; 1, 3, 4 to Centrum
In 1723–28, a Baroque complex was constructed on the site of an older church, built in 1683. The church has a dainty little Baroque interior with paintings in the archways. In front of the church, where the junction with Poštová ulica is today, was Anča Korzo, the meeting point and promenade start point for labourers, maidservants and other working-class people. The Korzo for merchants and businessmen started at the junction of Michalská, Ventúrska and Sedlárska.

CAPUCHIN CHURCH (Kapučínov sv Štefana) 222 B3; Kapucínska; services 06.00, 17.00, 19.00 Mon–Fri, 17.00, 19.00 Sat, 05.15, 06.00, 08.00, 09.30, 11.00, 17.00, 19.00 Sun; 9 to Kapucínska
This Baroque complex built in 1708–11 has a bare white interior with elegant arches and wooden tableaux. Right outside the church is a **plague column** with a saint on top and a halo of stars that some people call a 'helicopter'.

CHATAM SÓFER MEMORIAL 220 A6; Nabrežie arm gen L Svobodu; **m** 09 48 554 442; **w** chatamsofer.sk; book in advance; €6; 29, 30, 31, 37, 39, 50 or 4 to Chatam Sófer; 9 to Kráľovské údolie
A Jewish cemetery was buried when the road level was raised and the tunnel under Castle Hill was constructed in 1942. A black box was created in 2002 to give access to 23 graves of renowned rabbis, including that of Chatam Sófer, a great scholar, also known as rabbi Moshe Schreiber, who was born in Frankfurt am Main in 1762. In 1806, he accepted an invitation from the Jewish community of Pressburg (Bratislava) and became Chief Rabbi in the city. He remained in the post for 33 years during which time the yeshiva he headed became one of the most prominent centres for Orthodox Jewish learning in Europe.

FRANCISCAN CHURCH (Františkánsky kostol) 222 D4; Františkánske námestie 2; services 08.00, 09.00, 19.30 Mon–Sat, 09.00, 10.30, noon, 16.30, 18.30 Sun; 1, 3, 4 to Centrum
Built between 1280 and 1297, this is the oldest surviving religious building in the Old Town. After several fires, the choir and the adjoining Chapel of Saint John the Evangelist are the only remaining Gothic sections, with a Renaissance nave added in the 16th to 17th centuries, plus a Baroque altar and façade from 1760. There's a limited exhibition (mostly in Slovak) in the cloister, and upstairs you can visit the treasury and tower, and also take a virtual reality tour (all just €1).

HOLY TRINITY CHURCH (Kostol svätého Jána z Mathy) 222 C2; Župné námestie 1; services 07.00 & 17.00 Mon–Sat, 07.00, 09.00, 10.30, noon & 20.00 Sun; 1, 9 to Poštová
The Trinitarian church was built in the High Baroque style in 1717–27 by architects Franz Jangl and Johan Lucas von Hildebrandt, and was dedicated to one of the founders of the Order of the Most Holy Trinity, St John of Matha (Jána z Mathy). It should not be confused with the much more modest Holy Trinity Church beneath the castle in Podhradie.

The church is an imposing sight, with its bold curving façade in beige and cream colours and two low pointed towers. The highly ornate interior has typical Baroque overcrowding in gold and fake marble, while the oval dome is decorated with frescoes (1736–40) by Italian painter Antonio Galli Bibiena. On the gigantic main altar is a painting of John of Matha and Felix de Valois buying slaves out of Turkish captivity. The domes above the nave and choir show off some splendid trompe l'oeil painting. Both Franz Liszt and Johannes Brahms gave concerts in its cavernous space. From 1939 to 1994, the church housed the Slovak National Council until it moved to the new parliament building near the castle. The church was also the location for the signing of the Declaration of Independence of Slovakia on 14 March 1939, and also the Declaration of Independence on 17 July 1992.

NOTRE DAME CHURCH (Kostol Nanebovzatia Panny Márie-Notre Dame) 223 F7; Námestie Eugena Suchoňa; 08.00–18.00 daily; 50 or 1, 4 to Námestie Ľudovíta Štúra
A Baroque building from 1754 by N Jadot, located in a beautiful, quiet corner of Hviezdoslavovo námestie between the Reduta and the Slovak National Theatre (SND) Historic Building. In 2008 this 'corner', with seats in the shade of tall trees, was renamed 'Námestie Eugena Suchoňa' to commemorate 15 years since the death of Slovak composer Eugen Suchoň (1908–93), many of whose classical works have been performed at the Reduta.

POOR CLARES CHURCH AND CONVENT (Kostol klarisiek) 222 B5; Farská 1; 9 to Kapucínska
A Gothic single-nave church built in 1302 with a beautiful hexagonal tower. In 1782, the Poor Clares order was abolished in the Austrian Empire and

the building became a school, then a law academy and a Catholic grammar school where Hungarian composer Béla Bartók studied. It's no longer a convent, but you can go inside and explore – there are even concerts here on occasion (page 124).

GARDENS AND PARKS

Bratislava is a very green city, with 809ha of parks and forests and 34 protected reservations. Most of this is formed by the Bratislava Forest Park (Bratislavsk lesopark) to the north of the city. The hills above the city make an excellent cool getaway from the heat of the summer, and they are crisscrossed with hiking trails and cycle paths. Here are a few places to get some oxygen.

BOTANICAL GARDEN OF COMENIUS UNIVERSITY (Botanická záhrada) 220 A6; Botanická 3; 02 9010 8021; Apr–Oct 09.00–18.00 daily, greenhouses 09.00–15.00 Mon–Fri, 09.00–18.00 Sat & Sun; adult/child €4.50/1.50; 29, 32 or 4, 9 to Botanická Záhrada

The Botanical Garden, extending over 5ha, contains more than 5,000 species of exotic and domestic plants, as well as 650 woodland species. Established in 1942, the garden became an important centre for botanical study only after World War II, when scientists working at the Comenius University undertook much research work there. The rosarium boasts more than 120 species of roses, while the Japanese-style garden is also a highlight.

BRATISLAVA ZOO 220 A4; Mlynská dolina 1; 02 6010 2111; w zoobratislava.sk; Apr–Sep 09.00–19.00 daily, Mar & Oct 10.00–18.00 daily, Nov–Feb 10.00–16.00 daily; adult/concession €10/7; 31, 32, 37, 39, 92 to Zoo

The zoo, founded in 1948, is in a park in the hills west of town, and is a good day out for visitors with children. A sizeable collection of favourites ranges from fish, mammals, reptiles and birds to hippos, bears, big cats, monkeys, lemurs, kangaroos and chinchillas. New enclosures for boar and lynx, and a pool for the hippos, were under construction at the end of 2024.

CHAIR LIFT (Lanová dráha) map, page 196; Kamzík Hill; w lanovky.sk; 10.00–18.00 Thu–Sun, Jul & Aug Tue–Sun; one way €4.50, return €7; 42, 47 to Červený most or train to ŽST Železná Studienka then 43 to Lanovka; from the upper terminal, walk down through the forest to the Koliba stop for 44

This scenic ride takes 15 minutes (climbing 186m) and offers great views en route of the Železná Studienka Valley and picnic area (page 185). It's popular with mountain bikers, and also opens up pleasant walks and hikes in the wooded hills.

FOUR GATES OF THE OLD TOWN

The construction of the medieval fortifications in Bratislava started in the 13th century. By the end of the 14th century, there were three gates leading to the town: Michalská brána (Michael's Gate) in the north, Vydrická brána (Vydricka Gate) in the west and Laurinská brána (Lawrence's Gate) in the east. In the 15th century another, smaller, gate was built in the south: Rybárska brána (Fisherman's Gate), leading to the Danube. The suburbs gradually grew around the walls, which were fortified in the 15th century with embankments and dykes on the order of King Sigmund after a Hussite invasion. The town's outer line had five gates: Kozia brána, Suché mýto, Špitálska, Dunajská and Schöndorf, today called Obchodná.

FISHERMAN'S GATE (Rybárska Brána) 223 E6; 1, 3, 4 to Centrum
Built in the 14th century, jutting out into a filled-in moat, this was pulled down in 1776 to the orders of Maria Theresa so that it would not hinder the city's development. Between McDonald's and the Slovak National Theatre, a glass window offers a glimpse of 15th-century stonework, all that remains of this.

GOAT GATE CEMETERY (Cintorín Kozia Brana) 220 C4; Šulekova; m 09 03 752 897; Apr–Oct 07.00–20.00 daily, Nov–Mar 07.00–17.00 daily; 44, 47 to Kozia
A lovely, peaceful spot on the side of a hill and a good place for a sit-down and a breather after walking up to the Slavín Monument. Office workers and romantic couples sit by ancient graves in the shade of tall trees.

GOLDEN SANDS (ZLATÉ PIESKY) map, page 196; Zlaté Piesky; w starz.sk; Jun noon–18.00 Mon–Fri, 09.00–18.00 Sat & Sun, Jul & Aug 09.00–18.00 daily; adult/child €3.00/2.50; 4 to Zlaté Piesky
In the heat of the summer, Bratislava residents head off on the tram to 'Golden Sands', Zlaté Piesky, a 32ha artificial lake surrounded by campsites and stalls offering snacks. Even the roar of the Nitra highway nearby can't deter families from having fun, splashing about in the soft, clear waters of the lake. It has a little of a Socialist-era children's camp about it but it's worth a trip to see how Slovaks used to sunbathe in the 1960s. There's a campsite (page 88) at the resort where small cabins can be rented, and a free nudist beach on the far side of the lake (53, 56 to Dvojstudňové polia).

GRASSALKOVICH PALACE GARDEN (Grassalkovičova záhrada) 220 E3; Apr–May 10.00–20.00 daily, Jun–Sep 08.00–22.00 daily, Oct–Mar 10.00–19.00 daily; 42, 44, 47, 83, 84, 93, 212 to Hodžovo námestie; 44 to Prezidentská záhrada
Behind Grassalkovich Palace (page 155), the official residence of the Slovak president, this is a rather formal garden with little shade. Along the side are

LAWRENCE'S GATE (Laurinská Brána) 222 G4; 1, 3, 4 to Centrum
A municipal fortification gate with a tower and foregate built here in the 13th century and pulled down in 1778. A huge portcullis dangling above the street at Laurinská 15 marks the spot.

MICHAEL'S GATE (Michalská Brána) 222 C3; 1, 3, 4 to Centrum
This is the only gate of the medieval city fortifications still standing. Its Gothic foundations were laid in 1379; in 1529–34 its height was increased and in 1753–58 it was rebuilt into its present appearance with a statue of St Michael placed on the top of the 51m-tall tower. Behind the tower is a little Baroque pre-tower built in 1712 on top of a previous 15th-century bastion; the remains of the city moat can be seen just to the north.

VYDRICKA GATE (Vydrická Brána) 223 B7; Rudnayovo námestie; 1, 3, 4 to Centrum
The municipal fortification gate, along with the bastions Himmelreich and Leonfelderthurm, was built here in the 14th century. It was pulled down in 1777, leaving a bit of wall and a plaque.

trees planted by visiting heads of state. Visitors are not supposed to walk on the grass or bring dogs, but it's pleasant enough for a stroll.

HORSKÝ PARK 220 A1; 47 from Hodžovo námestie to Horský Park
Northwest of the town, Horský Park is a 20ha woody area with a network of paths. There is a 'Lourdes cave', recalling the grotto of pilgrimage in France, with a Kalvária pilgrimage site founded in 1694 by the Jesuits, the city council and the archbishop, who decided to build it where the Turkish guards had stood in the time of their raids. Another popular destination is a gamekeeper's lodge which has a café (10.00–20.00 daily; €). Near the café, a plaque in English marks the site of a house where Mozart stayed in 1764–65; there's now a small park of abstract sculptures here. The E8 hiking trail runs through the park, leading south to Slavín (15mins) and north to Kamzík (1hr 20mins), continuing along the length of the Small Carpathians.

JEWISH CEMETERIES 220 A6; Žižkova ulica to the west of town, beyond the Chatam Sófer Memorial & River Park; 09.00–17.00 Sun–Thu, 09.00–15.00 Fri; 37 or 4, 9 to Kráľovské Údolie
An enjoyable walk upstream along the Danube's northern bank. The walls of the cemeteries along Žižkova are a popular free rock-climbing venue and always filled with lithe youngsters and spider-Slovaks clambering all over. The Orthodox and Neolog graveyards contain graves of important

Jewish residents, who were removed from the Jewish cemetery at the Chatam Sófer Memorial and reburied when the tunnel was built and the road level raised. Can be visited by private arrangement; contact Chatam Sófer (page 179).

KOLIBA-KAMZÍK ♀ map, page 196; Kamzík vrch, north of the city; 🚌 44 from Hodžovo námestie to Koliba (terminus), then walk uphill through the forest for 25mins or, at w/ends except in winter, take 🚌 144 from Koliba to Kamzík

In Slovak, the chamois or small, goat-like mountain antelope is called *kamzík vrchovsk* (*Rupicapra rupicapra*), and the hilly area north of Bratislava bears the same name, although they're no longer found in this area. It's the best-known part of Bratislava Forest Park underneath the TV tower. Kamzík Hill (439m) offers cool woods and a range of trails to follow at the southernmost tip of the Small Carpathian mountain range. There are little triangular wooden huts, looking like chunks of Toblerone, offering draught beer or Kofola (a Czech version of Coca-Cola) on tap. At the top is a huge meadow with skiing in winter. In summer, a bobsleigh (*bobová dráha*) run follows the slope for 360m (page 136). The revolving Veža restaurant and café are at the top of the 200m-high TV tower (pages 101 and 116).

MEDICAL GARDEN (Medická záhrada) ♀ 221 H3; Blumentálska 10/a; ⏱ Apr–Sep 07.00–21.00 daily, Oct–Mar 10.00–18.00 daily; 🚌 47 or 🚋 3, 4 to Americké námestie; 🚌 42 to Špitálska

The Medical Garden is a pleasant park to the northeast of the city where people take their lunch break, walk the dog or play frisbee. There's a children's playground at one side and a statue to the Slovak writer Martin Kukučin by the Croatian sculptor Ivan Meštrovic. There's also a statue of 19th-century Hungarian poet and revolutionary Sándor Petőfi who lived in Bratislava for a while. This is often defaced by anti-Magyar protestors, especially following the 2006 election of some dubious extreme nationalist politicians, who whipped up anti-Hungarian sentiment (page 19). The garden once belonged to the Count of Aspremont, whose palace stands to the west of the park. It is a late Baroque palace in a delicate pink hue; commissioned in 1769, it was later owned by the Esterházy family, and Joseph Haydn gave concerts here. Since World War I, the palace has housed the Comenius University medical department, hence the name of the park.

ROHKATKA-KAKTUS DOWNHILL MOUNTAIN BIKE TRACK ♀ map, page 196; near the chair lift at Kamzík Hill (above); ⏱ all year except during ski season; 🚌 44 from Hodžovo námestie to Koliba terminus, then walk uphill through the forest for 25mins

Next to the chair lift is a steep 1,920m track with jumps, raised barriers, rocky sections and different levels of difficulty at varying stages of descent to Železná Studienka Valley. Bikers bring their wheels back up again on the chair lift.

SAD JANKA KRÁĽA 220 E8; 3 to Sad Janka Kráľa; 80, 83, 84, 88, 93, 94 to Aupark/Pri sade
South of the Danube, this spacious park seems like the first choice for those seeking a patch of green. The park was created in the time of Maria Theresa, and the eponymous Janko Kráľ (1822–76) was a revolutionary poet who used to walk there. There are several restaurants in the park and features of interest such as a 14th-century church tower that was removed from the Franciscan church in the Old Town and brought to the park in 1897. A plaque near the Einsteinova main road reveals that an 'anti-Napoleonic wall' stood here in 1809. The park is also decorated with 12 astrological star signs marked out along the circular pathway with a symbol, and a collection of benches to have a rest on; it's fun trying to find your sign. Toilets and furniture have recently been refurbished. The ground-breaking Aréna theatre (page 120) stands by the water near the Old Bridge. For mall rats, it's a pleasant stroll across the Most SNP and through this park to reach Aupark Shopping Center.

ST ANDREW'S CEMETERY (Cintorín Ondrejský) 221 H4; Ulica 29 augusta; Nov–Mar 07.00–17.00 daily, Apr–Oct 07.00–20.00; 42 to Ondrejskýcintorín
St Andrew's cemetery is a good place to pause while contemplating life (and death) on a shaded bench among elegant statues. It's a haven of peace and calm, except for the manic tidying leading up to All Saints' Day (1 Nov). The grave dedications are in Slovak, Hungarian and German.

SLÁVIČIE VALLEY CEMETERY (Cintorín Slávičie údolie) 220 A4; Staré grunty 47; 02 6542 3969; Nov–Mar 07.00–17.00 daily, Apr–Oct 07.00–20.00 daily; 31, 39 to Cintorín Slávičie
Just uphill from Bratislava Zoo, this is the final resting place of Alexander Dubček, First Secretary of the Communist Party of Czechoslovakia (1968–69). His grave is near the main entrance: a simple stone in dark pink marble with a bust of his kind, smiling face. You can also check out where he lived, at Mišíkova 46, when walking up to the Slavín Monument (page 159). The cemetery also contains a modern concrete and metal memorial to those who fought against fascism and died in the Mauthausen concentration camp in 1945.

SLAVÍN MONUMENT See page 159.

ŽELEZNÁ STUDIENKA VALLEY Northeast of Kamzík; 42, 47 to Červený most; train to ŽST Železná Studienka then 43 to Železná studnička; a more scenic alternative route is by 44 from Hodžovo námestie to Koliba, walk up to Kamzík, then sail down on the chair lift & walk through the beautiful meadow

At Železná Studnička (Iron Well), the water from the spring is rich in iron and a picnic and recreation area grew up around it in the sun-trap valley. There are many small terraces and snack bars offering beer and hearty dishes. At **w** lesy.bratislava.sk, you can find trail maps (in Slovak), including the *náučný chodník* (study trail).

SQUARES

Bratislava's squares are the perfect locations to soak up the sunshine, enjoy an ice cream or just hang out and watch the world go by.

HLAVNÉ NÁMESTIE (Main Sq) 222 D5; 1, 3, 4 to Centrum

You'll find everything on the Main Square: three great cafés, Art Nouveau buildings, the Roland Fountain, and statues of Schöne Naci, a guardsman and a Napoleonic soldier (page 191). The square originated in the 13th century and, from the start, was at the centre of the town's social life – a place of markets, festivities and executions – all well attended. Hlavné námestie is almost indistinguishable from Františkánske námestie (Square of the Franciscans) immediately north where there are little stalls with people selling folky souvenirs and an excellent Christmas market (page 142).

HVIEZDOSLAVOVO NÁMESTIE (Hviezdoslav Sq) 223 D7; 50 or 1, 4 to Námestie Ľudovíta Štúra

Another great square for eating ice cream, walking the dog or playing chess on a giant board. Two literary greats are honoured: Pavol Országh Hviezdoslav, the 'father of Slovak poetry', and Hans Christian Andersen, near Most SNP. This is the main location for the Christmas market (page 142) and there are always stalls offering folk souvenirs throughout the year.

NÁMESTIE ĽUDOVÍTA ŠTÚRA (Ľudovít Štúr Sq) 223 E9; 50 or 1, 4 to Námestie Ľudovíta Štúra

The development of this square only began in the 18th century after a branch of the Danube was filled in. Local sculptor János Fadrusz created a monument to Maria Theresa which was unveiled in 1897, but destroyed in 1921 during a period of unrest following the former Hungarian King Károly IV's attempts to return to the throne. In 1938, a statue of Štefánik was erected in the square incorporating a column topped with a lion holding the state coat of arms. Originally, the lion was to face the Danube and the Austrian border, but because of international tensions, a diagonal view was chosen. Allegedly, Hitler, observing Bratislava from Petržalka in March 1939, said 'the cat must go' and the lion disappeared a year later. Štefánik was not favoured by the communist regime and in 1972 they erected in its place a modernist statue (by Tibor Bártfay and Iván Salay) to Ľudovít Štúr, one of the leaders of the Slovak nationalist movement in the 19th century (page 208).

NÁMESTIE SLOBODY (Freedom Sq) ♀ 221 F2; 🚌 44 to Úrad vlády SR; 🚌 94 to Námestie slobody

During medieval times, this area was covered with vineyards. The square probably originated in the 17th century, along with the Archbishop's Summer Palace which was built there. A giant statue of communist president, Klement Gottwald, used to dominate the square but it was removed soon after the regime collapsed in 1989. The square was named after him but was one of the first squares in Bratislava to be renamed after the Velvet Revolution. A modern statue of a giant metal flower (page 190) now rises up in the centre. On one side is a building which claimed to be the largest post office in the world, although these days the imposing building is occupied by the Ministry of Transport, Post and Telecommunications. On the opposite side is the Slovak Technical University, with some great Soviet Constructivist reliefs all along the wall, with groups of happy workers, bucolic peasants and clever-looking scientists.

BRIDGES

I have listed the five bridges over the Danube at Bratislava in sequence from west to east. All have cycle/walkways but the first and last (as listed here) are basically motorways.

LANFRANCONI MOST (Lanfranconi Bridge) ♀ 220 A6

This four-lane expressway bridge, 766m long, runs about 2km west of the Old Town and into Austria, and is also cycle-friendly and with a separated side wall. Built in 1985–91 and named Most mládeže (Bridge of Youth) until 1989, the bridge was renamed – with incorrect spelling – Lafranconi Most, paying homage to the famous Italian engineer Count Grazioso Enea Lanfranconi (1850–95), who was responsible for regulating the Danube. Since 2020 the correct spelling has been used. Before Lanfranconi, Bratislava – or Pressburg as it was then called – was plagued by periodic floods. After Lanfranconi's projects, the flooding became much less frequent; however, the regulation of the riverbed has destroyed most of the inland delta of the Danube and turned the 'land of a thousand islands' into a straight and easily navigable and – some say – rather dull canal.

Before he went insane and killed himself, Lanfranconi donated his land on the riverbank to the city to be used for sporting and recreational activities. There was a sports ground, a marina and a botanical garden; however, the last was demolished to make way for the bridge and the marina was replaced by a housing estate. Lanfranconi's villa and small park still stand near the bridge.

MOST SNP AND UFO (SNP Bridge) 220 D7/8
SNP stands for 'Slovenské národné povstanie' ('Slovak National Uprising'). Pedestrians and cyclists use a level just below the traffic. It was completed in 1972 as the finishing touch to a highway barging straight through the centre of the city; the project required the destruction of 226 buildings, two-thirds of Bratislava's Old Town and the Jewish quarter. Under the north end of the bridge, a defaced inscription on a triple-flame plaque tells of a 'special friendship and brotherhood with the people of the Soviet Union'. Previously called 'Nový Most' (New Bridge), it was renamed when the newer Apollo Bridge was built.

The UFO-like spaceship hovering above the bridge was built at the same time and houses a restaurant with observation deck (page 101) which gives a magnificent view of the city from a height of 85m.

STARÝ MOST (Old Bridge) 221 G7/8
The tram to Vienna used to rattle across the ancient wooden-slatted spans of this bridge. At the end of the 19th century, Bratislava was an important part of the Hungarian Empire; however, it lacked a firm connection to the right bank of the Danube (though there was a pontoon bridge and paddle steamers crossed the river – until as recently as 2003). In 1889, Minister Baross persuaded the regional assembly to build a permanent bridge, with a toll house at each end. Designed by the French architect François Cathry-Saléz, the bridge was opened by Emperor Franz Joseph on the eve of the 1891 New Year's celebrations. It has borne many names throughout its life: Emperor Franz Joseph Bridge, Štefaník Bridge, Red Army Bridge and now Old Bridge. As it deteriorated due to age and neglect it was closed to cars in 2009, to buses in 2010, and to pedestrians and cyclists in 2013 when reconstruction finally began, funded by the European Union. The bridge was totally dismantled, rebuilt and reopened in 2015, in time for Slovakia's Presidency of the EU beginning 1 July 2016. The bridge now carries only pedestrians, cyclists and trams (line 3 goes just two stops south of the river but is being extended to the southern edge of Petržalka – it's unlikely to ever go all the way to Vienna again).

MOST APOLLO (Apollo Bridge) 221 K8
Opened in 2005, Most Apollo was named after the Apollo oil refinery situated on the left riverbank in this area before World War I, but perhaps its beautiful curved, white shape was also meant to be reminiscent of Apollo's

◀ **1** Take the lift from the Most SNP for spectacular views over the city from the UFO café. **2** The Most Apollo recalls the lyre of the Greek god Apollo. **3** One of several quirky statues around the city, the *Skateboarder Girls* take a break on a working post box. **4** *Čumil* has been peeping out from his manhole since 1997 and remains the city's favourite photo op.

STATUES – THE AMUSING, CREEPY OR JUST PLAIN WEIRD

Bratislava is filled with interesting and imaginative statues, which present great photo opportunities and an insight into the Slovak sense of humour. The eastern European tradition of public sculpture is particularly obvious along the Danube embankment, but the humorous statues elsewhere in the Old Town are what really mark Bratislava out. The Eurovea shopping centre in particular has tried to match these with a set of a dozen humorous statues of circus performers by the English artist Colin Spofforth (2013), but they seem less likely to catch people's hearts.

ČUMIL 223 E6; cnr Panská & Rybárska brána
Created by Viktor Hulík, this man peering out of a manhole cover 'looking up skirts' has been here since 1997 and is the favourite photo op in town.

DUCK FOUNTAIN (KAČACIA FONTÁNA) 221 G6; Šafárikovo námestie
The three naked little boys teasing ducks was, built in 1914 by the sculptor Robert Kúhmayer (who also created the 'Crutch-Breaker' statue at Piešťany Spa; page 202). According to legend, the three boys were playing with ducks when the water sprite Zeleniak appeared and ordered them never to peek under the water at his kingdom. They disobeyed and were turned to stone.

FOUR PEEING BOYS 222 D5; Hlavné námestie
The Roland (Maximilián) Fountain (page 147), erected in 1572 in the centre of Hlavné námestie, features four little boys having a wee – two are holding hands. In 1794 shocked Bratislava residents had it removed and replaced by more innocent boys holding fish! The peeing boys were hidden away in a courtyard of the Ruttkay-Vrútocký Palace off Uršulínska 6 until 2019, when the fountain was restored to its original site.

FRIENDSHIP FLOWER 221 F2; Námestie Slobody
At the centre of Freedom Square, laid out in 1980, is a fountain with this metal sculpture of a linden flower (*lipovy kvet*) at its centre, a symbol of friendship between the Slav peoples.

HANS CHRISTIAN ANDERSEN 223 C7; Hviezdoslavovo námestie
The Danish fairytale teller visited Bratislava in 1841 and the statue depicts a tall, skinny poet looking a bit bashful, with a huge snail gazing up at him in awe of his imagination. The emperor with no clothes and other characters from his stories are depicted on the rear. Created by Tibor Bártfay, whose father designed the soldier on the top of the Slavín Monument (page 159).

THE MOCKER (POSMIEVAČIK) 📍 223 C7; Panská 29
This is a grotesque gargoyle from the late Gothic façade of what is currently the Luculus ice-cream shop; a horrible dwarf squatting and flashing at the street. There are various theories about his significance – some say he is looking towards Vydrica, the former red-light district, and that's why he is aroused; others insist he represents a very nosy resident of the building who likes to spy on passers-by from a tiny bay window.

NAPOLEONIC SOLDIER 📍 222 D5; Hlavné námestie
Leaning on a bench, the soldier seemingly poses for photos behind those who sit down for a rest; watch out for photobombing!

SCHÖNE NÁCI 📍 222 D5; Hlavné námestie, on the corner by Kaffee Mayer
This statue, by Juraj Meliš, depicts a real person who was famous locally as a dandy. Ignác Lamár (1897–1967) was nicknamed Schöne Náci, meaning 'Handsome Ignatius'; he appears quite friendly and jolly on the statue, but his fiancée was deported to a Nazi concentration camp in World War II, where she died. He never recovered psychologically from the trauma and spent his days wandering along the Korzo in a top hat and tails, smiling at everyone.

SKATEBOARDER GIRLS 📍 222 E1; Poštova & Obchodná
One girl sits on a fence, while another girl sits below on a skateboard looking up. The post box is real and working – you can send your postcards from here.

TOWN GUARDHOUSE 📍 222 D5; Hlavné námestie 2
A statue of a guardsman standing in his sentry box arrived here in 2006. A wooden sentry box stood in the south of the square from the 1650s until the 18th century when it burnt down. In 1767, a new brick guardhouse was built by M Walch but removed in 1860.

lyre. The Apollo Bridge became the only European project named as one of five finalists for the 2006 Outstanding Civil Engineering Achievement Award (OPAL Award) by the American Society of Civil Engineers – it was selected for its 'bold aesthetic statement'.

PRÍSTAVNÝ MOST (Harbour Bridge) ♀ 221 K6

The 599m-long Prístavný Most was built between 1977 and 1985. Known until 1993 as Most hrdinov Dukly (Dukla Heroes' Bridge, after a battle of October 1944), the bridge carries the busy D1 motorway, with a railway on a lower level plus pathways for cyclists and pedestrians.

ALSO WORTH A VISIT

HOUSE OF THE GOOD SHEPHERD (Dom u dobrého pastiera) ♀ 220 D6; Židovská 3; ☏ 02 5441 1940; ⓘ Apr–Oct only 10.00–18.00 Thu–Sun; 🎫 adult/child €3/1.50; 🚌 50 or 🚋 4 to Most SNP; 🚋 9 to Kapucínska

This Rococo burgher's house dates from 1760–65 and got its name from a statue of Christ, the Good Shepherd, on the corner. The house was lucky to escape demolition during the construction of the Most SNP and highway, surviving today in its original state. After reconstruction in 1975, the City History Museum opened an exhibition of 60 historic clocks here (page 161). The lower part was once used for commercial and production purposes, the upper parts were a living area. A false window has been retained in the façade of the house; the moulded statue of the good shepherd in the niche under the baldachin is not original. The house is a small treasure of central European burgher architecture. There's a tiny café-bar in the lowest level.

PETRŽALKA 🚌 83, 84, 93, 94 or 🚋 3 to Petržalka

Petržalka (Ligetfalu in Hungarian, Engerau in German) is Bratislava's largest suburban district, with about a third of the city's population living here (114,000) – the most densely populated place in central Europe. It is in most part a residential area with blocks of flats known as *paneláky* or panels, owing to the prefab construction material. There are records of a settlement here from 1225, when it was inhabited by Pecheneg mercenaries on guard duty near the Danube. In the late 18th century when neighbouring Pressburg/Pozsony was the capital of Hungary, Petržalka was called Pozsonyligetfalu (Bratislava Park Village). In 1891, the first railway bridge was built, providing a link to the capital and in 1919, the village – the largest in Czechoslovakia – was renamed Petržalka ('petržlen' means 'parsley') acknowledging all the vegetables and herbs grown there. From 1938 to 1945 Petržalka was annexed by Germany (which then included Austria) and there were passport checks on the Stary Most. In 1944 a labour camp was established for Hungarian Jews forced to build fortifications; almost a quarter of them died. Construction of the housing blocks, or 'panelák', began in 1973; it developed a reputation for drugs and petty crime, but is now a green and pleasant area. It is being extended south towards the modern bypass with stylish modern apartment developments.

SLOVAK RADIO BUILDING (Slovenský rozhlas) 221 F2; Mytná 1; 1 to STU
It's well worth the walk out towards the northeast of town to see this bizarre creation – a huge brown inverted pyramid balancing improbably on its pointed tip, which looks like it has been rammed deep into the ground. It was built during 1971–85, and although it looks like it is made of wood, it is actually brown COR-TEN steel. The concert hall is on springs to reduce vibration and the acoustics are excellent. You will see this building on your left if you take tram 1 into town from the main railway station.

UNIVERSITAS ISTROPOLITANA 223 C6; Ventúrska 3; 1, 3, 4 to Centrum
This was the oldest university in the territory of present-day Slovakia, founded by Hungarian King Mátyás Corvinus in 1465. After his death in 1490 the university ceased to exist. The Academy of Performing Arts has its seat in the building, which is today a national monument.

10

Beyond the City

Bratislava is a neat and compact city, and perfect for a weekend break; however, its strategic location, almost on the border of three countries (Slovakia, Austria and Hungary), makes it an ideal base for exploring the surrounding region. Imposing castles, pretty villages, gorgeous countryside and the mighty River Danube offer a range of day-trip options. As well as the options covered in this chapter, it's also very easy to visit Vienna; see pages 46 and 50 for information on getting there, and the box on page 48 for ideas on what to see and do.

DEVÍN

Devín is a village 10km west of Bratislava along the Danube, considered a vital part of Slovak history. Its castle is an impressive sight when you arrive, probably by bus or boat – you see it rising up on a 212m-tall crag above the confluence of the Danube and Morava rivers. Occupied since Neolithic times, by both the Celts and Romans, a castle and church were built here in the Great Moravian period, and a palace was added in the 15th century. The old name, Dowina, derives from the Slavic word *deva* (maiden) and the Maiden's Tower is one of the most popular sights to photograph; there are many legends about lovelorn maidens, imprisoned in the tower, escaping by leaping to their deaths. In 1809, Napoleon's advancing troops blew up the fortress en route to the Battle of Wagram against the Habsburg forces. It later became a key symbol for the Slovak National Revival and Ľudovít Štúr organised a series of events here to whip up nationalist fervour. In summer, you can also take a ferry to Devín. Walking around, you'll discover hiking routes, cycle routes and even a lighthouse. You can also see the Iron Curtain memorial sculpture by Slovak artist Milan Lukáč. Unveiled by Queen Elizabeth II in 2008, it marks where the barbed-wire border fence with Austria used to stand. It is a memorial to the many people who died trying to swim across the Morava River to Austria.

◀ 1 Devín's spectacularly sited castle is of great historical importance to Slovaks; the area is a good base for cycling too. 2 Rusovce's imposing manor house is built in Baronial style with turrets and battlements.

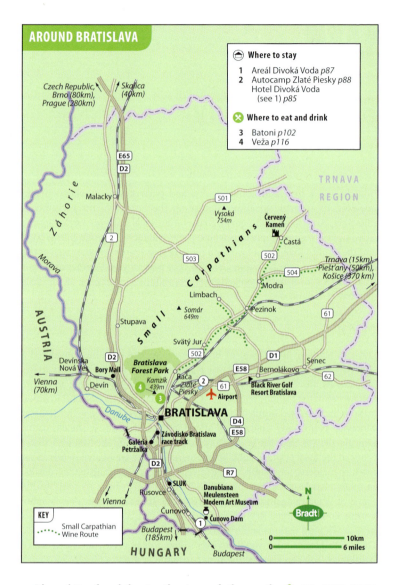

It's a bit of a hike to the top of the castle (\ 02 6573 0105; w muzeumbratislava.sk/en/devin-castle; ⏲ Mar & Oct 10.00–17.00 Tue–Sun; Apr, May & Sep 10.00–18.00 Tue–Sun; Jun–Aug 10.00–19.00 Tue–Sun; Nov–Feb 10.00–16.00 Tue–Sun (weather permitting); 💰 adult/concession €8/4, Nov–Mar €4/free, free with Bratislava City Card) but there are some modern walkways and viewpoints and the views are great. There's been almost 7,000 years of human occupation here, but the displays in the castle focus on Tertiary geology and the period from the 13th century on.

Devín's other claim to fame is its *ríbezlák* or blackcurrant wine, which you can buy from a stand (🕐 noon–18.00 Wed–Sun) near the restaurant in the castle car park. Alternatively you should find it in shops for about €8 a bottle. It's semi-sweet but often aged in oak barrels to give some depth and complexity of flavour.

GETTING THERE AND AWAY As a rule you'll have to take bus 29 (every 20mins) from Malá Scéna or on the main road under Most SNP and get off at one of the four request stops (I suggest Cyril a Metod – the church) in Devín village, then walk towards the castle. It's quite tricky (with winding roads and no signposts), but doable. If you continue to the Hrad Devín (Devín Castle) stop, you've overshot but can walk back on the riverside cycleway, past a petting farm.

From April to September, **ferry** boats cruise from the LOD dock to Devín (mid-Apr–mid-May 10.00 Tue–Sun, returning 13.30, mid-May–Aug 10.00 & 14.30 Tue–Sun, returning 13.30 & 18.00, Sep & Oct 10.00 & 14.30 Sat & Sun, returning 13.30 & 18.00). The trip to Devín takes 90 minutes, but the return sailing just 30 minutes, showing the strength of the Danube current. Single tickets cost €19/15 adult/child to Devín but only €16/14 back to Bratislava, and €2 to take your bike on board. Return tickets cost €21/16 adult/child, with a 2-hour stop in Devín. Tickets are available from LOD (Fajnorovo nábrežie 2; 📞 02 5293 2226; **w** lod.sk; 🕐 08.00–19.30 daily*)*.

ANCIENT GERULATA, RUSOVCE

There are a few sights in Rusovce, just 11km south of Bratislava, on the way to Čunovo. Here, you'll find a beautiful **manor house** (Kaštieľ Rusovce) built in 1840 on the site of an older manor house from 1521. The manor is in Baronial style with towers, battlements and a central terrace; at the time of writing it was fenced off for restoration, but the park remains open, if overgrown. It's also worth seeing the simple Romanesque Church of St Vitus, rebuilt in 1613, by the Kaštieľ Rusovce bus stop. But Rusovce's real claim to fame is the remaining foundations of **Gerulata**, a Roman military camp dating from the 2nd to 4th centuries, recently added to UNESCO's World Heritage List (page 166). Archaeologists discovered the ruins of a forum, a well, and fragments of furnaces, tombstones and altar stones. The finds are displayed in the **Ancient Gerulata Museum** (Múzeum Antická Gerulata; Rusovce Gerulatská 69; 📞 02 6285 9332; **w** muzeumbratislava.sk/en/ancient-gerulata; 🕐 Apr & Oct 10.00–17.00 Thu–Sun, May–Sep 10.00–18.00 Tue–Sun; 🎟 adult/child €4/2), part of the Bratislava City Museum, hidden behind Rusovce's Roman Catholic church.

GETTING THERE AND AWAY Buses 91 from Most SNP (towards Čunovo; every 20mins) and 90 from Nové SND (towards Danubiana; hourly) stop after 20 minutes at Gerulata then at Kaštieľ Rusovce; the stops are about 5 minutes' walk away from each other.

SENEC

Senec, 25km east of the capital, is a quiet town, known mainly for its water resorts. The **Sunny Lakes** (*Slnečné jazerá*) resort is popular with Bratislava families attracted by the mild climate, warm water and 2,200 hours of 25°C sunshine a year. The lakes are a collection of gravel pits covering a 116ha area and filled with clear, clean water. The resort has volleyball courts, minigolf, maxi-chess and toboggans as well as an open-air cinema in the summer. There's also the **Aquathermal Park Senec** (📞 02 4564 8021; w aquaparksenec.sk; ⏰ 09.00–21.00 daily; 🎫 all-day ticket €28.90, child/senior €23.90), a modern lido complex with four small and five large pools, waterfalls, slides, jets and sprinklers as well as saunas and massage. In the town of Senec itself, the synagogue at Mierové námestie 12 is to be a cultural centre, with an exhibition on the history of Jewish culture in the Bratislava region.

GETTING THERE AND AWAY Senec is on the D1 motorway heading east out of Bratislava. Bus 632 comes here hourly (35mins) from the main bus station, as well as buses 620/630 every 2 hours. There's also the hourly 529 to Pezinok and the 539 to Modra every 2 hours. Trains run hourly from both Bratislava main station and from Petržalka/Nové Mesto. Senec's station is immediately south of the Sunny Lakes and Aquathermal Park Senec; the bus station is a few hundred metres to the northwest. Integrated Transport System tickets are valid.

SMALL CARPATHIAN WINE ROUTE

Covering some 7,300ha, the Small Carpathian Wine region (Malokarpatská Vínna Cesta) is the largest in Slovakia. With Gothic churches and belfries, Baroque chateaux, walled towns, the aroma of roast goose and brass band music, it provides a great day out in the Slovak countryside. **The Days of Open Cellar Doors** (w mvc.sk) takes place in February when dozens of wine cellars along the entire 40km route, stretching from Rača in Bratislava's northern suburbs to Trnava, are accessible to the public. The main wine-producing villages and towns on the wine route are Svätý Jur, Limbach, Pezinok, Slovenský Grob, Vinosady, Modra, Dubová, Častá and Doľany. A **cycle route** (Malokarpatská cyklomagistrála) follows the southern part of the Small Carpathian range. Local tour companies (page 62) organise trips along the route.

PEZINOK AND MODRA Pezinok is one of the main towns on the Small Carpathian Wine Route and plays host to many events throughout the year, including wine festivals in February, May and September. During these, dozens of wine cellars, often little more than a family house with a barrel in the basement, throw open their doors to wine lovers and tourists. The **Small Carpathians Museum** (Štefánika 4; ☎ 033 641 3347; w muzeumpezinok.sk; ⏰ May–Oct 09.00–noon & 13.00–17.00 Tue–Fri, 10.00–17.00 Sat, 14.00–17.00 Sun, Nov–Apr 09.00–noon & 13.00–17.00 Tue–Fri, 10.00–16.00 Sat; 💰 adult/child/students & retired €7/4/6, free with Bratislava City Card) focuses on the wine business and the associated guilds, with a large collection of ancient wine presses; it's good but mainly set up for groups. Pezinok Castle – built in 1300 as a moated fortress – has been somewhat over-restored and now houses a rather kitschy hotel. The castle park is open, as long as you shut the gate to keep the peacocks in. There are many good restaurants and small pensions in the town if you want to linger. For more information, visit the tourist information centre (Radničné námestie 9; ☎ 033 6406 989; w pezinok.sk; ⏰ 09.00–13.00 & 13.30–17.00 Tue–Sat).

Modra is famous for its wine, and there are many little cellars that can be visited, especially during the Vintage Festival in September (w slovakia.travel/en/modra-vintage-festival), but they have also made ceramics and fine china here since the 16th century, in a style known as *habánská* after the Haban craftsmen who originally made it. The Habans, also known as Anabaptists or Hutterites, were a religious sect during the Reformation who rejected papal authority and lived in communes. They fled religious persecution in Switzerland and came to Modra in the early 1600s (although they did have to convert to Catholicism). The motifs on the ceramics use everyday images of flowers and patterns from hunting, dancing and wine pressing in yellow, blue, green and plum colours, and visitors can tour the **ceramics factory** (Slovenská Ľudová Majolika; Dolná 138; m 09 11 980 105; w majolika.sk; ⏰ tours 08.00–16.00 Mon–Fri, 10.00–16.00 Sat; 💰 for groups of 5–10 visitors €5, English-speaking guide €15) and buy from the shop (Štúrova 71; ⏰ noon–18.00 Mon–Sat).

Otherwise, the **Ľudovít Štúr Museum** (Štúrova 84; ☎ 033 647 2765; w snm.sk/?about-the-museum-18; ⏰ 08.30–16.00 Tue–Fri, Apr–Oct also 10.00–16.00 Sat, 1st Sun of these months 13.00–17.00; 💰 €3) remembers the leader of the Slovak nationalist movement (page 208) in the house where he died in 1856, having accidentally shot himself while hunting three weeks earlier (he'd moved here in 1851 after the death of his brother, headmaster of the Modra grammar school, to look after his children). There are very detailed information panels (in Slovak and English) on his life and the nationalist movement itself.

In addition to the wineries, there's a clutch of nice cafés, restaurants and places to stay here – perhaps the most interesting are the Cuvée wine and coffee shop (Štúrova 95; m 09 17 530 847; f; ⏰ 15.00–20.00 Tue,

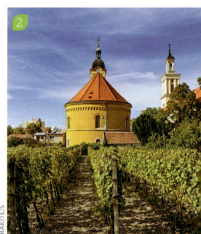

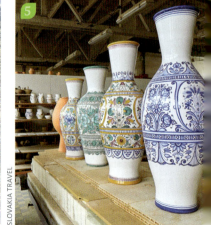

08.30–noon & 15.00–20.00 Wed–Thu, 08.30–22.00 Fri, 09.30–22.00 Sat, 09.30–18.00 Sun) and the Wild Kitchen restaurant (Moyzesova 27; **w** wildkitchen.sk; ⏰ 11.30–21.00 Thu–Sat, 11.30–15.00 Sun, no reservations), which specialises in fresh local produce, especially from their own garden.

For more on Modra, visit **w** modra.sk or **w** visitmodra.sk.

Getting there and away Pezinok is 21km and Modra 28km from Bratislava on route 502, the main highway northeast out of the city to Trnava. Regular buses (routes 506, 535, 540, 550, 565, 566, 576 & 650; 45–60mins) leave from the main bus station at Mlynské nivy and pick up in the suburbs, including at Bajkalská and Vinohrady station. Pezinok is on the main Bratislava–Trnava railway line with trains every 20 minutes from the city's main railway station (20mins), but you'll have to get a bus from there to Modra (or Červený Kameň; below). There are also buses from Pezinok and Modra to Trnava and (less frequently) Senec.

ČERVENÝ KAMEŇ

This is an impressive 13th-century castle (Hrad Červený Kameň; Častá; ✆ 033 690 5803; **w** hradcervenykamen.sk; ⏰ Jun–Aug 09.00–17.00 daily, Sep 09.00–16.00 daily, Oct–May 09.30–15.30 Tue–Sun; 🍵 adult/retired/youth/child from €10/5/5/1; tours in English from €8, May & Jun 11.30 & 15.30 Sat & Sun, Jul–Sep hourly) – the name 'Červený Kameň' means 'red rock'. You'll visit the 24 richly furnished rooms, walking through parlours, bedrooms, a dining room and a knights' hall, viewing the interior furnishings of nobility from the Renaissance until the Secession/Art Nouveau period. Tours finish in the spectacular cellars (the largest in central Europe), including a cavernous hall that once held wine for the 16th-century aristocratic Fugger family and subsequent occupiers such as the Pálffys. An antiques and popular flea market is held at weekends in the courtyard, where there's a café. Fairs, knight jousting, falconry displays, horseriding and pony trekking take place in the surrounding meadows between May and September.

As the castle is only 30km from Bratislava, the best way to see it is on a tour – the Bratislava Tourist Board (page 62) arranges group tours of the local area and provides guides (in 13 languages) for walking and sightseeing. The Small Carpathian Wine Route trip (page 198) usually combines a visit to Červený Kameň with a tour of the ceramics factory in Modra, and visits to wine-producing villages such as Pezinok.

◀ **1 & 2** The towns of Pezinok and Modra are both on the Small Carpathian Wine Route, with Pezinok playing host to many events including wine festivals throughout the year. **3** A beautiful sunset at Sunny Lakes in Senec. **4** Červený Kameň castle dates from the 13th century. **5** Modra has been producing beautiful ceramics for more than 400 years.

GETTING THERE AND AWAY There are regular buses (45mins) from the main bus station at Mlynské nivy (picking up north of the centre, eg: Bratislava Vinohrady station) to the village of Častá, from where it is a 20-minute walk uphill. Every hour or two, bus 550 makes a loop up to the castle from the city. You can also hike into the beech forests of the Small Carpathians, perhaps coming down to Modra in 2½ hours.

TRNAVA

Trnava, 20km beyond Modra, was the ecclesiastic capital of Hungary for almost three centuries, and today retains most of its medieval walls, along with some fine churches and museums. In addition to being the residence of the Archbishop of Esztergom from 1541 to 1820, it was also the seat of a Jesuit university from 1635 to 1777 which played an influential role in the Counter-Reformation; as a result, the town became known as Little Rome or the Slovak Rome. Although the archbishop returned in 1977 and a new university opened in 1992, it's nowadays a quiet, largely pedestrianised town (although FC Spartak Trnava did win the Slovak football championship in 2018).

The central crossroads is marked by the 16th-century Town Tower (containing the small, helpful tourist office, which contains tools for basic cycle repairs: Trojičné námestie 1; \ 033 323 6440; w regiontrnava.sk; ⏰ May–Sep 10.00–18.00 daily, Oct–Apr 10.00–17.00 daily) and Slovakia's oldest theatre, opened in 1831. The basilica of St Nicholas (the original cathedral, dating from 1380–1421) is a few hundred metres to the east, with a heavy exterior and a dark interior owing to having murals rather than windows on the north side of the choir. The 17th-century University Church of St John the Baptist (now the cathedral), a block to the north, is a stunner, though, with a gorgeous Rococo interior of pale apricot, white and gold. Just south of the cathedral, one of the town's synagogues now houses an attractive café (€). The people of Trnava love gelato! And pizza, but you won't find much gastronomic excitement otherwise.

GETTING THERE AND AWAY Trnava is 47km northeast of Bratislava, along the main road and railway towards Žilina and Košice. Fast trains get here in about 25 minutes once or twice an hour, and there are also Regional Express and suburban services – but Trnava is just outside the Bratislava Integrated Transport area (page 72; w regiontrnava.sk), so you will have to buy a ticket.

PIEŠŤANY

Piešťany, 85km northeast of Bratislava, is one of Slovakia's best-known spa towns, with a clutch of excellent hotels located on an island in the middle of the Váh River (the town is just to the west of this). This region is one of the warmest in Slovakia, with the sun shining for around 2,080 hours a year.

First mentioned for its healing waters in 1549, Piešťany's spas have long attracted visitors to their hot thermal springs and sulphurous mud. In 1912, local businessman Ľudovít Winter built the gorgeous Art Nouveau Thermia Palace hotel and Irma Spa. Since then another five giant hotel-spa complexes have sprung up on the island, turning the idyllic space into a year-round leisure and wellness centre. There's even a nine-hole golf course to the north and a network of cycle paths.

The resort has dozens of hotels, but the best are the four-star **Esplanade** (€€€€) and the five-star **Thermia Palace** (€€€€€), both part of the Ensana group (**w** ensanahotels.com).

GETTING THERE AND AWAY Piešťany is on the D1/E75 Bratislava–Žilina motorway and the main Bratislava–Žilina–Košice rail line; the stop is about 25 minutes beyond Trnava, with regular trains from Bratislava (50mins). There is also a regular bus service from Bratislava (1hr) and Vienna.

KOŠICE

Despite its distance from Bratislava (315km as the crow flies, but at least 400km by road or rail), Košice, Slovakia's second city, is included in this chapter because of its historical importance, fabulous range of cultural attractions, wealth of architectural treasures, superb collection of restaurants, bars and cafés, and – significantly – the fact that Wizz Air and Ryanair now fly there direct from London. Many people have not heard of this important Slovak city, but it is an exciting and rewarding destination, and it is included here in the hope that a brief description serves as a tempting introduction.

Košice is often called the 'gateway to eastern Slovakia' as it makes an excellent base for exploring this undiscovered, underrated part of central Europe. Eastern Slovakia is home to many UNESCO landmarks (notably its wooden churches) and four national parks. Many vineyards producing the legendary Tokaj wine are found here and it is known as the cradle of Pop Art, since the parents of Andy Warhol were born in this part of Slovakia. In 2013, Košice was European Capital of Culture, and since then, even more cultural venues and exciting artistic projects have sprung up.

There is so much to see and do in Košice and around, but here's just a taste.

GETTING THERE AND AWAY The best option is to hire a **car** in Bratislava (see page 76 for companies), so you can explore the 'wild east' at your leisure. Drive from Bratislava along route E58 (5hrs) via Trnava, Nitra, Zvolen and Lučenec.

Another possibility is to get the **train** from Bratislava (5hrs), though because of Slovakia's strange geography the train has to go in a loop right up to Žilina and Poprad before heading down to Košice. If coming from Hungary, the two daily trains from Budapest only take 3½ hours. Direct trains from Prague (via Ostrava and Žilina, not Bratislava; 8hrs) are provided by two private operators, Leo Express (w leoexpress.com) and RegioJet (w regiojet.sk). Unfortunately the station has been rebuilt as a shopping mall, with no signs to the platforms (one floor up) so allow plenty of time.

Flixbus (w flixbus.com) has daily buses from Prague (10hrs; from £28) and started less-frequent services from Vienna, Munich and Berlin in 2019. Czech Airlines (w csa.cz) no longer flies from Bratislava to Košice, but there are daily flights from Prague (CSA), Vienna (Austrian Airlines), Warsaw (LOT) and Zurich (Swiss). There are low-cost flights from London to Košice (2hrs 45mins) with Wizz Air (w wizzair.com; from Luton; 4 weekly; from €20 one way), and Ryanair (w ryanair.com; from Stansted; daily; from €30 one way; also Liverpool & Dublin).

TOURIST INFORMATION

MIC Košice Hlavná 32; m 09 11 567 423; w miskosice.sk; ⏲ 09.00–15.00 Mon–Fri
Regional Information Centre Hlavná 48; ☎ 055 305 0530; ⏲ 10.00–12.30 & 13.15–18.00 Mon–Fri, 10.00–12.30 & 13.15–16.00 Sat–Sun

Visit Košice Infopoint Hlavná 59; m 09 49 475 777; e visit@visitkosice.org; w visitkosice.org; ⏲ 11.00–17.00 Mon–Fri. Young, multilingual staff who love their city – their enthusiasm is infectious.

WHERE TO STAY AND EAT

Ambassador (23 rooms) Hlavná 101; m 09 05 220 430; w ambassador.sk. Comfortable hotel with a great location right on the promenade. €€€€
Sport Penzión (19 rooms) Protifašistických bojovníkov 9; m 09 11 917 551; w penzionsport.sk. Between the station & the centre, this is a clean modern hotel with AC & Wi-Fi; there's a good b/fast (extra). €€€
Košice Hostel (20 rooms) Jesenského 20; m 09 07 933 462; w kosicehostel.sk. A simple hostel in a good location without any frills (eg: no kitchen). *Dorm €17*. €€
Villa Cassa Wine Bar Pri Miklušovej väznici 2; m 09 07 916 566; w villa-cassa.sk; ⏲ 15.00–22.00 Mon–Thu, 15.00–midnight Fri–Sat, 17.00–22.00 Sun. Superb wine bar, a great place to try (& buy) Tokaj. €€€
Hostinec Pivovar Hlavná 65; m 09 02 58 0580; w pivovarhostinec.sk; ⏲ 14.00–midnight Mon–Thu, 14.00–01.00 Fri–Sat, 14.00–23.00 Sun. Perhaps the oldest restaurant in Europe, opened in 1542, this is also now a brew-pub, with a wide range of unpasteurised & unfiltered beers, including IPA & stout as well as Czech-style lagers. The menu is fairly meaty, but there's pasta & gnocchi too. €€
Porto coffee & wine Dominikánske námestie 1; m 09 08 500 881; ⏲ 07.00–20.00 Mon–Wed, 07.00–21.00 Thu–Sat. Facing the Dominican church on an attractive café-lined square, this serves tasty bagels as well as drinks. €

WHAT TO SEE AND DO Hlavná ulica ('main street') is Slovakia's longest promenade: an elegant pedestrianised street lined with beautiful historic buildings, cafés and restaurants. All Košice life centres on it, and it's a delight to sip a lemonade or local wine on a terrace and watch the world go by, or get an ice cream and admire the **Singing Fountain** – a watery concert, which chimes every hour. It's also worth exploring the courtyards to the west, leading to the pretty Dominikánske námestie.

Hlavná is dominated by the Gothic masterpiece **St Elisabeth's Cathedral** (Dóm sv Alžbety), built between 1380 and 1508. You'll probably be told that this is the easternmost Gothic cathedral in Europe, but in fact there are others in Ukraine and Transylvania. It's surprisingly short, but there are excellent frescoes both from the 14th to 16th centuries and from 1896. Climb 160 steps to the top of the 60m tower for an amazing view (€1.50). Outside, don't miss the carvings of the north portal and the nearby **tomb of Francis II Rákóczi** (1676–1735), leader of the last anti-Habsburg uprising and a great local hero. Also just north of the cathedral is the freestanding **Urbanova Tower**, built in the 16th century to bear the great bell of St Urban,

with an arcaded porch added in 1912. On the south side of the cathedral is the Gothic **Chapel of St Michael**, built in the first half of the 14th century and rebuilt in 1902–04 and 1998–2006. All in all, it makes a charming streetscape.

The new cultural centres arising out of Košice's time as European Capital of Culture are in repurposed buildings a short distance from the centre. At Rumanova 1, an old swimming pool has been converted into a great, light space, **Kunsthalle** (w k13.sk; ⏰ 11.00–18.00 Tue–Sun), for art exhibitions and concerts. Go there via the photogenic alley, Hrnčiarska ulička, filled with craftsmen's workshops and little cafés.

A 19th-century army barracks has been revitalised as a multi-cultural centre, **Kasárne/Kulturpark** (w steelpark.sk) at Kukučinova 2, where you will find art exhibits, theatre, sound and video studios, dance classes and a café (⏰ whole area 06.00–22.00 daily, exhibitions 10.00–18.00 daily; 🪙). Contemporary creations can also be found at a converted **tobacco factory** (Tabačka Kulturfabrik; w tabacka.sk) at Gorkého 2, which provides space for many artistic groups, and there's also a huge bar, bistro and concert/performance space.

For an insight into Košice's history, visit the high-security vault of the **East Slovak Museum** (Vychodoslovenské Múzeum; Hviezdoslavova ulica 3; 📞055 622 0309; w vsmuzeum.sk; ⏰ May–Oct 09.00–17.00 Tue–Sat, 11.00–18.00 Sun, Nov–Apr 09.00–17.00 Tue–Sat, 13.00–17.00 Sun; 🪙 adult/child €8/5) to see the Košice Gold Treasure, a collection of gold coins discovered in 1938 by building workers in the centre of town, having probably been buried in 1682. The museum's two massive buildings also house displays on history (good but only in Slovak) and natural history, as well as temporary exhibitions. Similarly, the **East Slovak Gallery** (w vsg.sk; ⏰ 10.00–18.00 Tue–Sun; 🪙 adult/seniors & schoolchildren €7/5.50, or 1 selected exhibition: €4/2.50, free on 1st Wed of the month) is spread between a couple of buildings, at Hlavná 27 and Alžbetina 22, and has a large collection mainly covering the strong central European tradition of plein-air landscape painting and the Košice avant-garde of the 1920s.

Košice is quite a treasure itself, just waiting to be discovered.

◀ **1** The centre of Košice, Slovakia's second city, is dominated by its Gothic cathedral, St Elisabeth's. **2** The Town Tower marks the centre of Trnava. **3** The Thermia Palace is one of the best hotels in the spa town of Piešťany.

Appendix 1

LANGUAGE

More than 5 million people speak Slovak in Slovakia and a few million more abroad. However, it hasn't all been plain sailing, or speaking, for the Slovaks.

In AD863, Greek missionary brothers Cyril and Methodius came from Thessaloniki at the invitation of the Great Moravian Prince Rastislav. They came to Great Moravia and created the Old Church Slavonic alphabet, the origins of today's Cyrillic alphabet. They also translated liturgical books into Old Church Slavonic.

Pastor's son and national hero Ľudovít Štúr codified the Slovak literary language in 1843; before that, everything written down was in Czech. Slovaks also had a hard time preserving their language as they were dominated for

ĽUDOVÍT ŠTÚR – MY COUNTRY IS MY BEING

Ľudovít Velislav Štúr was born in 1815 in Uhrovec. He was the leader of the Slovak national revival in the 19th century and the author of the Slovak language standard eventually leading to the contemporary Slovak literary language. Štúr organised the Slovak volunteer campaigns during the 1848 Revolution, he was also politician, poet, journalist, publisher, teacher, philosopher, linguist and member of the Hungarian Parliament. On 22 December 1855, Štúr inadvertently shot and wounded himself during a hunt near Modra. He died there three weeks later, aged only 40.

A national funeral was held there in his honour. Štúr is remembered throughout Slovakia in squares, streets, statues, and indeed Bratislava cafés, named in his honour. Visit his whitewashed birth house in the village of Uhrovec, between Trenčin and Prievidza, or his museum and grave in Modra (page 199), just 30km from Bratislava.

Štúr expressed his philosophy in one sentence, 'My country is my being, and every hour of my life shall be devoted to it.'

years by Hungarians and Austrians, both speaking (and forcing Slovaks to speak) languages with entirely different grammatical make-ups.

Slovak is a member of the Slavic group of languages, a large family including Russian, Ukrainian, Polish, Czech, Serbian, Croat and Slovenian, all of which have a devilish selection of possible endings, genders, declensions, conjugations and diacritical accents. The Slovak vocabulary is about half that of English (approximately 220,000 words to English's 450,000).

Slovak is not as tricky to pronounce as Czech and less tiring for the tongue. It doesn't have the horrendous Czech 'ř' for a start. Having said that, neither is it a doddle. However, a few choice phrases will not only endear you to the locals but also help decipher some of the tongue-twisting vowel-less words that litter Bratislava's streets. Try saying *zmrzlina* (page 110) after a few world-beating beers and you'll be amazed how easy it appears when wearing one's beer goggles. Good luck! (*Veľa šťastia*!)

PRONUNCIATION   Once you learn the rules, pronunciation is not so difficult as – unlike English – there are no peculiar irregularities in how you say what you see.

The vowels *a, e, i, o, u* are pure sounds, more like Spanish or Italian than English. Vowels can be either short (*a, äe, i, o, u, y*) or long (*á, é, í, ó, ú, ý*), basically pronounced with more emphasis but keeping the same sound. Those consonants not listed below (*b, d, f, g, l, m, n, s, v, z*) can be pronounced as in English, with the exception of *q* and *w*, which don't exist in Slovak except in some foreign words and names. The consonants *k, p* and *t* are as in English but not so aspirated.

a as in ah
á as in karma
ä as in hay
c like 'ts' in oats
č like 'ch' in cheeky
ď like 'dy' as in duty (as a capital it's written Ď); *d* followed by *e* or *i* is also softened
dz like 'ds' in heads
dž like 'j' in jam
e as in bed
é as in there
h quite breathily
ch like 'ch' in Scottish 'loch'
i/y as in spaghetti
í/ý as in believe
j like 'ye' in yes
ľ pronounced 'ly' like the *l* in lurid
ň pronounced 'ny' like the *n* in newt; *n* followed by *e* or *i* is softened

o as in hot
ó as in toe
ö pronounced 'ur'
ő as in whoah (you'll only find this on a few Hungarian signs)
r rolled, as in a Scottish accent
ř very rolled (but not followed by a *ž* as in the scary Czech version)
š 'sh' as in shandy
ť pronounced 'ty' as in tuna; *t* followed by *e* or *i* is softened
u as in root
ú as in school
ů pronounced more like a French 'u' with pouty lips
w only found in foreign words and pronounced as a 'v' (WC is *vay-tsay*)
ž like the 's' in leisure

WORDS AND PHRASES
Numbers

0 *nula*	5 *päť*	10 *desať*
1 *jeden*	6 *šesť*	20 *dvadsať*
2 *dva*	7 *sedem*	100 *sto*
3 *tri*	8 *osem*	1,000 *tisíc*
4 *štyri*	9 *deväť*	

Days of the week

Monday	*pondelok*	Friday	*piatok*
Tuesday	*utorok*	Saturday	*sobota*
Wednesday	*streda*	Sunday	*nedeľa*
Thursday	*štvrtok*	weekend	*víkend*

Months
In Czech the months are very poetic and bear no resemblance to English. Slovak months are easier to recognise.

January	*január*	July	*júl*
February	*február*	August	*august*
March	*marec*	September	*september*
April	*apríl*	October	*október*
May	*máj*	November	*november*
June	*jún*	December	*december*

Time

Yesterday/today/tomorrow	*Včera/dnes/zajtra*
Day/week/month/year	*Deň/týždeň/mesiac/rok*
Now/early/late	*Teraz/skoro/neskoro*

Basics

At your service (shops) — *Nech sa páči*
Excuse me (I'm sorry) — *Prepáčte*
Excuse me (Pardon?) — *Prosím?*
Good day — *Dobrý deň*
Good morning — *Dobré ráno*
Good night — *Dobrú noc*
Goodbye (familiar) — *Čau, ahoj*
Goodbye (polite) — *Dovidenia (adieu – zbohom)*
Hello (familiar) — *Ahoj, čau (ciao), servus*
Not at all! — *Niet za čo!*
How much? — *Koľko?*
Please — *Prosím*
Thank you — *Ďakujem Vám (Ti)*
Yes/no — *Áno/nie*

Meeting people

Do you speak English? — *Hovoríte po anglicky?*
Help! — *Pomoc!*
How are you? — *Ako sa máte? (máš)?*
I don't understand (Slovak) — *Nerozumiem (po slovensky)*
My name is… — *Volám sa…*
Pleased to meet you — *Teši ma*
Welcome! — *Vitajte!*
What's your name? — *Ako sa voláte?*

Questions

Can I help you? — *Môžem Vám pomôcť?*
Could you help me? — *Mohli by ste mi pomôcť?*
How far is it to…? — *Ako ďaleko je do…?*
What? — *Čo?*
What does…mean? — *Čo znamená…?*
What is the fare? — *Koľko stojí lístok?*
What is the time? — *Koľko je hodín?*
When is…? — *Kedy je…?*
Where is…? — *Kde je…?*
Which bus goes to…? — *Ktorý autobus ide do…?*

Transport and travel

airport — *letisko*
arrivals/departure — *príchod/odchod*
bicycle — *bicykel*
border check — *hraničná kontrola*
bus station — *autobusová stanica*

bus stop	*zastávka*
customs	*colnica*
delay	*mešká*
main (railway) station	*hlavná (železničná) stanica*
platform/direction	*nástupište/smer*
return (ticket)	*tam a späť*
seat reservation	*miestenka*
ticket(s)	*lístok (lístky)*
timetable	*cestovný poriadok*
toilet	*WC/záchod*
ladies/gents	*ženy/muži*
track	*koľaj*
train	*vlak*
tram	*električka*
trolleybus	*trolejbus*

Places

bank	*banka*	highway	*diaľnica*
bridge	*most*	hospital/	*nemocnica/*
bureau de change	*zmenáreň*	doctor	*lekár*
castle (fortress, ruins)	*hrad*	island	*ostrov*
castle (palace)	*zámok*	lake	*jazero*
cemetery	*cintorín*	monument	*(kultúrna)*
chateau, palace	*palác*		*pamiatka*
church	*kostol*	mountain	*hora*
consulate	*konzulát*	park	*sad, park*
embassy	*veľvyslanectvo*	river	*rieka*
exhibition	*výstava*	square	*námestie*
forest	*les*	street	*ulica*
garden	*záhrada*	town	*mesto*
gate	*brána*	village	*dedina*

Accommodation

first floor	*poschodie*	room	*izba*
ground floor	*prízemie*	shower/bath	*sprcha*
key	*kľúč*		

Do you have any vacancies?   *Máte voľné izby?*
I would like a double room   *Chcem dvojposteľovú izbu*

Shopping

antiques shop	*starožitnosti*	market	*trh/trhovisko*
bookshop	*kníhkupectvo*	police	*polícia*
chemist	*lekáreň*	theatre	*divadlo*

How much is it?	*Koĺko to stojí?*	May I pay with a credit card?	*Môžem platiť kreditnou kartou?*
Can you change this bank note?	*Môžete mi zmeniť túto bankovku?*		

Post

airmail	*letecká pošta*	postcard	*pohľadnica*
letter	*list*	stamps	*známky*
post office	*pošta*		
Australia	*Austrália*	Hungary	*Maďarsko*
Austria	*Rakúsko*	Ireland	*Írsko*
England	*Anglicko*	New Zealand	*Nový Zéland*
Canada	*Kanada*	USA	*Spojené štáty americké*
Great Britain	*Veľká Británia*		

Food and drink

Another beer, please	*Ešte jedno pivo, prosím*
Bon appétit	*Dobrú chuť*
Cheers! Your health	*Na zdravie!*
Could I see the menu?	*Môžem dostať menu/jedálny lístok?*
Do you have a table for 1, 2, 3?	*Máte stôl pre jedného, dvoch, troch?*
The bill, please	*Účet, prosím/Zaplatím*
Two beers, please	*Dvakrát pivo, prosím*
Waiter (male/female)	*Čašník/čašníčka*
Daily menu	*Denné menu*
Food menu	*Jedálny lístok*
Drinks menu	*Nápojový lístok*
Coffee to go	*Káva so sebou*

apple	*jablko*	cheese	*syr*
apricot	*marhuĺa*	chicken	*kuracie*
bacon	*slanina*	coffee	*káva*
baked	*zapečený*	deep-fried giant doughnut(s)	*langoš(e)*
beef	*hovädzie*		
beer	*pivo*	dinner	*večera*
beer hall	*piváreň*	dry/sweet (wine)	*suché/sladké*
boiled	*varený*		
bread	*chlieb*	duck	*kačica*
breakfast	*raňajky*	eggs	*vajíčka*
butter	*maslo*	fish	*ryba*
cabbage	*kapusta*	frankfurters	*párky*
café	*kaviareň, cukráreň*	fresh	*čerstvý*
carp	*kapor*	fried	*vyprážané*

Appendix 1 LANGUAGE

A1

fruit and vegetables	*ovocie a zelenina*	poultry	*hydina*
game	*divina*	restaurant/canteen	*reštaurácia/jedáleň*
garlic	*cesnak*	rice	*ryža*
a glass	*pohár*	roasted	*opekaný*
grapes	*hrozno*	salad	*šalát*
green pepper	*paprika*	salmon	*losos*
grilled	*grilovaný*	salt/pepper	*soľ/korenie*
ham	*šunka*	sausages	*klobásy*
ice cream	*zmrzlina*	seafood	*plody mora*
jam	*džem*	sheep's cheese	*bryndza*
juniper spirit (local)	*borovička*	side dishes	*prílohy*
light/dark beer	*svetlé/tmavé pivo*	soft curd cheese	*tvaroh*
lunch	*obed*	soup	*polievka*
meat	*mäso*	stuffed	*plnený*
menu	*jedálny lístok*	sugar	*cukor*
milk	*mlieko*	take-away	*vziať si so sebou*
mushrooms	*huby, šampiňóny*	tap/mineral water	*voda z vodovodu/minerálna voda*
mustard	*horčica*	tea (with milk/with lemon)	*čaj (s mliekom/s citrónom)*
onion	*cibuľa*	tomato	*paradajka*
orange	*pomaranč*	trout	*pstruh*
pancakes	*palacinky*	turkey	*morčacie*
peach	*broskyňa*	vegetarian dishes	*vegetariánske jedlo*
pear	*hruška*	white/red/rosé	*biele/červené/ružové*
pies	*buchty*	wine	*víno*
pork	*bravčové*	wine bar	*vináreň*
potato-pancake	*lokša*		
potatoes/chips	*zemiaky/hranolky*		

Other useful vocabulary

cheap/expensive	*lacný/drahý*
east/west	*východ/západ*
entrance/exit	*vchod/východ*
good/bad	*dobrý/zlý*
hot/cold	*horúci/studený*
large/small	*veľký/malý*
left/right	*naľavo/napravo*
no smoking	*zákaz fajčiť*
north/south	*sever/juh*
old/new	*starý/nový*
open/closed (shops)	*otvorený/zatvorený*

push/pull (on doors)	*tam/sem*
red/yellow/green	*červený/žltý/zelený*
white/black/blue	*biely/čierny/modrý*

Appendix 2

FURTHER INFORMATION

BOOKS
History and culture

Brock, Peter *The Slovak National Awakening* University of Toronto Press, 1976

Chapman, Colin *August 21st. The Rape of Czechoslovakia* Cassell, 1968. On-the-spot reporting of the Russian invasion of August 1969, published just a few months later.

Fonseca, Isabel *Bury Me Standing* Vintage, 1996. A fine account of the Roma of central-eastern Europe.

Henderson, Karen *Slovakia: The Escape from Invisibility* Routledge, 2002. A good introduction to contemporary Slovak history and politics.

Kirschbaum, Stanislav J *A History of Slovakia: The Struggle for Survival* (Updated paperback) Palgrave Macmillan, New York, 2016

Musil, Jirí (editor) *The End of Czechoslovakia* Central European University Press, 1995

Petro, Peter *A History of Slovak Literature* McGill-Queen's University Press (US)/Liverpool University Press (UK), 1996

Shawcross, William *Dubček and Czechoslovakia* (2nd edition) Touchstone Books, 1990

Literature

Dobšinský, Pavol, adapted by Ann Macleod *The Enchanted Castle, and Other Tales and Legends* (1880–83) Hamlyn, 1967

Hviezdoslav, Pavol Országh, translated by John Minahane *The Bloody Sonnets* Slovak Literary Centre, 2018. Also known as *Song of Blood*, a sequence of anti-war sonnets from World War I.

Jašík, Rudolf, translated by Karol Kornel *Dead Soldiers Don't Sing* Artia, Prague, 1963

Kráľ, Janko, translated by Jaroslav Vajda *Janko Kráľ 1822–1972* Tatran, Bratislava, 1972

Kramoris, Ivan J *Anthology of Slovak Poetry* Obrana Press, Scranton, PA, USA, 1947

Leigh Fermor, Patrick *A Time of Gifts* John Murray, 2004. Fermor's evocative walking journey from the Hook of Holland to the Middle Danube en route to Constantinople, with 15 pages on Bratislava.

Mikszáth, Kálmán, translated by Dick Sturgess *The Siege of Beszterce* (1894) Corvina, Budapest, 1982. Short stories by a Hungarian who set many of his stories in Slovakia.

Mullek, Magdalena and Sherwood, Julia (eds) *Into the Spotlight: New Writing from Slovakia* Three String Books (US)/Parthian (Cardigan, UK), 2017

Naughton, James (editor) *Eastern & Central Europe, Traveller's Literary Companion* In Print Publishing, 1995

Pynsent, Robert B (editor) *Modern Slovak Prose: Fiction since 1954* Macmillan, 1990. Critical essays on writers between 1954 and 1988.

Šimečka, Martin M, translated by Peter Petro *The Year of the Frog* (1985–90) Louisiana State University Press, Baton Rouge, LA, and London, 1993. Mostly autobiographical account of a young Slovak intellectual, son of a well-known dissident, living in Bratislava during the last years of communism.

Šmatlák, Stanislav, translated by M Hunningenová *Hviezdoslav: A National and World Poet* Obzor-Tatrapress, Bratislava, 1969

Sommer-Lefkovits, Elizabeth *Are You in this Hell Too?* Menard Press/Central Books, 1995. Harrowing Holocaust experience told by a Slovak Jewish woman.

Guidebooks and maps

Barta, Vladimir *Hrady, Burgen, Castles* Ab Art Press, Bratislava, 1994

Freytag & Berndt *Automapa Slovenská republika* (1:250 000; w freytagberndt.com)

Gresty, Jonathan and Andričík, Marián *Anglicko-slovenský, slovensko-anglický slovník* Pezolt PVD, 2005

Kallay, Karol *Slovensko-Slowakei-Slovakia* Slovart Ltd, Bratislava, 2012. Divided into four chapters covering nature, architecture, culture and sports. Available in Slovak, German or English.

Lazistan, Eugen *Slovakia: A Photographic Odyssey* Neografia, 2001

Lorinc, Sylvia and John M *Slovak–English–Slovak Dictionary and Phrasebook* Hippocrene Books, 1999

Mapa Slovakia *Slovensko autoatlas* (1:200 000) Bratislava, 2005 (w mapa.sk)

Martin *Slovakia 2001* (w neografia.sk)

WEBSITES

w **airbnb.com** Accommodation rentals, from single rooms to entire houses.

w **bratislava.sk/en** Bratislava City Hall's site is an excellent introduction to the city.

w **bts.aero/en** Website for Bratislava Airport.

w **busy.sk** Timetables for buses, trains, planes, town transport (Slovak only).

w dpb.sk Bratislava public transport – excellent site, but only in Slovak.
w enjoyslovakia.com Hotels, city breaks, tourist information.
w greenpages.sk Online version of the *Slovak Spectator*'s business directory.
w heartofeurope.co.uk Good introduction to Slovakia by expat James Ault.
w imhd.sk/ba/public-transport Public transport in Bratislava explained clearly and in English.
w inakost.sk Portal for LGBTQIA+ websites and advice.
w inba.sk Bratislava information and listings magazine.
w kamdomesta.sk Online edition of the listings monthly *Kam do Mesta*.
w lod.sk Boat trips up and down river from Bratislava.
w modra.sk Website for the wine-producing town of Modra.
w mpba.sk/en Hip map of cool venues in Bratislava.
w muzeum.bratislava.sk Links to all the museums run by the city of Bratislava.
w muzeum.sk Excellent store of museums, castles, churches and more.
w panorama.sk Mainly useful for links to webcams.
w pezinok.sk Website for the wine-producing town of Pezinok.
w ryanair.com Cheap flights to Bratislava and Košice.
w slovakia.travel/en The well-put-together tourist website of the Slovak government.
w slovakspectator.sk Online edition of the *Slovak Spectator*; registration and payment required for many articles.
w slovnik.sk Good English–Slovak–English dictionary.
w tour4u.sk/en One of Slovakia's leading incoming tourism companies.
w twincityliner.com/en Provides information on the Vienna–Bratislava high-speed catamaran.
w visitbratislava.com The Bratislava tourist office's website, with full information on the Bratislava Card.
w visitkosice.org Excellent introduction to Slovakia's second city.
w welcometobratislava.eu Travel information on Bratislava.
w wizzair.com Cheap flights to Košice.
w zoznam.sk Slovak search engine and information portal.
w zssk.sk/en Slovak State Railways; timetables, information, tickets and reservations.

The Baroque gardens on the north side of Bratislava Castle have been restored to their 1780 state – although with a modern car park beneath them. ▶

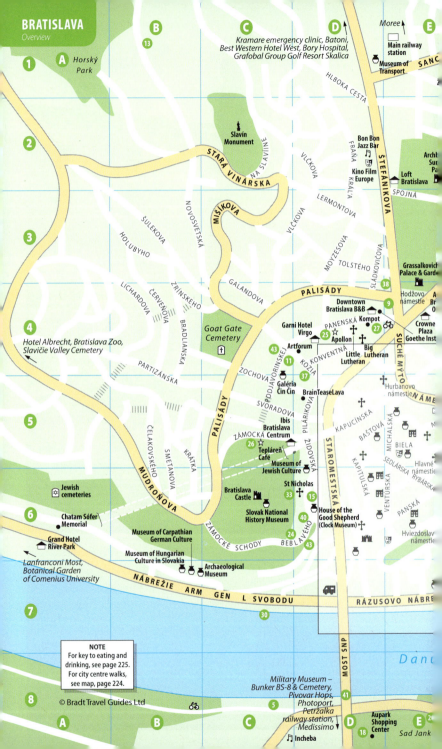

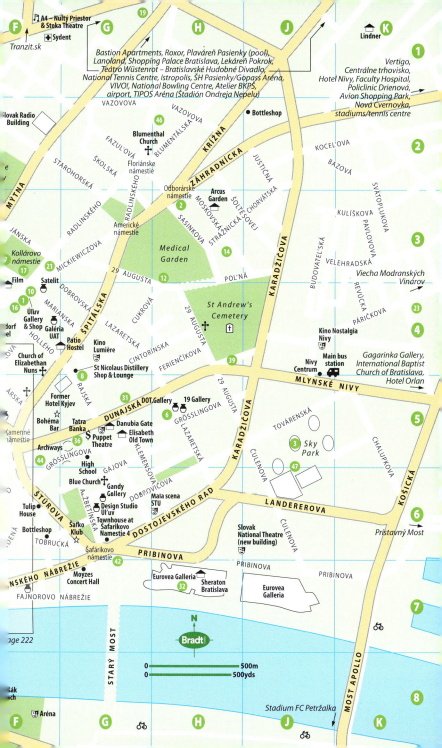

BRATISLAVA Overview
Map, page 220

Where to eat and drink

Name	Grid ref	Page ref
1 1 Slovenská krčma	F4	116
2 Allakaj bakery & caffe	H3	109
3 Amfora	J5	114
4 Au Café	E8	101
5 Aušpic	C8	102
6 Avra Kehdabra Literárna čajovňa	H5	109
7 Balans Bistro	F3	109
8 Bistro St Germain	G5	109
9 Café Le Petit	E4	109
10 Chutney	F4	104
11 Cozy Coza	C4	103
12 Domček Medická	H3	103
13 Funus	B1	117
14 Hostinec Opapa	H3	117
15 Jasmin	D6	99
16 KGB	F4	115
17 Kollarko	F3	115
18 Kubu	D8	102
19 La Putika	G1	107
20 Leberfinger	E8	101
21 Mestský pivovar Alžbetka	F3	115
22 Mešuge Craft Beer Pub	F4	117
23 Mint Pradiareň	K4	102
24 Modrá Hviezda	C6	98
25 Moshi Moshi	D4	103
26 Nervosa	C5	113
27 Next Apache	D4	112
28 Olive Tree	E4	104
29 Papaya	F3	103
30 Pink Whale	C7	117
31 Pivovarská Reštaurácia	G5	116
32 Primi	H7	99
33 Reštaurácia Hradná	C6	98
34 Savage Garden	F3	102
35 Skupinová Terapia All Day Bar	F3	116
36 Soho	G5	104
37 Soupa Bistro	D5	105
38 Štefanka by Pulitzer	E4	103
39 Sushi Time	H4	103
40 U čerta	D6	113
41 UFO	D8	101
42 Umelka	G7	116
43 Viecha malých vinárov	C4, D6	113
44 Vegan Kiosk	F5	104
45 Viecha Drevená Dedina	E1	118
46 Viecha Modranských Vinárov	H2, K4	114
47 Werk	J5	102

Off map

Moree	E1	103
Pivovar Hops	D8	117
Roxor	G1	105

BRATISLAVA City centre
Map, page 222

Where to eat and drink

Name	Grid ref	Page ref
1 10 Prstov	F5	114
2 17s Bar	C7	117
3 100 Pív	G6	117
4 Alchymista u veľkých Františkánov	D4	100
5 Arthur	E6	110
6 Bánh Mi Huy Vege	G2	104
7 Beer Palace	F6	114
8 Bodega	F4	108
9 Bratislavská Flagship reštaurácia	F2	101
10 Bratislavská Pekáreň a mliekareň	E2	108
11 Bratislavský Meštiansky Pivovar	D1	114
12 Brixton House	D4	102
13 Café L'aura	B7	109
14 Café Opera	F7	109
15 Café Verne	D7	115
16 CarneValle	C7	102
17 Cork	D6	112
18 Da Vinci Bistro&More	B4	100
19 Enjoy Bistro	C4	98
20 Fach Bistro	C6	109
21 Foodstock	F4	100
22 Foxford (see Martinus)	E1	112
23 Funki Punki Palacinky	B4	105
24 F X Messerschmidt Café & Museum	F2	110
25 Góvinda	F1	103
26 Grand Cru Wine Gallery	D3	113
27 Habibi Café	D6	107
28 Houdini (see Marrol's)	H7	100
29 I Nonni Craft Gelato	E5	110
30 Irin	B6	100
31 Kaffee Mayer	D5	107
32 Kaviareň Radnička	E5	108
33 KeP's Caffetteria	F5	112
34 Kláštorný Pivovar	F2	113
35 Kogo	D7	101
36 Koliba Kamzík	C4, C6	99
37 Koun	D8	110
38 La Putika	D6, F4	107
39 Lab	G4	108
40 Luculus	C7	110
41 Lux Flavour	C5	99
42 Malewill Café Bistro	F4	107
43 Martineum Café	A7	107
44 Mondieu	B8, C7, E5	107
45 Nibble & Sip House	C5	99
46 Orbis Street Food	F5	104
47 Pane e Olio	G6	103
48 Patisserie Kormuth	C5	107
49 Pinch Bistro	H6	109
50 Pod Kamenným Stromom	C5	113
51 Prazdroj	E8	107
52 Pressburg Bajgel	C7	108
53 Pulitzer	B3	102
54 Savoy	E7	101
55 Schokocafé Maximilian Delikateso	D5	108
56 Sky Bar & Restaurant	C8	114
57 Sladovňa House of Beer	C6	113
58 Spaghetti Leviathan	H6	105
59 Sushi Bar Tokyo	C7	100
60 Urban Bistro	C4	100
61 Urban House	F5	100
62 Viecha malých vinárov	F4	113
63 Vinopolitan	E2	113
64 Výčap U Ernőho	F4	114

225

Index

Page numbers in **bold** indicate major entries and those in green indicate photos.

accommodation 78–88
  camping 87–8
  four-star hotels 82–4
  hostels 87
  luxury hotels 80, 81–2
  pensions 85–7
  price codes 79
  private apartments 86
  three-star hotels 84–5
airport 39, 45–6
Ancient Gerulata, Rusovce 197–8
  getting there and away 198
antiques 140
Archbishop's Summer Palace 152, 156
Aréna theatre 120, 122
art 26–7 *see also* galleries
Art Nouveau 175, 176
ATM machines *see* money
Aupark 139, 143
Austria 1–3, 7–8, 14–15, 48–9
Austro-Hungarian triangle 142
Authentic Slovakia 62–3, 168

banks 66
bars, pubs and clubs 112–18
  further afield 114–18
  Old Town and Castle District 112–14
Bartók, Béla 27, 125, 181
beach sports 135
beer 96–7 *see also* drink
Beethoven, Ludwig von 27, 124, 147, 158
Beneš, Edvard 10, 15, 145

Bernolák, Anton 7, 14, 25
beyond the city 195–207
  Ancient Gerulata, Rusovce 194, 197–8
  Červený Kameň 200, 201–2
  Devín 193–5, 194
  Košice 203–7, 206
  Modra 199–201, 200
  Pezinok 199–201, 200
  Piešťany 202–3, 206
  Senec 198, 200
  Small Carpathian Wine Route 198–201, 200
  Trnava 202
bicycles *see* cycling
Blue Church 40, 42, 57, 148, **152–3**, 154, 175
boat trips *see* Danube boat trips
bobsleigh 136, 184
books 25–6, 140–1, 216–17
bookshops 108, 140–1
borovička 35, 40, 95
Botanical Garden 181
bowling 136, 140, 143
Bratislava, names of 9, 12, 13
Bratislava Castle 2, 14, 15, 17, 31, 32, 41, 42, 59, 98, 124, 150, **153–4**, 167–70, 218
Bratislava City Card 71
Bratislava Tourist Board 47, **62**, 71
Bratislava Zoo 181
bridges 38, 187–92
  Lafranconi Most 187
  Most Apollo 189–92, 188

226

Most SNP i, 38, **188**, 189
Pristavný Most 192
Starý Most 38, 189
Brothers of Mercy Church 179
bryndzové halušky 40, 90, **91**
Buda, fall of 7, 14
Budapest 23, 39, 46, 48, 51, 63, 65
budgeting 59–60
bunkers 63, 162, 166
Bush, George W 1, 3
business hours 66

cafés and tearooms **91**, 104–12, **106**
　further afield 109–12
　Old Town and Castle District 107–8
canoeing and rafting 137
Capuchin Church 179
Čaputová, Zuzana 16, 19
car factories 21
car hire 76
car parks *see* parking
Casanova 1
casinos 129
castle *see* Bratislava Castle
Celts 5, 13, 92, 153, 195
cemeteries 182–5
　Goat Gate Cemetery 182
　Jewish 183–4
　St Andrew's Cemetery 185
　Slávičie Valley Cemetery 185
Červený Kameň **200**, 201–2
chair lift 181
charities 36
Chatam Sófer 25, 179, 184 *see also* Jewish history
chemists *see* health
children, travelling with 56–8
Christmas 95
　market 33, 95, **142**, **142**, 186
church services *see* religious services
churches and religious buildings 179–81 *see also* individual entries
cinema 27, 130–1

classical music 27–8, 123–6
climate 4
climbing 136, 183
clinics, travel 53
coat of arms 6
coffee stalls **111**, 115
communication 67–70
communism 10, 15–16
Compromise (Ausgleich) 8, 15
concert venues 124–6
contexts 1–36
coronation 14, 31, 39, 154, 157, 158, 160
coronation route 31, 40, 157, **160**
credit cards 67
crime 54–5
cultural etiquette 33–5
cultural institutes 131
culture 25–8, 120–8, 130–1
Čunovo 5, 16, 32, 43, 51, 74, 77, 85, 87–8, 137, 162, 197–8
customs regulations 45
cycling 74, **75**, 132–3
　hire 133
　maps 133
Cyril and Methodius, Saints 6, 208
Cyrillic alphabet 6, 208
Czech food and drink 89, 93, 94, 95, 96, 98
Czech language 8, 14, 25, 130, 208–9
Czech people 7–12, 15–16, 20, 23
Czech Republic 3, 5, 18
Czechoslovakia 5, 9–12, 15, 144–5, 168, 185, 216

dance houses 126
Danube boat trips 51, 63, **64**, 65, **75**, 77, 197
Danube River 3, 5, 14, 38
Devín 6, 13, 15, 30, 39, **64**, 73, 74, 77, 95, 132–3, **194**, **195–7**
Devínska Nová Ves 16, 21, 73, 74, 133
disability, travelling with a 58

227

discos 128–9
discount card *see* Bratislava City Card
Dohnányi, Ernő 123, 125
drink 35, 92–3, 94–5, 96–7 *see also* cafés and tearooms, bars, pubs and clubs
drugs 35
Dubček, Alexander 10, 15, 159, 163, 185, 216
Dzurinda, Mikulaš 16, 18, 21

Easter 30, 138, 178
eating out *see* restaurants
economy 20–2
electricity xiv
embassies 45, 66
emergencies 53–6, 69
English-language press 68
entertainment 120–45
entry requirements 44–5
escape room 136
essential information xiv
ethnicity 23–4
etiquette 33–5
EU membership 16, 18
euro currency 59, 66
European Union 16, 18, 22, 38, 45, 59, 189
Eurovea 130, 138, 139, 143
events *see* festivals and events
exchange rate xiv, 66

fashion stores 137, 141
Felvidék 6, 8, 26
female travellers 56
Fermor, Patrick Leigh 23, 150, 153, 217
festivals and events 28–33, 29, 41
Fico, Robert 16, 18–20
fitness centres 136
folk crafts 29, 141
folk music 28, 126
  venues 126

folksong and dance heritage 28, 29
food 89–94, 91 *see also* restaurants
  healthy 139
  shops 139, 143
football 135
formalities *see* greetings
Franciscan Church 180
further information 216–18

Gabčikovo-Nagymaros hydro-electric dam 5, 43, 77
galleries 170–9
  19 Gallery 170
  A4 Space for Contemporary Culture 170–1
  ABC (Art Books Coffee) 171
  Bibiana 57, 171
  Bořek Šípek Gallery 171
  Bratislava City Gallery, Mirbach Palace 171
  Bratislava City Gallery, Pálffy Palace 171
  Central European House of Photography 172
  Cit Gallery 172
  Design Studio Úľuv 172
  Dot.Gallery 172
  F7 172
  Flatgallery 172
  Gagarinka Gallery 172
  Galéria Čin Čin 174
  Galéria UAT 174
  Gallery of the Slovak Union of Visual Arts 174
  Gandy Gallery 174
  Kunsthalle Bratislava/Dom Umenia 174
  Medium Gallery 174
  Nedbalka Gallery 173, 174–5
  Photoport 175
  Primate's Palace 173, 177
  Pro Art Gallery 177
  Roman Feck Gallery 177
  Satelit 177

Slovak National Gallery 26–7, 169, **173**, **178**
Steinhauser Gallery 178
Tranzit.sk 178
Úľuv Gallery 178
Umrian Gallery 179
gardens and parks 181–6
Gasparovič, Ivan 18
gates, Old Town 182–3
gay travellers *see* LGBTQIA+ Bratislava
geography 3–4
Gerulata 6, 13, 32, 166, **197–8**
    Museum of Ancient 166
getting around 72–7
    by bicycle 74, **75**
    by boat **75**, 77
    by bus 72–3
    by car 76–7
    by night bus 73
    by public transport 72–3
    by taxi 76
    by train 73
    by tram 73, **75**
    by trolleybus 73
    by wheelchair 74
    local transfers 46–7, 49
    tickets 72
getting there and away 45–51
    airport transfers 46–7
    by air 45–7
    by boat 51
    by car 51
    by coach or bus 50–1
    by train 47–50
    flights to Košice Airport 47
    flights to Vienna International Airport 46–7
    transfer from Vienna to Bratislava 47
golf courses 133–4
government 18–20
grape varieties 92–3

Grassalkovich Palace **149**, 151, **155**, 182
Great Moravian Empire 6, 13, 195, 208
green spaces 181–6
greetings 34–5
guidebooks 217
Gypsies *see* Roma

Habsburgs 7–8, 14–15, 153, 195
Havel, Václav 10–12, 83, 163
Haydn, Franz Joseph 27, **124**, 184
health 51–4
    clinics 53
    dentists 54
    EHIC card 53
    hospitals 54
    insurance 53
    pharmacies 53–4
    spas 54
    ticks 52–3
highlights 40–3
hiking 134, 163, 184
hire cars *see* transport
history 5–20
Hitler, Adolf 9, 15, 186
Hlavná stanica (main railway station) **11**, 47–9
Hlinka Party 9, 10
holidays, national xiv
Holocaust 24, 167
    memorial wall 164
Holy Trinity Church 180
home visits 35
horseracing 136
Hotel Kyjev 168, 169
hotels *see* accommodation
House of the Good Shepherd 150, **165**, **192**
how to use this guide xii
Hummel, Johann Nepomuk 27, 124–5, 164
Hungarians 9, 19, 21, 26, 166 *see also* Magyars

Hungary 1, 3, 5, 6–9, 13–15, 19, 21, 132, 159, 202
Hviezdoslav, Pavol Országh 26, 148

ice 34
ice cream 106, 110
ice hockey 134
identity of Bratislava 12
International Women's Club 36
internet 70
István, Szent *see* St Stephen
itineraries 40–3

jazz 28, 32
    venues 126–8
Jewish cemeteries 179, 183–4
Jewish history 9–10, 24, 101, 164, 167, 179, 198
Jewish people 24
Jewish quarter (former) 38, 147, 150, 168, 189
Jewish tours 65

Kiska, Andrej 18
Koliba-Kamzík 42, 56–8, 136, 184
Korzo (promenade) 146, 179, 191
Košice 203–7, 206
    Airport 47, 204
    getting there and away 203–4
    tourist information 205
    what to see and do 205–7
    where to stay and eat 205
Kováč, Michal 13
Kuciak, Ján 19

Lanfranconi, Count Grazioso Enea 187
language, Slovak 7–8, 14, 26, 208–15
Lechner, Ödön 148, 152–3, 175
Leopold De Pauli Palace 146
LGBTQIA+ Bratislava 35, 130
Lipa, Peter 28
Liszt, Franz 123, **125**, 146, 158, 180
literary tea houses 108

literature 25–6, 216–17
'little big city' 40

M R Štefánik Airport **45–6**, 76
Magyarisation 8, 15
Magyars, invasion by 6
maps 133, 140–1, 217
    list of vii
Maria Theresa, Empress 7, 14, 49, 93, 155, 182
markets 138, 139
Martin Declaration 9, 15
Martin Memorandum 8, 14
Masaryk, Tomaš 9, 15, 144–5, 148
Matyáš Corvinus, King 7, 14, 25, 193
Maximilián *see* Roland statue/fountain
Mečiar, Vladimír 12–13, 18–19, 24
media 67–8
Medical Garden 41, 103, 151, **184**
Messerschmidt, Franz Xaver 163–4, 171, 178
Michael's Gate and tower 146, **155–7**, 156, 164, 183
Michalská (street) 60, 137, **146**, 179
Middle Ages 6
Miklós, Ivan 21
Milan Dobeš 171, 175, 177
Mirbach Palace 42, 124, **157**, 165, 171
mobile phones 69
Modra 7, 14, 32, 65, 93, 114, **198–201**, 200
Mohács, Battle of 7, 14
money 59–60, 66–7
    exchanging currency 66 *see also* exchange rate
mountain biking *see* cycling
Mozart, Wolfgang Amadeus 27, 123, 124, 127, 146, 157, 183
museums 160–70, 165
    Apponyi Palace Museum of Viticulture and Period Rooms 160–1
    Archaeological Museum 161

City History Museum *see* Old Town Hall
Clock Museum 161–2
Danubiana Meulensteen Modern Art Museum 162–3, 173
F X Messerschmidt Café and Museum 110, **163–4**
Hummel Museum 164
Jewish Community Museum 164
Michael's Gate 164
Military Museum 166
Museum of Ancient Gerulata 166
Museum of Carpathian German Culture 166
Museum of Hungarian Culture in Slovakia 166
Museum of Jewish Culture 167
Museum of Pharmacy at the Red Crayfish 165, 167
Museum of Transport 165, 167
Slovak National History Museum 154, **167–70**
Slovak National Natural Science Museum 148, **170**
music 27–8, 123–8 *see also* festivals and events
  live music bars and clubs 126–8
  gig venues 128
musical heritage 124–5, 127

name days 34
names 34
Námestie Slobody 151, 152, 169, **187**, 190
Námestie SNP 38, 175
Napoleon 14, 31, 101, 147, 157, 158, 185, 191, 195
national holidays xiv
NATO 16, 18, 56
natural history 4–5
Natural Science Museum *see* Slovak National Museum
nature tours 44

Nazis 9–10, 15, 191
newspapers 67–8, 140–1
nightclubs and discos 128–9
Notre Dame Church 180

Old Town centre 1, 2, 7, 35, 146–7
Old Town Hall 147, 156, **157**, 161
opening hours xii, 66, 69, 97 *see also* business hours
opera 121, 123
Opera House *see* Slovak National Theatre
orientation 38–9
Ottomans 7, 14, 152

Pálffy Palaces 124, 146, 147, **157**, 171, 174
parking 77
parks 181–6
  Horský 183
  Medical Garden 41, 103, 151, **184**
  Sad Janka Kráľa 75, 185
Pellegrini, Peter 16, 19–20
people 23–4
Petőfi, Sándor 8, 151, 184
Petržalka 15, 38, 47, 49, 73, 74, 132, 135, 137, 140, 143, 162, 166, 169, 175, 189, **192–3**
  Railway Station 47, 50
Pezinok 30–2, 199–201, 200
  getting there and away 201
  Wine Cellars 30
Piešťany 54, 190, **202–3**, 206
plague column 179
planning 38–60
poetry 26, 216–17
point zero 146, 149
police 55
politics 18–20
Poor Clares Church and Convent 124, 146, **180–1**
popular music 28, 126–9
post offices 69, 169, 175, 176
practicalities 62–71

231

Prague Spring, the 10, 15
Prešporáčik little red bus 40, **64**, 65, 74
Pressburg 7, 9, 12, 14, 104
    Peace Treaty 14, 158, 177
price codes, accommodation 79
price codes, restaurants 98
prices, shopping 60
Primate's Palace 124, 147–8, **158**, **173**, 177
pronunciation, Slovak 209–10
public transport 72–4

quirky sights 162–3

Radičova, Iveta 19
radio 68
rail passes 50
railway station, main *see* Hlavná stanica
Red Cross 36
red tape 44–5
Reduta 123, 125, **127**, 148, **158**
Regiojet 47, 48, 50, 51, 204
religion and beliefs xiv, 24–5
religious services 70
restaurant names 99
restaurants 95–104
    further afield 100–4
    Old Town and Castle District 98–100
    swift snacks 104–5
revolutions 8, 10
River Park 79, 81–2, 143, 150
Rohkatka-Kaktus downhill mountain bike track 184–5
Roland statue/fountain 147, **149**, 186, 190
Roma, the xiv, 19, **24**, 216
Romans, the 6, 13, 32, 92, 153, 166, 195, 197
running 30, 33, 134
Rusovce 32, 103, 126, 166, **194**, **197–8**
Ruthene minority 24

Sad Janka Kráľa **75**, 185
safety 54–6
St Elizabeth 153, **155**
St Martin's Cathedral 7, 14, **37**, 124, 125, 147, **156**, **158**
St Stephen, King 6, 13, 147, 158
Samo 6
Schreiber, Moshe *see* Chatam Sófer
Schwechat Airport *see* Vienna International Airport
seasons 4, 39
Senec 198, **200**
shopping 137–45
shopping centres 143
sightseeing 152–93
skiing 184
Sky Park **17**, 103, 114, **150**
Slavic tribes 6, 13
Slavín Monument **11**, 40, **159**, 169
Slota, Ján 18
Slovak independence 12–13, 16
Slovak National Awakening 7–8, 14–15, 26
Slovak National Council 8, 14, 15, 154, 180
Slovak National Theatre (SND) 121, **122**, **159**
Slovak National Uprising xiv, 10, 15, 24
Slovak Philharmonic 125, **127**
Slovak Radio 68
    building and concert hall **64**, 123, 125–6, 163, 169, 193
Slovak State Railways 47–50, 218
Slovak Tourist Board 40, 62
Slovaks 1–3, 5–25, 33–5, 89
Slovenia 1–3, 16, 18, 33
Small Carpathian Wine Route **57**, 198–201, **200**
Smer 16, 18, 19
snacks 104–5
SNP *see* Slovak National Uprising
Socialism retro tours 168–9
Socialist architecture *see* architecture

souvenirs 143
Soviet invasion 10, 15
spas 54, 136–7, 202–3
sports 132–7
   where to watch 132
squares 186–7
   Hlavné námestie 147, **186**, 190–1
   Hviezdoslavovo námestie 71, 120, 148, **186**, 190–1
   Námestie Ľudovíta Štúra 186–7
   Námestie Slobody 151, 152, 169, **187**, 190
stag parties 35, 39, 43, 58–9, 63, 65
Stalinism 10, 26
statues 27, 152, **190–1**
   humorous 149, 188, 190–1, 191
Štefánik, Milan Rastislav **144–5**, 186
Štúr, Ľudovít 8, 14, 26, 148, 186–7, 195, 199, **208**
suggested itineraries 40–3
summer bobsleigh 136
swimming 136–7
synagogues 25, 38, 65, **70**, 147, 164, 168, 198, 202

Tatars, invasion by 6, 13
Tatra Tiger 20–2
tax 21–2, 81
taxis 46, 49, 55, 60, **76**
telephone 69
   emergency numbers 69
television 68
tennis 134–5
terrorism 55–6
theatre 120–3
ticket offices 121
tipping 60
Tiso, Jozef 9–10, 15
toilets, public 71
Tokaj wine 92–3, 203
tour operators, local 62–5, 64
tour operators, worldwide 43–4
tourist information 62
traffic regulations 51

transport 72–7 *see* getting there and away
travelling positively 36
Trianon, Treaty of 9, 93
Trnava 206, 202
TV tower 57, 101, 116, **168**, 184
Twin City Liner 51

UFO café i, 38, 42, 60, 65, **101**, 150, 151, 154, 159–60, 169, 188, 189
unemployment 13, **22**, 24
Universitas (Academia) Istropolitana 7, 14, 25, 147, **193**

Vallo, Matúš 16
vegan and vegetarian food 94
Velvet Divorce 12–13, 16, 20
Velvet Revolution 12, 16, 163
Ventúrska (street) 137, 146–7
Vienna 1, 3, 7, 8, 9, 14, 22, 23, 38, 39, 45–8, **48–9**, 50, 51, 63, 65, 76, 77, 104–5, 132, 142, 153, 158, 189, 203, 204
   day trip 48–9
   International Airport 46–7
Visa TravelMoney 67
visas 44–5
Vivo! 121, 130, 140, 143
vocabulary 39, 210–15

walking tours 146–51
   Castle and beyond 150–1
   Old Town 146–50
Warhol, Andy 3, 203
water, drinking 51
watersports 137
weather *see* climate
websites 217–18
weight and gravity measures 70
what to take 58–9
wheelchair access 58, 74
when to visit 39
wildlife *see* natural history

wine 92–3, 95, 97–8, 143–5 *see also* drink
Wine Route, Small Carpathian 32, 33, 57, 198–201, **200**
wine shops 143–5
wine-tasting 28–33, 65, 143–5, 198–201
women travellers 56
words and phrases 39, 210–15

World War I 8–9, 144–5
World War II 9–10, 15, 24, 25

Záhorie 4–5, 63
Železná Studienka Valley 181, **185–6**
Zichy Palace 99, 146
Zlaté Piesky 32, 56, 72, 88, 137, **182**
zoo *see* Bratislava Zoo